Retire
Worry-Free

W7/06
W8/09
W1/12
W3/15
W3/18

Fifth Edition

Retire Worry-Free

MONEY-SMART WAYS TO BUILD THE NEST EGG YOU'LL NEED

From the Editors of
Kiplinger's Personal Finance

Dearborn™
Trade Publishing
A **Kaplan Professional** Company

President, Dearborn Publishing: Roy Lipner
Vice President and Publisher: Cynthia A. Zigmund
Acquisitions Editor: Mary B. Good
Senior Managing Editor: Jack Kiburz
Cover Design: Design Solutions
Typesetting: the dotted i

Published by Dearborn Trade Publishing
A Kaplan Professional Company

Fifth edition. Printed in the United States of America

05   06   07   10   9   8   7   6   5   4   3   2   1

Library of Congress Cataloging-in-Publication Data

Retire worry-free : money-smart ways to build the nest egg you'll need / by the editors of Kiplinger's personal finance.— 5th ed.
    p.   cm.
Includes index.
ISBN 1-4195-0515-7 (7.25x9 pbk.)
   1. Retirement income—United States—Planning.   I. Kiplinger's personal finance magazine.
HG179.R3946 2005
332.024'014—dc22

                                   2005005377

Contents

Contents

Strategy #7: Avoid these investment potholes • Portfolio tracker: How are your investments deployed?

A few generations ago, the very idea of retirement was foreign to the vast majority of Americans. Retirement was for the well-to-do. Most people worked until they couldn't physically (or legally) work any longer. They lived a few more years in greatly reduced circumstances—often with their adult children—and then they died. Social security was in its infancy, and anyhow, it was just a minimal safety net for the last couple of years of life. Company-paid health insurance and pensions were uncommon. Most people's lifetime earnings didn't allow for much retirement savings, and the elderly were the poorest age group in America.

In the last 30 years or so, all of this has been turned topsy-turvy by simultaneous revolutions in health care, employment rights, pensions, and government policies that encourage tax-deferred saving. Today most workers are protected from mandatory retirement by the Age Discrimination in Employment Act (ADEA) that covers workplaces of more than 20 employees and most occupations other than some such as highly paid executives in policy-making positions, tenured university faculty, fire fighting and law-enforcement personnel.

On the other hand, many people who saved aggressively while they were young are able to retire much earlier than age 65.

Today millions of elderly Americans now live comfortably in retirement, with income from a combination of social security, private pensions, and their own savings. Many retirees have significant health care coverage from their previous employees.

While there is still much poverty among the elderly, as there is in every age segment, older people have a higher median net worth than any other age group, thanks in part to the rising value of their homes in recent decades.

Even as today's retirees are living far better than their predecessors, there is a lot of anxiety among younger Americans—those in their 20s, 30s, and 40s and 50s—about their prospects for a comfortable retirement. They may believe that social security will "be there" for them (which it certainly will), but they also recognize that they won't get as rich a return on their payroll taxes as today's retirees are getting. Young workers also see that many companies are replacing the traditional employer-paid, defined-benefit pension with some kind of retirement plan to which they must contribute, with future benefits determined by chancy investment results.

The Economic Growth and Tax Relief Reconciliation Act of 2001 benefited workers by raising the maximum contributions for various types of retirement plans, making it possible to accumulate a larger retirement nest egg, but there is still the problem of coming up with the money to set aside for retirement.

Because many Baby Boomers married later and had children later than used to be normal, they find themselves paying college tuition bills while they're in their early 50s—at an age when people used to be devoting major parts of the career-peak earnings to retirement saving. For many of today's middle-aged parents of young children, it won't be sufficient to save first for college expenses and then for retirement. To achieve both savings goals, they must do it simultaneously— which means heavy saving and deferred gratification.

What this all adds up to is more uncertainty, more choices, and—most of all—a clear sense that people must take responsibility for their own future. Early-middle-aged Americans still have the opportunity to enjoy comfortable retirements—if they accept personal responsibility for their own financial security and start the investment process early enough.

This book is not about living in retirement; it's about planning for retirement. It's for people still young enough to do something about it.

Written by the staff of *Kiplinger's Personal Finance, Retire Worry-Free* will give you a head start on many of your contemporaries. We hope it is useful to you as you embark on creating a retirement plan, and our best wishes to you on making that plan a reality.

KNIGHT A. KIPLINGER
Editor in Chief
Kiplinger's Personal Finance

A few generations ago, the very idea of retirement was foreign to the vast majority of Americans. Retirement was for the well-to-do. Most people worked until they couldn't physically (or legally) work any longer. They lived a few more years in greatly reduced circumstances—often with their adult children—and then they died. Social security was in its infancy, and anyhow, it was just a minimal safety net for the last couple of years of life. Company-paid health insurance and pensions were uncommon. Most people's lifetime earnings didn't allow for much retirement savings, and the elderly were the poorest age group in America.

In the last 30 years or so, all of this has been turned topsy-turvy by simultaneous revolutions in health care, employment rights, pensions, and government policies that encourage tax-deferred saving. Today most workers are protected from mandatory retirement by the Age Discrimination in Employment Act (ADEA) that covers workplaces of more than 20 employees and most occupations other than some such as highly paid executives in policy-making positions, tenured university faculty, fire fighting and law-enforcement personnel.

On the other hand, many people who saved aggressively while they were young are able to retire much earlier than age 65.

Today millions of elderly Americans now live comfortably in retirement, with income from a combination of social security, private pensions, and their own savings. Many retirees have significant health care coverage from their previous employees.

While there is still much poverty among the elderly, as there is in every age segment, older people have a higher median net worth than any other age group, thanks in part to the rising value of their homes in recent decades.

Even as today's retirees are living far better than their predecessors, there is a lot of anxiety among younger Americans—those in their 20s, 30s, and 40s and 50s—about their prospects for a comfortable retirement. They may believe that social security will "be there" for them (which it certainly will), but they also recognize that they won't get as rich a return on their payroll taxes as today's retirees are getting. Young workers also see that many companies are replacing the traditional employer-paid, defined-benefit pension with some kind of retirement plan to which they must contribute, with future benefits determined by chancy investment results.

The Economic Growth and Tax Relief Reconciliation Act of 2001 benefited workers by raising the maximum contributions for various types of retirement plans, making it possible to accumulate a larger retirement nest egg, but there is still the problem of coming up with the money to set aside for retirement.

Because many Baby Boomers married later and had children later than used to be normal, they find themselves paying college tuition bills while they're in their early 50s—at an age when people used to be devoting major parts of the career-peak earnings to retirement saving. For many of today's middle-aged parents of young children, it won't be sufficient to save first for college expenses and then for retirement. To achieve both savings goals, they must do it simultaneously— which means heavy saving and deferred gratification.

What this all adds up to is more uncertainty, more choices, and—most of all—a clear sense that people must take responsibility for their own future. Early-middle-aged Americans still have the opportunity to enjoy comfortable retirements—if they accept personal responsibility for their own financial security and start the investment process early enough.

Redefining "Retirement"

Chapter 1

Retirement is dead. That seems like an odd way to start a book about retirement planning. But then, what is "retirement," anyway? One thing's for sure—it's not what it used to be. Several generations ago, the very notion of retirement was non-existent. People simply worked until they were physically incapable of doing so. When they stopped working, they subsisted on savings they had scraped together over a lifetime, or accepted help from relatives. Then they died.

During the Great Depression, with unemployment running rampant, the Roosevelt administration devised "social security." This program forced workers to set aside a portion of their income—matched by their employers—to create a public-pension nest egg. The social security money withheld from those currently working would be used to pay those who no longer did. The government also hoped that social security would prompt people (overwhelmingly men) to stop working sooner, thereby opening up much-needed jobs for the young.

Corporate America—especially the financial-services and leisure industries—seized on this concept and began promoting a new American dream: "Retirement in The Golden Years," a period chock full of good times. The hours and days once filled with drudgery could now be spent sipping iced tea on the front porch, traveling, or playing golf. "Retirees" had earned this leisure time. But for many among the first generations of social security recipients reality fell far short of the mark: They barely scraped by.

For the most part, the parents of today's Baby Boomers had it better. Many, if not most, were able to retire to "the good life." Private pension plans had taken off, social security provided a higher payout than before, and real estate values soared. When they reached the mandatory retirement age of 65, they were set financially, so they simply stopped what they were doing for a living and "relaxed."

But the tide has begun to turn. While 65 is still the traditional retirement age, we're living much longer. Now, instead of a few years of retirement, we face the prospect of being healthy and living another 20 or more years. That's a lot of time—a lot of iced teas and golf. And it takes a lot of money to finance it. What happens when we either don't want to stop working, because we find work fulfilling (and still have much to offer), or simply cannot afford to stop working? And what about those of us who are entering retirement in our 50s, by choice or due to circumstances beyond our control? To further complicate matters, the full retirement age for social security is going up.

Reassessing Retirement

What happens is that society crafts a new system, taking what worked from the old one and adding it to the realities of today's lifestyles. A new definition of retirement has emerged. Where retirement once stood for the brief period between your work life and death, now it can also mean a new post-job career or business, part time work, volunteerism, or going back to school. "Retirement" certainly stands for a more active and diverse lifestyle than ever.

The march toward retirement is no longer a type of race or game, with age 65 as the goal or finish line. Rather, it is a life phase that begins at a different age for each person and is more like a new beginning or subtle shift that opens doors to vast new opportunities for a post-career life.

Recognizing things have changed—that your retirement will be vastly different from your parents'—is an essential first step toward making certain your future years are financially secure, whether you call that time "retirement" or something else. Planning how to pay for those years is what this book is all about.

Living and Working Longer

Today 65 is no longer "old." When social security was first implemented, Americans lived to an average age of 63 years. Now the average life span is 74.4 for a man and 79.8 for a woman. What's more, the average man who has survived to 65 can now expect to live until age 81.4; the average 65-year-old woman is likely to make it to 84.4. And according to the U.S. Census Bureau, Americans born at the beginning of the 21st century are expected to live almost 30 years longer than those born at the turn of the 20th century. And while logic would dictate that if we're living longer, we'll need to work longer to pay our way, be honest: Are you really thinking of retiring at 80? In fact, Americans are, on average, retiring earlier than ever before. According to the Ways and Means Committee of the U.S. House of Representatives, about 60% of workers retire by age 62, although not always voluntarily.

There are many factors contributing to this new idea of retirement. In addition to living longer and healthier lives (although we worry that at some point in the future we won't be), we're having children later in life than ever before, and we're more active.

Old thinking about retirement—and especially how to pay for it—simply won't work for everyone anymore. Unlike many current retirees, we can't assume that the house we own will increase tremendously in value over the years. On the other hand, the equity you realize when you do sell your home will likely be completely tax-free. Many companies are converting from defined-benefit pensions, which companies fully funded, to defined-contribution plans, which rely on employee contributions for at least some of the funding, or cash-balance accounts, which pay retirees a fixed monthly benefit based on their

Today, "retirement" stands for a more active and diverse lifestyle than ever before.

salary and length of service. And remember, we are looking at 20 to 30 years of retirement.

Which means one of two things:

1. **Either you'll need to inherit** or win a mountain of money to pay for a retirement that could stretch into decades; or
2. **You'll have to start thinking about retirement,** and planning for those years, in a different way.

The new retirement—or non-retirement—requires a new kind of plan, because a "worry-free" retirement doesn't necessarily mean a "work-free" retirement. While you might not be saving and planning for a traditional retirement, you will still need to save and plan for your future—whatever it holds. You might need to pay for your own school tuition, finance a new business, or supplement the income you'll generate from a part-time job. These are common life choices for today's retirees. Or maybe you'll try a straight leisure lifestyle for a few years, then return to work or start a business. Whatever you're going to do, you've got to get your financial house in order first.

Serious Planning a Must

Sadly, many of us seem gloomy about facing this fast-changing and potentially exciting future, especially after the stock market drop in 2000 and 2001 and plunge following the tragedies of September 11. Perhaps because of these financial uncertainties, many people are not saving and investing as they should.

According to the 2004 Retirement Confidence Survey conducted by the Employee Benefit Research Institute, fewer American workers were saving for retirement. After years of growth, the number of Americans workers who said they were saving for retirement dropped from 62% in 2003 to 58% in 2004. The survey stated that ". . . the aggregate level of worker confidence in having enough money to retire comfortably seems to remain unrelated to whatever economic conditions exist. . . . America appears to be a nation of optimists when it comes to retirement, but for some people the retirement dream may turn into a nightmare."

The reality is that the more you save now, the more options you'll have later. Even if you won't be able to stop working completely, by building a big nest egg now, you'll have to work less later. You still need to know the best places to put your money and how much risk you can afford to take with it. You have to figure out what you can expect from your pension plan at work and where social security fits in. It's crucial that you know how to protect yourself with insurance, what investment strategies work best, and how to make adjustments along the way. The one thing you can count on is that the rules of the game will change before you are ready or able to retire.

The good news is that you needn't despair. Your dream of a financially secure future is attainable, but how you make that dream a reality will be different from the way your parents got there.

Relax. Some helpful tools remain, and recent congressional action has made some even more attractive: The power of tax-deferred growth inside an individual retirement account (IRA), 401(k), or Keogh retirement plan is a fantastic force working in your favor. And the Roth IRA offers tax-free interest. Contrary to what you may have heard, social security will still be around and will provide payback for future retirees that's even higher than that of current retirees. The record number of dual-income couples today also will lead to retirement households with two full social security allowances and possibly two or more job-based pensions as well. Once you've determined both what you have and what you'll need, you can start thinking about how to fill the gap you'll probably find between the two.

Piecing Together Your Puzzle

Devising a plan for a financially worry-free future is like putting together a jigsaw puzzle that, once assembled, will give you a clear picture of financial self-sufficiency and security. Because lifestyles

> **Your dream of a secure future is attainable, but how you make that dream a reality will be different from the way your parents got there.**

are becoming so diverse, one person's puzzle will look quite different from another's.

Now is the time to ask yourself these critical financial questions:

■ **How much money will I really need** to maintain the lifestyle I want, and where will it come from?

■ **What can I do now** to make sure I'll have enough?

■ **What will social security provide?**

■ **How can I get started?**

■ **Do I really want to quit work altogether?** Can I afford to?

■ **What investment, tax, savings, credit,** and insurance strategies will help me put together the best worry-free plan?

■ **How can I keep medical costs** from wiping me out?

■ **When will it be financially safe** for me to retire?

You'll find the answers here, piece by piece. But keep in mind, there are no secret formulas or get-rich-quick schemes. No book, no matter how helpful, can plan and fund your future for you. A successful plan requires active participation on your part.

We'll help you bring your goals into focus, spell out your options and strategies, show you where you stand, and help jump-start your money-motor if it's stalled.

Overcoming Financial Worries

A litany of financial worries and complaints creates a mental barrier that keeps many of us from doing the kind of planning needed to get us where we want to go. Yet breaking through this wall of worries may be easier than you think. Many of the pieces of your worry-free retirement puzzle may already be in place; others can be added along the way. If a few are missing, don't panic—perhaps you can substitute something else. We'll show you how to shake off retirement worries such as these:

We worry that education costs for our kids and perhaps medical care for aging parents will crimp, if not obliterate, our ability to save. Couples are waiting longer to have children, so those expenses are pushed further into the critical retirement nest-egg-building years.

THE GOOD NEWS: We'll show you how to find the missing money in your household budget, reduce the cost of your debts, and get started on a savings program for retirement.

We worry that social security will do little for us and that the system will go broke.

THE GOOD NEWS: Despite all the dire talk in Washington about social security, it remains on firm footing until 2042. Even if social security goes broke then, there will still be enough tax revenue coming in to cover about 75% of benefits. We'll show you what you realistically will get from social security, what changes are in store, and how to make the most of it.

We worry because we have no idea what we'll really need to retire. How much money will it take? Where will it come from? Many of us take what amounts to a cross-your-fingers-and-hope approach.

THE GOOD NEWS: We'll show you how to accurately calculate your retirement-income needs and your available resources. Then we'll show you, step by step, how to go about filling any gap between the two.

We worry that inflation will erode our retirement savings—and it will. At a 4% annual inflation rate (that's higher than the rate's been for several years, but lower than it's been at other times), today's $1 will be worth only 52 cents in ten years. Few private pensions are indexed to inflation.

THE GOOD NEWS: We'll show you how to confront inflation to make certain you stay even or ahead.

We worry that we'll be overwhelmed by rising medical costs. Employers are cutting back on the amount of health insurance they provide to current employees and especially to retirees. Medicare will pick up no more than half of your total post-retirement medical costs, and Congress may restrict it even more as it works to cut federal spending.

THE GOOD NEWS: By knowing what to expect from medicare, what your employer's plan will or won't cover, and how supplemental health coverage can fill any gaps, you'll rest assured that health care costs won't threaten your retirement nest egg.

We worry that frequent job switches can make participating in a company pension impossible.

THE GOOD NEWS: That's less true today than it once was. We'll show you why—and how to get the most from employer-sponsored plans.

We worry that our goal of retiring early is only a pipe dream.

THE GOOD NEWS: We'll show you why even an early retirement is not out of the question if you make the right moves ahead of time.

It's never too early or too late to start planning for a worry-free retirement. Sure, earlier is better. But starting any time is still better than not starting at all—any financial decision you make before regular paychecks stop can be crucial.

The message here is that it can be done; you can take control and plan for a financially secure future regardless of where you stand right now.

Your best move to wipe away the worries is to take stock of where you stand, reconsider what retirement really means, compile your personal financial-freedom plan, and put that plan into action. By reading this book, you're already on your way.

Estimate How Much You'll Need

First things first: You have to know where you're going before you can plan how to get there. But peering into the future to arrange your finances for a worry-free retirement is tricky. Circumstances are always changing:

- **Your spouse** gets a higher-paying new job with new benefits.
- **Your investments** do well (or don't).
- **Your house** rises (or falls) in value.
- **Your company** merges and the pension plan changes.
- **College costs** buffet your bank book.
- **You go into business** for yourself.
- **Old Uncle Albert remembers** you kindly in his will.

Factors like these can complicate planning for your retirement but shouldn't deter you from beginning. To start building a realistic financial plan for retiring worry-free, start with five basic dynamics.

WHERE YOU STAND NOW. That includes your personal savings, pension plans, investments, and income prospects, as well as your debts and spending patterns.

HOW MUCH MONEY YOU'LL NEED TO RETIRE. We'll help you tote that tab right here.

WHERE THAT MONEY WILL COME FROM. We'll show you the range of possibilities and some typical case studies.

HOW MUCH TIME REMAINS UNTIL RETIREMENT. The strategy to achieve a worry-free retirement depends on the target date you've set and the progress you've made so far. Even fortysomethings who've procrastinated on their savings program have time to lay a solid foundation. You'll find that it's also possible to shoot for an early retirement with the right planning.

HOW MUCH RISK YOU ARE WILLING TO TAKE TO HELP YOUR NEST EGG GROW. When it comes to investing retirement money, risk is a balancing act. Take too little and your nest egg may not grow as fast as you'd like— or as needed. Take too much and you could find a crack in the egg that will be difficult to repair. The further away you are from retirement, the more risk you may be able to take; the shorter the time, the more risk you may *need* to take. Chapter 9 details the investment choices you have available, while Chapter 10 offers specific retirement investment strategies for putting the right balance into play.

Your Numbers Are Unique

Because so many variables play a role, everyone's retirement planning scorecard is different. The numbers you plug into your plan depend heavily on your age now, your projected retirement age, your income level, the benefits you and your spouse have at work, the lifestyle you have now, and the lifestyle you want to have in retirement. An employer pension, for example, may be the foundation of a financially secure retirement for some people but a minor contributor or nonexistent for others. A 401(k) retirement plan at work or a do-it-yourself, tax-favored individual retirement account (IRA) or Keogh plan is at the heart of some retirement plans. Perhaps a piece of real estate or a block of inherited stock will play a major role in yours. But one thing is certain: A secure retirement can be achieved only by understanding and managing the interactions among the five retirement-planning dynamics above. Your success in managing them from this point on will determine how financially worry-free your retirement becomes.

Start Here:
Figuring Your Future Income

This is the scary part, and it's important to confront it and conquer your fear at the outset. Figure that you'll need 80% of your preretirement income to maintain your lifestyle after the regular paychecks stop. Some people may be able to get by on 70% to 75%, but you should aim for the higher figure to be better assured of achieving your ideal retirement lifestyle.

That's not 80% of today's income. It's 80% of your income at the point you are ready to retire. In other words, that's future dollars.

Of course, you can't be sure what your income will be years down the road, but you can make an educated guess based on the two main influencing factors:

1. **The constant grind of inflation** will both boost your income and erode its purchasing power. Assuming a 4% annual inflation rate, something that costs $1,000 today will cost $1,480 in ten years and $1,800 in 15 years. At the same time, a $35,000 salary that increases in line with 4% annual inflation will reach $63,000 in a decade and a half.

2. **Job promotions may increase your income** even faster than the inflation rate between now and retirement. For example, if that $35,000 salary increases 3% annually over and above inflation (for a total of 7%), it will hit $96,600 in 15 years.

You can easily account for both cost-of-living increases and merit raises by using the Money Growth and Inflation Factors table on page 12.

Here's how it works: Say you have a current household income of $60,000 and plan to retire in 15 years. If you were retiring today on 80% of $60,000, you would need $48,000 a year to maintain your lifestyle. That's in today's dollars—dollars that will be worth considerably less 15 years from now.

For long-term-planning purposes, a good estimate is that inflation will average about 4% annually

Figure that you'll need 80% of your preretirement income to maintain your lifestyle after the regular paychecks stop.

MONEY GROWTH AND INFLATION FACTORS

Years to Retirement	4%	5%	6%	7%	8%	9%	10%	11%	12%
5	1.22	1.28	1.34	1.40	1.47	1.54	1.61	1.69	1.76
6	1.27	1.34	1.42	1.50	1.59	1.68	1.77	1.87	1.97
7	1.32	1.41	1.50	1.61	1.71	1.83	1.95	2.08	2.21
8	1.37	1.48	1.59	1.72	1.85	1.99	2.14	2.30	2.48
9	1.42	1.55	1.69	1.84	2.00	2.17	2.36	2.56	2.77
10	1.48	1.63	1.79	1.97	2.16	2.37	2.59	2.84	3.11
11	1.54	1.71	1.90	2.10	2.33	2.58	2.85	3.15	3.48
12	1.60	1.80	2.01	2.25	2.52	2.81	3.14	3.50	3.90
13	1.67	1.89	2.13	2.41	2.72	3.07	3.45	3.88	4.36
14	1.73	1.98	2.26	2.58	2.94	3.34	3.80	4.31	4.89
15	1.80	2.08	2.40	2.76	3.17	3.64	4.18	4.78	5.47
16	1.87	2.18	2.54	2.95	3.43	3.97	4.59	5.31	6.13
17	1.95	2.29	2.69	3.16	3.70	4.33	5.05	5.90	6.87
18	2.03	2.41	2.85	3.38	4.00	4.72	5.56	6.54	7.69
19	2.11	2.53	3.03	3.62	4.32	5.14	6.12	7.26	8.61
20	2.19	2.65	3.21	3.87	4.66	5.60	6.73	8.06	9.65
21	2.28	2.79	3.40	4.14	5.03	6.11	7.40	8.95	10.80
22	2.37	2.93	3.60	4.43	5.44	6.66	8.14	9.93	12.10
23	2.46	3.07	3.82	4.74	5.87	7.26	8.95	11.03	13.55
24	2.56	3.23	4.05	5.07	6.34	7.91	9.85	12.24	15.18
25	2.67	3.39	4.29	5.43	6.85	8.62	10.83	13.59	17.00
30	3.24	4.32	5.74	7.61	10.06	13.27	17.45	22.89	29.96

between now and the time you retire. (That's the figure the government uses to project the long-term effects of inflation on social security.) If you expect raises and promotions to boost your income beyond cost-of-living increases, you can estimate how much the raises will be on a percentage basis and add that to your inflation estimate.

Say you anticipate your salary increases will average 3% annually above the rate of inflation. (Raise or lower this figure, depending on your expectations.)

Add this figure to your inflation expectation for a total annual increase—7% in this example.

Now go to the table to quickly calculate the amount of income you'll be earning in 15 years. Find 15 in the left column, follow it over to 7%, and you'll see another number: 2.76. That's your multiplier.

Multiply $60,000 by 2.76 and—voila—you come up with nearly $165,600. That's what you will be making come retirement day.

Taking 80% of that as the postretirement income you'll need leaves a target annual retirement income of $132,480. That's what you can realistically expect to need to maintain your lifestyle.

Don't Panic!

Now you know why we say this is the scary part.

But the figure you come up with is not as bad as it first appears. For one thing, those are future, inflation-cheapened dollars. What's more, the same forces that make your needs grow will help your nest egg grow, too.

Social security, pension plans, IRAs, Keogh plans, 401(k) plans and your personal savings and investments can rise to meet your needs at retirement, with a little planning. Here's what the numbers look like for a two-income couple in their mid-40s who plan to retire in 22 years.

Planning Profile:
A Dual-Income Couple, Both 45 Years Old

These partners have a combined income today of $100,000 ($60,000 for one; $40,000 for the other) and expect their income to increase an average of 7% per year (including promotions and cost-of-living raises). That means their projected income in 22 years will be about $443,000. They'll need 80% of that, or $354,400, to maintain their lifestyle in retirement.

Eeeeooowm!

That figure sounds humongous, but look at how various pieces of a retirement-planning puzzle can fit together to make even that amount manageable. Consider some of the resources—shown on page 14—this dual-income couple will probably have.

CLOSING THE GAP

TWO-INCOME COUPLE; BOTH AGE 45
- Retiring in 22 years
- Current combined income: $100,000
- Inflation assumption: 4%
- Additional income gains: 3%
- Projected income at retirement: $443,000

Target retirement income

(80% of $443,000):	$ 354,400
– expected social security:	– 76,000
– expected pensions:	– 84,000
– past 401(k), IRA savings:	– 90,000

Remaining income gap:

current $	$ 44,000
future $	104,400

Total additional savings needed to produce steady stream of income to fill gap for 20 years, with nest egg earning 8%:

current $	$ 438,350
future $	1,039,000

Built-in inflation cushion raises needed savings to:

future $	$1,298,750 to $1,454,600

Monthly savings target now to reach retirement goal:

current $	$ 513 to $575
future $	rising 4% a year

First, there's social security—not one monthly check but two, because there are two wage earners. Together, the social security incomes could total about $76,000 a year in future-value dollars 22 years from now, according to Social Security Administration estimates that include annual benefit increases tied to inflation. (It seems like there's always talk in Washington of cutting back on those cost-of-living adjustments, or COLAs. It appears unlikely that there will be a significant cut, but this is an area that you must watch carefully.) Social security checks narrow the retirement-income gap for this couple to about $278,400. (Chapter 5 will tell you more about what to expect from social security.)

Pension plans will provide another chunk of income, possibly even larger than social security. Because not all workers are covered by a defined-benefit pension plan (the kind that promises a set monthly benefit), we'll be conservative and say that only one spouse has a pension coming. But, because many future retirees will draw pensions from two or more firms, we'll say this individual will receive two pensions—one from a current employer, and a smaller one from a previous employer. Together they promise to produce about $84,000 per year in postretirement dollars. (Pensions are discussed in detail in Chapter 4.)

The somewhat mountainous target income for this two-income couple has now been whittled down to a more climbable hill of $194,400 (in future dollars). But we're not finished yet. If spouse #2 has been participating in a 401(k) retirement plan at work, another puzzle piece has fallen into place. (Chapter 4 discusses 401(k)s.) By the time retirement arrives, income from the assets already tucked away in that plan could lop another $55,000 off the needed annual income figure, slicing it to about $139,400.

Things are looking up. Since this couple also have managed to contribute regularly to their IRAs and other savings and investments earmarked for retirement, they can count on another $35,000 of annual income from what they already have in these sources after retirement. (Chapter 7 is devoted to IRAs.)

Tote up all the available sources of retirement income and you see that the remaining gap has been reduced to $104,400 in future money. In today's dollars, that would be around $44,000.

Hey, that's doable! In order to draw $44,000 a year for 20 years after retirement, the couple needs to start with about $438,350 of current dollars, assuming the money earns 8% annually. (We'll show you how to make such a calculation in the next section.) In future

HOW BIG A NEST EGG YOU'LL NEED TO COVER AN INCOME GAP

Years in Retirement	Savings Needed to Permit Monthly Withdrawals of $1,000 at Each Rate of Return							
	5%	6%	7%	8%	9%	10%	12%	14%
5	$ 52,990	$ 51,730	$ 50,500	$ 49,320	$ 48,170	$ 47,060	$ 44,960	$ 42,980
10	94,280	90,070	86,130	82,420	78,940	75,670	69,700	64,410
15	126,460	118,500	111,250	104,640	98,590	93,060	83,320	75,090
20	151,530	139,580	128,980	119,550	111,140	103,620	90,820	80,420
25	171,060	155,210	141,490	129,560	119,160	110,050	94,950	83,070
30	186,280	166,790	150,310	136,280	124,280	113,950	97,220	84,400

dollars, this couple should aim to sock away additional savings—in their IRAs, 401(k) account, and other savings and investments designated for retirement—of $1,039,000 to produce $104,400 annually for 20 years starting 22 years from now.

But there's one more hurdle to jump—the continued effects of inflation. To play it safe, the couple needs to boost their future savings target by 25% to 40%. That would increase their target from $1,039,000 to between roughly $1,298,750 and $1,454,600 in future dollars.

That's a rough estimate, because the actual amount depends on what portion of the couple's retirement income is provided by social security, which automatically rises with inflation, as well as on the actual inflation rate and the number of years they'll draw on their nest egg. The middle of the range—adding 33%—figures on about a 20-year retirement and 4% inflation. If longevity runs in their family and their retirement stretches 25 to 30 years or more, they should figure on the high side.

What does that mean for our hypothetical couple today? Basically, if they can manage to set aside $513 to $575 a month in IRAs, Keoghs, 401(k)s, and so on, and they increase that amount each year to match inflation, they'll reach their retirement-income goal, assuming that the money grows at an average annual rate of 10%. That's a little less than 7% of this couple's monthly pay.

How Long You— and Your Nest Egg—Will Last

An essential element of knowing how much money you'll need when you retire is something you can't know with certainty: the date of your ultimate demise. Will your retirement last five years? Or 30?

The best you can do is bank on what we do know: that healthier lifestyles and better medical care are helping Americans live longer. The average woman retiring today at 65 is expected to live another 19.4 years; men average 16.4 years. Life expectancy is on the rise, so today's 40-to-55-year-old crowd can expect to survive even longer than today's retirees. Retirements that last 25 to 30 years or longer will become more and more common.

What's more, since many people retire at a young age, some of them will spend nearly as many years in retirement as they did working.

Just how big a nest egg do you need at retirement to generate the income that isn't covered by social security, pensions, or other sources? How long will that chunk of retirement money hold out if you start hacking into it each month? The table on the opposite page lets you do some quick figuring. Here's how it works:

Say you estimate you'll need $21,000 per year ($1,750 per month) for 20 years and you think the nest egg will continue to earn 9% annually. The point where the 9% and 20-year columns intersect is $111,140. That's the amount of money needed to produce $1,000 per month for 20 years.

Since your monthly requirement is 1.75 times that amount ($1,750 ÷ $1,000), multiply $111,140 by 1.75 and you find a total nest-egg requirement of $194,495— the amount you need to start with to produce $1,750 per month for 20 years if the money earns 9% annually. However, you still need to account for inflation over those 20 years, as the value of that $1,750 diminishes. A safe rule of thumb is to add 25% to 40% to the total nest egg as an inflation cushion. In this example, that would bring the total to between $243,119 and $272,293.

The same dynamics that make your future income requirements look so huge will also help your investments grow.

And inflation isn't the only thing that can affect how much you'll need. If your investments are hit by a declining market—as just about all retirees were beginning with the market decline in 2000 and intensified following the events of September 11, 2001—you may find your nest egg is no longer enough to last as long as you had planned. Of course, the reverse is also true: If we enjoy another boom market as we did through most of the '90s (which for many helped lessen the effects of the market tumble), you might find yourself with a bigger—possibly much bigger—nest egg. That uncertainty concerning the market's performance is one of the reasons you should be conservative in deciding the average annual earnings percentage of your investments.

Still, all things being equal, in the early years of your retirement, your nest egg's growth should more than offset your withdrawals. But as you take out more and more each year to keep up with inflation, you will begin to eat into your principal and ultimately deplete it.

Calculating Money Growth

Some of the best panic-busting news about how much money you'll need is this: The same dynamics that make your future income requirements look so huge will also help your retirement savings and investments grow.

To see how, go back to the Money Growth and Inflation Factors table on page 12. Assume you let $25,000 grow at 10% for 15 years. Find the number where the 10% and 15-years columns intersect (4.18). Multiply $25,000 by 4.18, and you get $104,500.

A $40,000 nest egg growing at 8% for 20 years would produce $186,400. At 12% growth you'd wind up with a whopping $386,000.

These figures don't allow for taxes that you might have to pay on earnings. If the money is inside a tax-sheltered retirement plan such as an IRA or Keogh, you needn't take taxes into account. If the nest egg is taxable, however, lop two to three percentage points off your earnings assumption to make a rough approximation of how taxes will gobble up a portion of earnings. Since the money to pay those taxes may come out of a different pocket, however, it may not have a direct impact on the size of your nest egg. Also, note that the retirement-income needs projected in this chapter are for taxable income. To the extent that your retirement needs will be met by income that has already been taxed (such as the principal portion of savings or investments made outside of a traditional IRA or other tax-deferred plan, or inside a Roth IRA, where your contributions are initially taxed but the earnings grow tax-free) or is only partially taxable (such as social security benefits), the calculations here actually overstate your need.

Toting Your Own Retirement Tab

The Worry-Free Retirement Worksheet on pages 20 through 23 will help you prepare a personalized what-will-I-need-and-where-will-it-come-from analysis. (You can also go to our Web site, www.kiplinger.com, and use the retirement-planning calculator there. It's a little different from the one in this book, but you should get satisfactory results if you use it instead of the one shown here.) To get the clearest picture of your financial future, you'll need to gather some current numbers on your income, savings, investments, pensions, and social security. By plugging those numbers into the worksheet, you can estimate the income you'll need at retirement, the amount you can expect from various sources, the remaining gap to be filled, and the retirement savings you'll need to fill that gap.

You begin by pinpointing your retirement-income needs in future dollars—as discussed earlier in this chapter. Then figure out how much will be provided by social security and any employer-provided pension. (Chapters 4 and 5 tell you what you need to know about pensions and social security and how to get estimates of your benefits.)

continued on page 24

WORRY-FREE RETIREMENT WORKSHEET

HOW MUCH WILL YOU NEED TO RETIRE IN STYLE?
A. First, decide what portion of current income (yours and your spouse's, if you're married) you want to replace in retirement (80% is recommended).

$_____ x _____% = $ _____
  current income   target retirement income in today's $

B. Now adjust that figure to account for 4% inflation between now and the time you call it quits. Use an inflation factor from the table below. If you plan to retire in 20 years, for example, multiply your target income by 2.19. That tells you how many future dollars you'll need to reach your goal.

Years to Retirement	10	15	20	25
Inflation factor	1.48	1.80	2.19	2.67

$_____ x _____ = $ _____
  target income in today's $ inflation factor   target retirement income in future $

WHAT SHOULD YOU EXPECT FROM SOCIAL SECURITY AND YOUR PENSION?
C. Find what part of your need will be met by social security and any defined-benefit pension. Chapters 4 and 5 tell you where to get estimates of those benefits.
■ Projected social security benefit (today's $)　　　　　$ _____
■ Projected defined-benefit pension benefit (today's $)　　$ _____

D. Adjust those amounts for inflation between now and when you retire, using the same inflation factor from the table above.

$_____ x _____ = $ _____
  social security (today's $)   inflation factor   social security (future $)

$_____ x _____ = $ _____
  pension (today's $)   inflation factor   pension (future $)

CALCULATE YOUR PRELIMINARY RETIREMENT GAP
E. Subtract what you can expect from social security and company defined-benefit pensions from your target retirement income (future dollars) to see how much must be provided from other sources.

Target retirement income (future $)　　　　　　　　$_____
– Social security and pension benefits (future $)　　–_____
= Preliminary Retirement Gap (future $)　　　　　　$_____

F. Now divide by 12 to find the preliminary monthly shortfall.

$ _____ ÷ 12 = $ _____
   preliminary retirement gap   *preliminary monthly shortfall*

HOW BIG A NEST EGG WILL YOU NEED?

G. Use the table below (an abbreviation of the one presented earlier in this chapter) to determine the size of the nest egg you'll need to generate enough income to cover the monthly shortfall determined above. The table shows how much you need to produce $1,000 of monthly income over various time periods, assuming different investment returns. Assume, for example, that your monthly shortfall is $2,700 and you want the nest egg to last 25 years. If you expect to earn a 10% annual return, find where the 10% and the 25-year columns meet. Now multiply the number there ($110,050) by 2.7 (your shortfall divided by 1,000). The result, approximately $297,000, is the size of the nest egg you need when you retire.

AMOUNT NEEDED TO GENERATE $1,000 PER MONTH

Years in Retirement	Annual Rate of Return		
	6%	8%	10%
10	$ 90,073	$ 82,420	$ 75,670
15	118,504	104,640	93,060
20	139,581	119,550	103,620
25	155,207	129,560	110,050

$ _____ x _____ = $ _____
   amount from table   *monthly shortfall divided by 1,000*   *preliminary nest-egg goal*

H. Now you need to adjust that preliminary nest-egg goal (which assumes you'll need the same amount month after month) to account for the reality that inflation will not stop when your paychecks do. As the cost of living rises, you'll need to draw more from your nest egg each year to maintain your lifestyle. How much you need to increase the target depends on how long you will live in retirement and what happens with inflation. Another variable is the percentage of your retirement income that is provided by social security (which rises each year to keep up with inflation). For a rough estimate, increase the preliminary nest-egg goal by 25% (multiply by 1.25) if you expect a retirement of less than 20 years; by 30% (multiply by 1.3) for a 20-year retirement; and by 40% (multiply by 1.4) for a longer retirement.

$ _____ x _____ = $ _____
   preliminary nest-egg goal   *inflation protection factor*   *inflation-adjusted nest-egg goal*

continued on next page

WORRY-FREE RETIREMENT WORKSHEET (continued)

HOW CAN YOU FILL THE GAP?

I. Current savings. Don't let that figure scare you. You probably have already made a start—perhaps a good start—toward that goal. Add what you (and your spouse, if you're married) have currently set aside for retirement in 401(k) plans, profit-sharing or any other company-sponsored defined-contribution plan, individual retirement accounts, Keogh plans, and any other savings you've earmarked for your retirement.

$ _____
current retirement savings

Now adjust that figure for expected growth between now and when you retire. You can choose a multiplier from the abbreviated table below or see the Money Growth and Inflation Factors table on page 12. If you plan to retire in 25 years and expect your retirement investments to grow at a rate of 10% a year, for example, you would multiply the current total by 10.83.

	Expected Annual Return		
Years to Retirement	**8%**	**10%**	**12%**
10	2.16	2.59	3.11
15	3.17	4.18	5.47
20	4.66	6.73	9.65
25	6.85	10.83	17.00

$_____ × _____ = $_____
current retirement savings *growth factor* *projected future value of current savings*

Subtract that amount from the inflation-adjusted nest-egg total to see how much you still need to save.

$_____ − _____ = $_____
inflation-adjusted nest egg *future value of current savings* *adjusted nest-egg goal*

J. Don't forget the house. If you own a house and plan to use the equity in it to help finance your retirement, you're further along to your goal. To estimate the value of your home when you retire, multiply its current value by a factor in the inflation-adjustment table in the first step of this worksheet. That will give you a conservative estimate that assumes your home's value will rise 4% a year.

$_____ × _____ = $_____
current home value *inflation factor* *estimated home value at retirement*

Now subtract any mortgage you expect to still owe at retirement. If you file a single return and you've lived in the house for at least two of the last five years, all equity up to $250,000 is tax-free! For those who file a joint return, the tax-free amount doubles. If there is any tax due, subtract it and any part of proceeds of the sale you'll use for the down payment on a retirement home. Add whatever is remaining to your nest egg.

$\underline{\hspace{4cm}}$ − $\underline{\hspace{4cm}}$ = $ $\underline{\hspace{4cm}}$

estimated home value at retirement   remaining mortgage, tax on profit,   home's contribution to nest egg

                                                & down payment for retirement home

K. What you need to save. To see how much you need to save between now and a worry-free retirement, subtract your home's contribution to the nest egg from the adjusted nest-egg figure determined in (I).

$\underline{\hspace{4cm}}$ − $\underline{\hspace{4cm}}$ = $ $\underline{\hspace{4cm}}$

adjusted nest egg   home's contribution   NEST-EGG GOAL

CALCULATE YOUR SAVINGS TARGET

Don't panic. Remember, that's future dollars, and you've got a long time to build that nest egg. To see how much you need to start saving each month to reach that goal, find the factor in the table below where the number of years to your retirement intersects with the annual return you expect to earn on your future retirement savings. Assume, for example, that the worksheet shows that you need to have an extra $275,000 saved by retirement in 20 years. If you expect that your investments will return an average of 10% a year, multiply your nest-egg goal by 0.001381. The result—$380—tells you how much needs to be saved each month to build your nest egg for a worry-free retirement. It may not all have to come out of your pocket, either: It includes future employer contributions to a 401(k) or profit-sharing plan.

Years to Retirement	Annual Compounded Rate of Return						
	6%	7%	8%	9%	10%	12%	15%
5	0.014322	0.013967	0.013621	0.013285	0.012958	0.012330	0.011449
10	0.006125	0.005813	0.005516	0.005233	0.004964	0.004464	0.003802
15	0.003469	0.003196	0.002943	0.002708	0.002490	0.002101	0.001622
20	0.002195	0.001959	0.001746	0.001554	0.001381	0.001087	0.000754
25	0.001471	0.001270	0.001093	0.000939	0.000804	0.000587	0.000363

$\underline{\hspace{4cm}}$ × $\underline{\hspace{4cm}}$ = $ $\underline{\hspace{4cm}}$

final nest-egg goal   savings-target factor   MONTHLY SAVINGS NEEDED
TO MEET GOAL

Once you know how much of your monthly income needs to come from other sources, you can figure just how big of a nest egg you need to produce that cash flow during your retirement years.

The first step toward that goal is toting up what you already have saved for retirement, in 401(k) plans at work, variable annuities, IRAs, and Keoghs. This also includes any other savings you have specifically earmarked for retirement. Figure what today's total will be worth when you retire—assuming reasonable investment gains—and subtract that from your nest-egg need. If you own a home and plan to use it as a source of retirement income, by selling it or borrowing against its value, you're further along the road to a worry-free retirement. Chapter 9 has more on how home equity fits into a retirement plan.

MONTHLY SAVINGS NEEDED TO REACH $200,000	
Years to Retirement	**$ per Month***
5	$2,631
10	1,026
15	525
20	297
25	177
30	108
	* Assumes 9% annual return

Filling the Retirement-Income Gap

Seeing the size of the remaining income gap can be disheartening. But your ace in the hole is the savings and investments you sock away for your retirement from this point forward. Remember, the calculations so far are based primarily on the growth of what you've already accumulated for retirement, along with anticipated pension and social security growth. They don't include those all-important future savings, which will make the real difference in the quality of your postretirement years. The options include IRAs, 401(k) plans, Keogh plans, and your own savings and investments such as stocks, bonds, mutual funds, and certificates of deposit (CDs).

The alternatives to saving more for retirement are certainly less attractive, and they should provide incentive enough to get your program going:

- **Work beyond your hoped-for retirement age.**
- **Lower your postretirement living standard.**
- **Stake your retirement dreams on high-risk investments in hopes of higher returns.**

Saving more is the surest route to filling a gap and achieving a worry-free retirement. Some of the most dedicated post-40 retirement savers are putting away 20% to 25% of their salaries. That's impressive and even scary if your savings rate seems paltry by comparison.

But saving a relatively small dollar amount regularly can put you in good shape if the power of compounding has two decades or so to work in your favor. For example, suppose you want to accumulate $250,000 on top of what you've already put away. You have 20 years to go, and you think you can earn an average 10% on your investments. You can reach your goal by putting aside just $328 per month in the investment account you've earmarked for retirement. The worksheet includes a section that pinpoints the monthly savings needed to meet your nest-egg goal.

As a rule of thumb, aim to save 15% of your after-tax income from now on; a bit less will do if you already have a head start on your nest egg. Remember that you may get some help: The 15% figure includes any employer contributions to your retirement account.

If you can't meet that 15% goal now, you may be able to exceed it as you get older and other financial demands—such as putting children through college—diminish. The key is to start saving what you can now.

The Power of Compounding: Big Gun in Your Corner

The sooner you get going, the better. Why? One word says it: compounding. When you invest money and reinvest the earnings so that they feed on themselves, the money grows faster than you might imagine. How fast? The most dramatic illustration (even if it's not terribly realistic) is the story of doubling a penny.

Start with one penny and double your investment each year. How long will it take that penny to become $10 million? A hundred years? A thousand? (Here's a hint: After 14 years, you're already up to $164!)

The answer is . . . drum roll, please . . . 30 years. Yep. By the 30th year you will have reached $10.7 million.

Of course, no investment can provide a 100% return on your money every year. But the same basic wizardry applies even on much more modest returns of 6%, 8%, or 10% annually. The compounding effect makes money work hard for you—even if you invest a level amount, or start with a single sum and never add another penny. But it works hardest if you give it time.

For example, if you invest $100 per month for 30 years, earning 5% annually, your total will be $83,570 (not subtracting any taxes). That includes $36,000 of principal you invested, plus $47,570 in earnings on that money. If you invest that $100 per month at 10% annually, your total in 30 years will be $227,930. That's $191,930 of earnings—four times the earnings at a 5% rate of return. The difference is due mainly to the money-boosting effect of compound interest—a kind of financial snowball that grows ever larger and faster as it rolls toward your retirement date

Say you're aiming for a nest egg of $200,000 to cover an anticipated retirement-income gap in 25 years. Assuming a 9% annual return, you'll have to stash away about $53,100 of the hard-earned money you saved, plus $146,900 in compounded earnings that the money generated on its own at 9% annually. The longer the power of compounding has to work in your favor, the less you'll need to save monthly to reach your retirement goals.

But what if you had only ten years to reach your $200,000 goal, again assuming a 9% annual return? In that case, you would have to save $1,026 per month in order to reach your goal. In the end you'll have contributed $123,000 of the total, with compounded earnings accounting for the rest.

The Benefits of Regular Saving

If starting as early as possible is top priority in creating your worry-free retirement savings plan, then investing regularly runs a close second. No matter when you start, if you can manage to keep it up, you'll find yourself well on your way toward completing your retirement-income puzzle.

The table below illustrates how rapidly money grows through the combination of regular saving and the powder-keg power of compound interest. For example, saving $200 per month for 20 years at a 5% annual return produces $82,560. Up the return rate to 10% and the result soars to $153,140. And remember, over those 20 years that $200 will become easier and easier to save or—better yet—you're likely to steadily hike the amount you're setting aside to guarantee your worry-free retirement.

HOW REGULAR SAVINGS WILL GROW

You invest $200 per month for:

| Years | At This Annual Growth Rate | | | |
	5%	8%	10%	12%
5	$ 13,660	$ 14,800	$ 15,620	$ 16,500
10	31,180	36,840	41,320	46,460
15	53,680	69,660	83,580	100,920
20	82,560	118,580	153,140	199,820
25	119,600	191,480	267,580	379,520

Manage Your Spending and Debts

Now that you have an idea of how much money you'll need for a worry-free retirement, you can begin searching for answers to the eternal question. No, not the meaning of life. The question here is: Where the heck am I going to find the money for this personal retirement savings plan?

Today's acute financial pressures, from high health-care and tuition costs to the steady grind of inflation and taxes, make it difficult to put away money for retirement. Single people, one-income couples, and dual-income couples all face the same retirement-savings conundrum: Before you can put away money, you have to find some money to put away, and that's where the best of intentions run awry.

There is a solution to this retirement riddle. Locating money requires a three-pronged attack:

1. Getting a grip on where your money is going

2. Getting serious about saving

3. Using debt sensibly

It's Not What You Earn, It's What You Save

Do you regularly find yourself in a cash crunch just before payday? If so, it's time to embrace the "B" word. You need a budget to find the missing money that is somehow eluding your grasp. After all, it's not what you earn that will guarantee a comfortable retirement, but rather what you are able to save.

All you need to track your spending is a notebook, ledger pad, pocket calculator, and a sharp pencil.

The first step is to pinpoint where your money goes now. And that means keeping records. You may think the records you already keep are enough. Check stubs, receipts, and charge-account statements do paint the big picture, documenting rent or mortgage, utilities, car payments, furniture, and other major purchases. But the clues you really need are smaller. What about your pocket money? How did you spend those $100 withdrawals from the automated-teller machines? What were the department-store and credit card charges for? What do these sums tell you about your spending?

If you don't really know, it's because you don't accurately keep track. Yet doing so is surprisingly easy and will help immeasurably as you begin or accelerate your plan to put money away regularly for retirement. By keeping track of your outgo you'll be able to analyze spending patterns and stick to a realistic budget that includes saving for your worry-free retirement. Preparing a meaningful budget (as opposed to a wishful one) depends largely on this first step: accurate records.

You don't need a computer for this, just some simple materials. First, a daily expense log—a notebook small enough to fit in your pocket or purse works fine. Second, a simple ledger book or pad with one wide column on the left and at least six narrower columns ruled for entering figures. Add a pocket calculator and a sharp pencil and you're ready to start hunting the missing money.

You'll need to set up expense categories. They should be narrow rather than broad because the purpose is to develop a detailed picture of monthly spending. Catchall categories like "household expenses" aren't useful. You want to discover what those household expenses consist of—groceries, furnishings, maintenance, maid service, gardening supplies, and the like. You can consolidate later.

On the first ledger sheet, list spending categories down the left-hand column. Every family's spending habits will vary to some degree, but many categories are common to all households. Use the money-tracking worksheets on pages 34–35 and 36–37 to get going, adding as many categories as you want. Each column of figures will represent one month's spending, so label them accordingly.

Consider Retirement Savings a Fixed Monthly Expense

Don't forget to set up a monthly expense category for regular retirement savings. After all, the goal here is to track down and lasso some savable funds. Consider your personal retirement savings a fixed expense—shoot for 15% of your net income if you can swing it. You may need to start small and build toward that goal. But the nearer you are to retirement (and the longer you've procrastinated about saving for it), the higher the percentage of income you should save. Think of it as paying yourself first.

Fixed expenses—those that change little or not at all each month—will be recorded directly into the ledger. You can do the same with variable expenses that are paid in one monthly sum (utilities, for instance). Use the daily journal to list out-of-pocket expenses. Label a page for each category of expenses and record each outlay under the appropriate category. This means every purchase, from clothing and groceries to furniture and pine-bark mulch—each movie or dinner, all gas, oil and other auto expenses, haircuts and dry cleaning, books, compact disks, postage stamps, magazine and newspaper subscriptions, and so on.

Each evening, jot down the day's expenses while they're still fresh in your mind. Receipts can help jog your memory, but remember to separate the expenses into categories. The supermarket receipt, for example, may reflect not only groceries but also lawn chairs and medicine.

At month's end, sit down with your journal and checkbook. First, total the outlays for each category in your journal. Then assign each check you've written to one or more categories, using credit card statements and receipts as reminders. Finally, combine the journal and checkbook numbers, and record the month's total spending by category in your ledger. Remember, a $200 check to MasterCard tells you nothing. If at all possible (and it may not be, if you're simply paying off a large outstanding balance), break it down into $112 for clothing, $36 for yard supplies, and $52 for that fancy dinner out. This may sound intimidating but should take less than 30 minutes a month.

You now have an accurate picture of one month's spending. It's early yet for analysis, but if outgo exceeds income, zero in on the discretionary spending—clothing, entertainment, gifts. What can you cut back or eliminate next month?

To gain a fuller understanding of your spending patterns, you need a longer perspective. So repeat the process. Three months is good; six months is better because your outlays will fluctuate from month to month. Some fixed expenses are spaced over long intervals—insurance premiums, taxes, and car-registration fees, to name a few. Then come surprise expenses, such as medical bills and car repairs. All of these are as much a part of your overall spending profile as utilities and mortgage payments are. They just don't occur as often.

Some Recordkeeping Nuts and Bolts

For this exercise, "income" is anything used to pay expenses and could include bonuses, investment gains, gifts, loans, or an inheritance. If you spent it, it had to come from somewhere. Record as income savings withdrawn to pay expenses, and classify as an expense money put into savings.

SALARY. It's simpler to include only your take-home pay. That way you can skip expense categories for taxes, health insurance, and other deductions from your paycheck. A self-employed person would record gross income and all expenses.

ACCURACY. You want to be accurate, not fanatical. Amounts need not add up to the penny, and if you forget an outlay, don't get suicidal. Aim for 98% accuracy—for $2,500 in monthly expenses to match $2,500 in income, plus or minus $50. Round off subtotals and totals to the nearest dollar. Dropping the extra cents will make the numbers easier to analyze later.

CONTINUITY. This simple expense-tracking system is built on what accountants call the cash method of accounting—income and expenses are recorded when they are received and paid, not when they come due. So if you defer one regular monthly expense into the next month, record it in the month it was actually paid. Likewise, if you pay off a credit card bill in installments, record only the amount paid each month. We'll show you how to reduce those credit card costs later in this chapter.

What It All Means for Your Retirement Plan

After a few months of record keeping, you'll know within a few dollars how much you spent and on what. If you stick with it, keeping track of spending will become second nature, and so will your new expense category earmarked for retirement savings.

You will develop a gut feeling about where the money goes each month and the best places you can nab even more dollars for your retirement nest egg. This sounds simplistic, and it is. But if you have chronic problems saving money for retirement, a realistic idea of your spending and saving may be just what you need to put your program on track. Following each dollar builds discipline that will translate into a more financially secure retirement.

After three to six months of recording monthly expenses, your ledger page will have become a spreadsheet, which is a mathematical model of your finances over time. You can follow rows across the page to see how particular categories of spending change over time. You can calculate average amounts for variable expenses—in effect, turning them into fixed expenses, which are much easier to use for planning your finances.

A MONTH-TO-MONTH BUDGET WORKSHEET

Month _____

Income

Take-home pay $ _____

Other _____

Total $ _____

Fixed Expenditures	Projected	Actual	(+) or (-)
Mortgage or rent	$ _____	$ _____	$ _____
Property taxes			
Income and social security taxes			
not withheld by employer			
Alimony, child support			
Installment and			
credit card payments			
Insurance:			
auto			
homeowners			
life			
health and other			
Savings and investments:			
emergency fund			
investment fund			
vacation fund			
other			
Subtotal, Fixed Expenditures	$ _____	$ _____	$ _____

At this point a personal computer, if you have one, can become a helpful tool. With a simple spreadsheet program, like the one in Microsoft Works, or one of the popular off-the-shelf money management programs, such as *Quicken* or *Microsoft Money*, you can plug

Variable Expenditures	Projected	Actual	(+) or (-)
Food	$ _____	$ _____	$ _____
Utilities:			
gas or oil	_____	_____	_____
electricity	_____	_____	_____
telephone	_____	_____	_____
water and sewer	_____	_____	_____
Home maintenance, furnishing, and improvement	_____	_____	_____
Automobile:			
gas and oil	_____	_____	_____
repairs	_____	_____	_____
Public transportation	_____	_____	_____
Day care	_____	_____	_____
Pocket money:			
hers	_____	_____	_____
his	_____	_____	_____
kids'	_____	_____	_____
Clothing (including dry cleaning):			
hers	_____	_____	_____
his	_____	_____	_____
kids'	_____	_____	_____
Personal care (haircuts, gym membership, etc.)	_____	_____	_____
Medical and dental bills not covered by insurance	_____	_____	_____
Educational expenses	_____	_____	_____
Entertainment, recreation, gifts	_____	_____	_____
Charitable contributions	_____	_____	_____
Miscellaneous	_____	_____	_____
Subtotal, Variable Expenditures	_____	_____	_____
Subtotal, Fixed Expenditures	_____	_____	_____
Total	$ _____	$ _____	$ _____

your numbers into the program and ask "what if" questions, instantly manipulating income, spending and saving categories to analyze different approaches. You can do the same with a paper and pencil, of course, but a computer makes it a breeze.

continued on page 38

WHERE YOUR MONEY IS

NET WORTH

Assets

	Amount
Checking account	$ _____
Savings accounts	_____
Savings certificates	_____
Savings bonds	_____
Market value of home/apartment	_____
Market value of other real estate	_____
Cash value of life insurance	_____
Surrender value of annuities	_____
Equity in pension or profit-sharing plans	_____
IRA and Keogh plans	_____
Market value of:	
stocks	_____
bonds	_____
mutual funds	_____
Other investments	_____
(including collectibles	
and precious metals)	_____
Current value of:	
automobiles	_____
household furnishings and appliances	_____
furs and jewelry	_____
Loans receivable	_____
Other assets	_____
Total Assets	$ _____

Liabilities

	Amount
Current bills	$ _____
Mortgage balance	_____
Credit card balance	_____
Auto loans	_____
Student loans	_____
Check-overdraft line of credit	_____
Home-equity loan	_____
Margin loan	_____
Other debts	_____
Total Liabilities	$ _____
Current Net Worth (assets minus liabilities)	$ _____

CASH FLOW

Income	Annual Amount	
Take-home pay	$	_____
Bonuses		_____
Self-employment income		_____
Net income from rental properties		_____
Interest		_____
Dividends		_____
Other (specify)		_____
Total Income	$	_____

Outgo

Mortgage or rent	$	_____
Property taxes		_____
Income and social security taxes not withheld by employer		_____
Alimony, child support		_____
Installment and credit card payments		_____
Insurance:		
auto		_____
homeowners		_____
life		_____
health and other		_____
food		_____
utilities		_____
Furnishings and home improvements		_____
Transportation (gas, repairs, commuting)		_____
Day care		_____
Pocket money		_____
Clothing and personal care		_____
Medical and dental bills not covered by insurance		_____
Educational		_____
Expense		_____
Entertainment, recreation, vacations, gifts		_____
Contributions		_____
Miscellaneous		_____
Total Outgo	$	_____
Surplus or Deficit (income minus outgo)	$	_____

Automating your savings program could be the single most productive action you can take toward reaching your goal.

As you play the "what if" game, you'll find yourself setting goals and building the framework of a realistic retirement-savings plan that will work wonders for you in the years ahead.

Get Serious about Saving

With a firmer fix on where your money is going and how much of it might be diverted to savings, you can get serious about building your retirement nest egg. Once you're under way it gets easier, and you'll get better at it, too. Keep pressing. Your goal now is to live not only within your means but beneath them. Here are a few tips and tricks that will help you get serious and stay serious about saving money for retirement.

Automate Your Savings Program

This may be the single most productive action you can take toward ensuring you'll have enough money for retirement. You can bootstrap your way toward a bigger retirement nest egg by establishing an automatic savings plan that sets aside a fixed amount of money on a regular (probably monthly) basis. Don't underestimate the power of this simple strategy. Sure, anyone could do this on his or her own by simply writing a check each month. But it takes discipline to keep it going year after year, and that's where many savers come up short.

Savings institutions offer these "pay-yourself-first" plans, as do the major mutual fund groups. They'll pluck the amount you specify directly out of your checking account on the day you choose, automatically. Just sign up and select the amount. Another powerful version of this saving method is your company's 401(k) retirement plan, if it has one, through which money is deducted from your paycheck and squirreled away in a special tax-favored account.

Consider a single 42-year-old angling for an early retirement at age 62. She's making $40,000 now. To ensure the success of her retirement-income target, she wants to have a $350,000 cushion by retirement day. So she signs up for the automatic-investment plan offered by a top-performing equity mutual fund that has averaged annual returns of 10% for the past 20 years. (Funds often waive initial-investment minimums if you sign up for automatic plans, so not having a large enough amount to start is no excuse.) If the fund continues to post the same 10% average annual gain for the next 20 years, this self-employed woman will need to systematically invest $457 per month in order to reach her $350,000 goal.

If $457 a month seems out of reach, don't throw up your hands in despair. That $350,000 goal can also be reached through monthly savings deposits that start much smaller and grow each year along with income. If our worker expects 7% annual increases in salary and plans to boost her savings amount by 7% each year, for example, deposits during the first year could be a more modest $225 a month. She'd hike the amount by 7% the next year, saving $241 each month. Another 7% boost for year three raises the deposits to $258 a month. She'd continue to raise her savings each year along with her salary during the 20 years until retirement. At that point, her account would hold $349,400.

Chapter 10 offers more details on putting an "autopilot" strategy to work in your financial plan for retirement.

Be Discerning on Discretionary Buys

Scrap one major discretionary outlay per year and put the money toward retirement. When you don't buy a new video camera, cancel your tennis-club membership (try the free public courts), or give up a winter trip to the Caribbean, the money you save now will be worth thousands more down the road. If you smoke, the best thing you can do for your bank account, not to mention your health, is quit and use that money fruitfully. That's exactly what a couple in Lake Placid, N.Y., did. They cut back on cigarettes and are adding the $69-a-month savings to their mortgage payment. Once their home loan is paid off—11 years early—cash that used to go to the mortgage company will be sluiced into their retirement account. We'll tell you more about mortgage prepayments later in this chapter.

Avoid the Urge to Splurge

Save your next bonus or an unexpected windfall instead of splurging for something you've been wanting. Or, try saving any salary increase you or your spouse gets this year. Try to resist the urge to buy a bigger house if you don't really need the space. A major upward move could cost you big bucks and crimp your retirement savings. You may not be able to count on rising home prices to bail you out later.

Refinance Your Mortgage When Rates Are Low

If the interest rate on your mortgage is relatively high, refinancing may lop $100 to $300 or more off your monthly payment. When you switch to a cheaper mortgage, don't let the savings slip away. Each time you write a check for your mortgage payment, write a second check for money saved and add it to your retirement nest egg. (If you're among the hundreds of thousands of Americans who refinanced to lower rates in recent years, what happened to your savings? Make a commitment now to reclaim part of the extra cash for your retirement fund.)

Tap Tax Breaks for the Self-Employed

If you are self-employed, consider arranging your business to take advantage of home-office tax deductions. Then put the money you save into your retirement plan. If you aren't self-employed, consider starting a for-profit sideline (not a simple hobby) that lets you capture the same home-office deduction while creating extra income. An added bonus: You can open a Keogh retirement plan and make tax-deductible contributions of up to 100% of your self-employment income. Chapter 8 will show you how Keogh plans work.

Good Debt, Bad Debt: Be a Sensible Borrower

Yes, debt is a four-letter word, especially when it comes to saving money for retirement. But not all debt is bad. The idea is not to run willy-nilly away from debt, but to pay the least you can for debt that is necessary and to eliminate debt that is not necessary.

Necessary debts can include a mortgage, a car loan, and money you borrow to pay for your kids' education. These debts, managed wisely, can be strategic financial moves aimed at helping you get what you need now.

Then there's the other kind of debt—the unnecessary, discretionary variety that tends to show up as creeping credit card balances, installment loans, and other revolving-door debt. As you plan for your retirement, your debt-management strategy should have two key aims:

1. **Keeping the cost of necessary debt as low as possible** by using the simple strategies that we describe in this chapter

2. **Keeping discretionary debts to a minimum**—zero is your goal

Being in hock can be damaging in several ways. It costs you money and thwarts your ability to save for retirement. And continuous debt causes stress that you can do without. Before you can get serious about a retirement-savings plan you need to do something about unnecessary and costly debt. No matter what your own circumstances—moderately in hock or deep in the hole—breaking out of the cycle is a vital step toward launching your retirement savings plan.

It used to make more sense to borrow. You could deduct every penny of interest payments on consumer debt from your taxable income. When inflation was running at 8% to 12% a year, you could repay loans with "cheaper" bucks years later. You could count on steadily higher income, too. Those days are gone.

Before you can get serious about a retirement savings plan, you need to do something about unnecessary and costly debt.

Although you can still deduct your mortgage interest, tax deductions for interest on consumer or installment debt have been erased. (A tax deduction for interest paid on student loans elbowed its way back into the law starting in 1998.) Inflation is relatively low, meaning "expensive" dollars remain expensive. And credit card interest rates are stratospheric compared with what you can earn in a savings account or money-market fund.

The moment you start paying down debt, you'll notice benefits. You owe less money, so the finance charges drop. Less of future earnings is spoken for, freeing up cash for retirement savings. The rewards can quickly, and lucratively, translate into a nest egg that you otherwise might never have been able to build. Plus, you gain peace of mind, both now and later.

Depending on your financial circumstances, eliminating all debt may not be possible, or even desirable. Borrowing does have strategic advantages at times—you can use it as an asset to boost your wealth through leverage, to handle a financial emergency, or to speed up a necessary purchase. What's crucial is that you manage credit wisely.

Four Ways to Keep Your Debt Costs Down

There are four ideal ways to slash interest costs on your mortgage, credit cards, car loans, and virtually any other high-interest debt you may have. These strategies involve a minimal effort on your part and only a tiny financial sacrifice now in exchange for what could be gigantic savings long term. Savings from this one source, invested for retirement, could single-handedly erase a majority of the retirement-income gap you calculated in Chapter 2.

Pay Off Your Mortgage Early

Would you spend less than $100 a month to save yourself tens of thousands in interest costs on your home loan, and at the same time pay it off as much as five, ten, or 15 years early? Would you like to invest some of your retirement savings at the same rate (guaranteed and with no risk) that you're being charged on your home mortgage—8%, 9%, or more? Here's the big-gain, low-pain secret to accomplishing both ambitions: Pay off your mortgage a little faster than you have to.

That's it. No fancy formulas or funny-money investments. Simply paying a little extra principal each month on your mortgage gets you there. Any amount will do— $25, $50, $100, or $200. Each time you make such a mortgage prepayment you are, in effect, investing the money at the same rate the bank, savings and loan, credit union, or other lender has been charging you.

On an 8% mortgage, the effect is like earning a risk-free, guaranteed 8% on your money.

It's tough to earn that kind of return with no risk these days, so prepaying a mortgage can be a terrific use for some of your retirement-savings dollars.

Don't get hung up on the tax deduction you get for mortgage interest. True, the interest you save by pre-paying would have been tax deductible. But if you invested elsewhere rather than prepaying, what you earned would have been taxed. So, the tax issue is basically a wash. Also, don't imagine that prepaying will bring a sudden drop in your mortgage-interest tax deduction. It will decline gradually, almost impercep-tibly at first.

WHAT YOU CAN SAVE. The savings generated by pre-paying a mortgage are dramatic. Consider a 40-year-old couple who just bought a house with a 30-year, $100,000 mortgage at 8% interest. Their monthly pay-ment is about $733, not counting any set-aside for taxes or insurance.

By adding a paltry $38 a month to their payment, this couple can reduce the term of the mortgage by five years. The extra $11,400 they invest over 25 years through those $38 monthly additions will knock $32,600 off what they'd otherwise have to pay in inter-est over the life of the loan.

The moment you start paying down debt, you'll notice benefits.

There's no major lifestyle change involved in prepaying a mortgage— just a system for funneling a few extra dollars a month toward your mortgage principal.

If the same couple could manage to pay an extra $222 each month, they would pay off the mortgage in just 15 years, saving a beefy $92,200 in interest.

What's more, they would be free of mortgage debt at age 55. The $955 monthly payments ($733 plus the extra $222) they were making on the mortgage could start going into their retirement nest egg. If the money grows at 7% a year, after taxes, and the couple retires at 65, this "found money" will total $166,260 at retirement. They will not only get to burn their mortgage a decade and a half early but also build a substantial cushion for their retirement.

These calculations are for a fixed-rate mortgage. The same basic principles apply to variable-rate loans, although the precise savings and early-payoff dates depend on how much interest rates rise or fall over the course of the loan.

You can start prepaying at any time, regardless of your age or whether you're in the early or late stages of paying off your mortgage. Work it into your plan from the beginning, or add this feature later on after your regular savings program is already in place. The flexibility is all yours. Many homeowners, for example, devote the savings from refinancing at a lower rate to prepaying the new mortgage. There's no major lifestyle change involved here, just a system for funneling a few extra dollars a month toward your mortgage principal.

You could, for example, customize your prepayment strategy so your mortgage is fully paid by the time you retire. Consider a 55-year-old couple with 15 years remaining on a 9.5% mortgage loan that was originally $90,000. Their payments are about $757, and principal has been reduced to around $72,000.

By adding $180 a month to their payment, this couple can eliminate 60 monthly payments (five years' worth) and save more than $23,000 in interest costs. They then can retire at 65, mortgage-free.

Alternatively, if the couple were to refinance the $72,000 balance at 7% (and roll $1,500 of closing costs into the new loan), they could pay off the new loan in ten years with payments of just $853—less than $100 a month more than they're paying now.

Without refinancing, the extra amount this couple needs in order to lop five years off their mortgage is relatively large, by prepayment standards, because they have only 15 years to go on the loan. The earlier you start, the smaller the extra amount needed to cut five, ten, or 15 years off a loan. If the couple had started prepaying at the beginning of their loan, for example, $29 a month extra would have been enough to cut five years off the term of the loan. With a financial calculator, you can quickly determine how prepaying different amounts will shorten the term of your loan or how much extra you need to prepay each month to retire the debt at a certain point in the future. *The Banker's Secret* by Marc Eisenson (GoodAdvice press) is a book filled with tables that show how prepaying speeds up mortgage payoffs; a companion software program allows computer users to prepare customized prepayment scenarios. Call 800-255-0899 or go online at www.goodadvicepress.com for current pricing and ordering details.

Saving interest costs and freeing up funds for retirement savings are only two of the reasons that mortgage prepayment is appealing. If rates on interest-bearing investments are low, it's hard to beat the guaranteed return you get by using this strategy. And if you are hesitant to tie up extra money in home equity, remember that the easy availability of home-equity loans (discussed later in this chapter) has all but eliminated the liquidity problem. You can always borrow the money back again, with tax-deductible interest.

THE MECHANICS OF MORTGAGE PREPAYMENT. The reason this works so well centers on the total interest cost of a 30-year mortgage. For example, the total amount you would pay on a $100,000 loan at a fixed rate of 8% is roughly $264,100. That's $100,000 of principal and—most borrowers are shocked to learn—$164,100 of interest. By paying just a little more than you have to each month, you dramatically reduce the amount of interest you pay over the life of your loan.

If you have any extra money in a liquid account, such as checking or savings, paying off high-interest credit card debt should be a top priority.

How? Each month, the bank calculates how much interest you owe based on your mortgage balance. If you paid off an extra $25 in January, that's $25 less that you owe interest on in February. Do that every month and the advantage grows rapidly, in much the same way that the compounding effect helps build your investment and savings-account returns.

You say your mortgage has a prepayment penalty built in? Some do. But check again. Penalties are often waived when you prepay in small installments. In most cases, homeowners can prepay as much or as little as is convenient. Some mortgage lenders even make it easy by including a fill-in-the-amount excess-payment line on the monthly payment coupon. Before you begin prepaying, you may want to touch base with your lender to see whether any special procedures should be followed. Make sure your prepayments are applied against principal; unless you specify, some lenders will stick the extra cash in an escrow account.

Remember that there's no obligation on your part to keep the program going. You needn't keep to any particular prepayment schedule, though doing so will be to your advantage.

Mortgage prepayments actually cost you nothing—you're just paying sooner rather than later—so don't think of them as an additional expense. By coughing it up a little early, you ultimately save a small fortune in interest while filling in another piece of your worry-free retirement puzzle.

Save a Bundle on Credit Card Interest

Among all types of consumer debt, credit card debt stands as king of the high-cost hill and the most damaging to even the best retirement-saving intentions. The real cost of running big balances on credit cards should be an eye-opener: If you're making the minimum 2% payment on a card charging a $20 annual fee and 19.8% interest, it will take you 31 years—and a total of $7,700—to pay off a $2,000 balance.

If you have any extra money in a liquid account, such as checking or savings, paying off high-interest credit card debt should be a top priority. For example, if your money is now earning 5%, you can immediately boost your return to 18% by paying off a card balance that costs you 18% annually.

To get an idea of where you stand, look at last month's credit card bills—not the minimum payments, but what you actually owe. Add it all up and ask yourself: If I had to pay it all back in one year, could I? If the answer is no, you're a good candidate to go on a debt diet. Keep in mind that plastic is not a paycheck extender. It actually gives you less money to spend because, unless you pay the bill in full each month, you must pay interest, too.

If you have balances on several different cards, begin by trying to pay one off in full. If you can't manage that right now, at least concentrate the bulk of your efforts on a single card (preferably the one with the highest interest rate) so you can get the psychological boost of seeing the balance drop. Each month, pay all new charges on your cards, plus interest and a portion of the previous balance. It will get easier as finance charges begin to abate.

Also, try to shift your debt to credit cards offering the lowest interest rate on outstanding balances. There's no reason to pay 18% or 19% when you could be paying around 9% to 12%. Many credit card companies offer extremely low introductory rates and rates for balance transfers from other credit cards. If you think you can pay off all or most of the money you would transfer to the low-rate card, you can save money that way. But don't continue moving balances from one introductory-rate card to another; you probably won't save that much, and your credit report might suffer.

Remember, though, your goal is to pay credit card balances in full each month. That way, none of the money that could go to fund your nest egg is flying away to pay interest. There's no need to give up the convenience of charge cards as long as you pay the balance in full each month. Doing so means there's no finance charge—one of the best credit bargains around.

Tap the Tax Advantage of Home-Equity Credit

When borrowing is necessary, your plan should be to find the cheapest possible source of credit. And for anyone who owns a home with enough built-up equity, the least expensive credit source is almost certainly a home-equity loan or line of credit. Whether fixed-term loans or revolving lines of credit, these loans are today's debt of choice because rates are among the lowest available and the interest you pay is usually fully tax-deductible for loans up to $100,000.

To qualify for the tax break, the loan must be secured by your home, and that means, of course, that your home is on the line if you can't repay the loan. That's a sobering thought, but because home-equity debt is likely to be by far the cheapest source of credit when you need to borrow, its use can be a responsible part of your financial plan.

Rates can be fixed or variable, often floating 1% to 3% above the prime rate, which is what banks charge their best corporate customers. Imagine the benefit if you use a home-equity line to pay off high-interest credit card debts. Say you have $5,000 of debt on a credit card that charges 19.5% interest, or $975 a year. Shifting that $5,000 debt to a home equity loan at 8.5% knocks the carrying charge down to $425 a year. Since that's deductible, in the 25% bracket your real cost falls to $319. The $656 savings could go into your retirement fund.

There are some pitfalls. For one thing, to make the loan-consolidation strategy work for your retirement-savings plan, you'll have to put the brakes on credit card use. Running the balances up again will saddle you with an even steeper debt burden than before. Also, you will have to go through an application process, including a credit check and scrutiny of your ability to pay off the maximum amount of the credit line (even if you aren't actually borrowing that much).

Be careful about calculating the true cost of the loan, which includes fees, points, and closing costs to set up an equity line or loan, and perhaps an annual charge as well. Some lenders even charge you for not using the loan account. This is where careful shopping for a home-equity loan can pay off handsomely. As you compare offers, look past the initial interest rate and focus on the rate that will apply when the introductory period ends.

Repayment terms can be quite flexible, leaving it up to you to be prudent in use of the funds. Low-minimum and "interest only" repayment schedules can let you stretch the loan almost forever. But that's a trap you don't want to fall into because it will only damage your financial plans for a worry-free retirement nest egg. For bill consolidation, set up a tough repayment schedule that will eliminate the debt in no more than five years. The money you save on interest will help you do that.

Step Off the Auto-Loan Treadmill

A car loan is probably your biggest debt outside of a mortgage (unless you're using debt to help finance a child's college education). But with auto loans being stretched to four or five years, by the time you pay the loan off it's time to step right back into another one. Getting off this auto-loan treadmill can be a big step toward freeing still more money for your own retirement savings account.

One way to break free is to use home-equity credit to pay for your next car. Assuming a prime rate of 6%, for example, you could buy your vehicle with a 7.5% home-equity loan, making your after-tax cost just 5.62%, assuming you're in the 25% tax bracket. That might be around half the cost of a regular, nondeductible car loan from the bank. Set your payments at a level that will retire the debt in no more than three years.

Chances are you'll still be driving your vehicle after the loan is paid. But don't stop making monthly payments. Steer that $300 to $400 into your nest-egg account each month.

Size Up Your Retirement Plan at Work

A pension plan where you work will play a major role in your retirement-planning strategy. The more generous the plan, and the more effectively you tap its benefits, the more easily you can attain your goal of a worry-free retirement. And, with 78% of working-age couples bringing home two paychecks, a record number of future retired couples will enjoy a double dose of postretirement pension income.

Nearly all large companies—those with 500 or more employees—have tax-deferred retirement plans of some kind. The most common type is an excellent plan called a 401(k), which we'll explain in detail later. Most of the biggies offer a 401(k) in addition to a cash-balance plan, which replaces the traditional "defined-benefit" plan that pays retirees a fixed monthly benefit based on their salary and length of service at the company.

Every employer, whether it's General Motors, city hall, or a small local company, puts a little different spin on its retirement-benefits package. If you participate in several employers' plans over the course of your working career, which is becoming more and more common, you may be entitled to collect from more than one plan.

Take a Look at Two Plans

F or an idea of the scope of what's available, here's what two of the biggest corporate pension packages are offering these days. The details presented here about these plans are the kinds of things you need to know about your own plan.

IBM

This company was long noted for offering its workers some of the best retirement benefits going. But the company's fortunes soured in 1992. The stock tumbled. IBM posted its first-ever loss. Jobs were cut.

By 1995, the IBM roller coaster had turned the other direction. Profits soared and the stock price rebounded, restoring confidence. And although the company's outlook is once again bright, the tougher competitive environment forced IBM to take a hard look at the way it did business—even in the area of providing retirement benefits.

In 2004, IBM announced that it was closing its traditional pension plans to new employees and would provide only a 401(k) plan. Employees can contribute up to 10% of eligible compensation each pay period on a tax-deferred basis, up to amounts permitted by tax laws. IBM matches 50 cents on every dollar contributed, up to the first 6%. Employees are fully vested in these company matching funds immediately. The plan lets employees choose from a broad selection of investment options.

Another IBM feature—an employee stock-purchase plan—illustrates both an opportunity and a worry-free plan pitfall. Employees can use up to 10% of their pay to buy shares of the company's stock at a 15% discount (that is, $100 worth of stock for $85). The stock does not have to be held for retirement—employees can sell it after holding it for one year. The discount is a terrific deal if the stock does well. If not—and the employee has invested a large portion of his or her nest egg in company shares—it can be a disaster.

Just consider what happened at Enron, where many employees had most or all of their retirement savings in company stock. Even IBM shares have had their ups and downs. Over a one-year period from early 1992 to early 1993, shares plunged from about $100 to below $50, less than what their value had been ten years earlier. But the IBM example shows that timing and patience can be crucial. From January 1995 through January 1997 its price had ranged from around $70 to $156. Those who bought shares at the low point in 1995 would have more than doubled their money in two years if they had sold in 1997. Those who bought in 1997 would not have been too happy a few years later when the shares had dropped to around $115. And in early 2005, shares hovered around $100 each.

Aetna

Aetna Life & Casualty offers a cash-balance plan (see details regarding cash-balance plans later in this chapter) as well as a 401(k). The Aetna 401(k) is a good deal, with the company's 50% match of contributions, up to 6% of salary. In other words, employees who earn $50,000 and contribute $3,000 get an instant 50% return on their investment, thanks to the company's matching $1,500 contribution. In addition, in 2002 and 2003, the company kicked in an additional 3% based on company performance targets. This contribution is not guaranteed for future years, however.

Employees also have the opportunity to contribute an additional 5% of unmatched funds if they meet certain IRS guidelines. That's a giant boost over the long term for a worry-free retirement program.

Trend Toward "Self-Directed" Programs

These plans reflect an important change that started in the '90s that may affect your retirement thinking. There has been a wholesale shift away from traditional pension plans in which employers assume all responsibility for making contributions and managing the money, and toward self-

For self-starters and plan-ahead people the move is a major plus.

directed programs that force you into an active role on both counts.

For people unaccustomed to taking charge of their future finances, that shift has pitfalls. But for self-starters and plan-ahead people—including you—the move is a major plus. Traditional pension plans are mysterious animals to employees who have nothing to do with how much is contributed or where the money goes. The move toward greater self-direction makes the process more clear-cut. You and your employer put money into an account with your name on it, and you call the shots on where you want it invested. What's more, if you leave your job you can probably take the money with you.

How Does Your Employer's Plan Work?

Sizing up your own pension plan will give you the tools to fit this important piece into your retirement puzzle. If you and your spouse are employed by small companies that don't offer pension plans, don't panic. You're each entitled to create your own tax-deductible, do-it-yourself pension plan with an individual retirement account (IRA). Even if you're not eligible to establish a deductible IRA, you can still have a nondeductible one, particularly the Roth IRA, which taxes contributions but in which earnings grow tax-free. We'll explore the phenomenal potential of IRAs, especially the Roth, in Chapter 7. And if you're self-employed, see Chapter 8 for the glad tidings about the additional opportunities available to you.

If you and your spouse are covered at work by "qualified" retirement plans (so called because they must follow government rules in order to qualify for special tax treatment), they probably fall into at least one of three categories:

1. a defined-benefit plan (includes both traditional defined-benefit plan and cash-balance plans);

2. **a defined-contribution** or profit-sharing plan;
3. **a 401(k) plan,** also known as a deferred-pay or salary-reduction plan.

More than 80% of large employers have two-part plans. Part one is a defined-benefit plan paid for by the company. This traditional plan, which was once considered the pension cornerstone, has been replaced by many companies with the cash-balance plan. A cash-balance plan is a hybrid type pension plan that meets the funding and legal qualifications for a defined-benefit plan, with some important differences. Part two—the self-directed portion—allows employees to boost retirement benefits through their own savings, often magnified by matching contributions from their employers.

Briefly, here's how these different plans work, the key elements you should know, and how you can find out the specifics of your own plan.

What You Should Know about Cash-Balance or Hybrid Plans

Cash-balance plans, which combine the protections of a traditional pension with the portability of a 401(k) plan, have been sweeping corporate America from Avon to Xerox since 1999. Their proponents hail them as being more in keeping with conditions in the modern workplace. Funds are held in individual interest-bearing accounts for each participant and translated into a defined benefit at retirement. You make no contributions to a cash-balance plan; the company contributes all the money and assumes all of the investment risk. Like traditional plans, it is insured by the Pension Benefit Guaranty Corporation.

Because few people today remain with one company for their whole career, traditional defined-benefit (DB) pension plans that reward employees for long service—the bulk of their benefits are earned during their final years—are less attractive than they once were. Today, fewer than 10% of employees work for the same company for 20 years or more, according to the Employee Benefit Research Institute. Many people don't stay long enough to become vested in a company's defined-benefit plan or to build substantial retirement benefits.

Unfortunately, when a company switches from a defined-benefit plan to a cash-balance one, those 10% or fewer workers may get hurt. Mid-career workers are particularly vulnerable because they may end up with a smaller pension than was promised under the old plan.

In a cash-balance plan, each year an amount equal to a percentage of your salary goes into the account—5% of pay in IBM's plan—and is guaranteed to earn a predetermined interest rate, which is usually tied to an index, such as the consumer-price index or Treasury-bill rate. If plan investments earn less than the promised interest rate, the employer has to make up the difference. If the investments earn more, the excess counts toward the next year's contribution and reduces the employer's out-of-pocket cost.

HOW LONGER SERVICE BOOSTS A PENSION $200,000*	
Years on job	**Income replacement**
5	6%
10	12%
15	18%
20	24%
25	30%
30	37%

*Replacement percentages for services of less than 30 years may be reduced further by early-retirement reductions.

When an employee leaves, he or she can take a lump-sum payout of the account balance and roll it into an IRA. If he or she is of retirement age, the payout can be made into an annuity. Because the employer's contribution is based on a percentage of your current salary, benefits in a cash-balance plan grow more evenly over the years than do those in a traditional pension plan, in which benefits are weighted more heavily toward your last years on the job.

One study comparing traditional pensions with cash-balance plans found that two-thirds of plan participants—mainly those who hopped from one job to another—would receive a larger benefit with a cash-balance plan than with a traditional pension. Women, the study showed, who often interrupt their careers to take care of children, may have the most reason to cheer a switch to a cash-balance plan.

When companies convert to a cash-balance plan, they set an opening balance for each employee, based on the benefits accrued in the pension plan up to the time of the change. The law forbids companies to take away any benefits earned up to that point. The Retirement Security and Savings Act of 2000 was passed to insure that when a traditional defined-benefit plan is converted to a cash-balance or other hybrid plan, it must provide that the employee's normal retirement benefit always equal the benefit earned under the old plan formula prior to the conversion, *plus* the benefit earned under the new (cash-balance) plan formula.

What You Should Know about Defined-Benefit Pensions

Some 44 million Americans are covered by private-sector defined-benefit pension plans. Traditional defined-benefit plans guarantee to pay you a specified amount when you retire, based on your salary, age, and years of service. Both traditional defined-benefit and cash-balance pension plans are backed by a government insurance agency called the Pension Benefit Guaranty Corporation (PBGC).

Traditional plans are designed so that the pension benefit plus social security benefits will replace 60% to 70% of an employee's preretirement income—not bad, considering that you are shooting to replace 80% of that income. A typical replacement percentage is figured like this: 50% of income at retirement minus 50% of social security. Bottom line: the typical defined-benefit pension will replace about 37% of income for a 30-year worker retiring at a salary level of $50,000.

HOW TO CALCULATE THE BENEFIT. A standard formula for calculating a defined-benefit pension looks like this:

final average monthly earnings x 1.5% x
years of service - monthly benefit due

"Final average earnings" would likely be the average of the five consecutive years you earned the most—probably your last five. For someone with 25 years on the job and final average earnings of $54,000 ($4,500 per month), the monthly retirement benefit would come to about 37.5% of preretirement income and be figured as follows:

$$\$4,500 \times 1.5\% \times 25 = \$1,687.50$$

To receive the maximum pension, most plans require that you work at the company for 30 years and wait until "full retirement age." That's usually 62 or 65, but some companies use a point system that lets you retire at full benefits once your age plus years of service total a certain number of points. Kodak's traditional retirement plan, for example, allows employees to retire at age 60 with full benefits if they've put in at least 30 years or at age 65 with any amount of service.

What percentage of your preretirement income will your pension replace? The answer varies greatly from employer to employer. Generally, the longer you stay with the same employer, the bigger your pension. Because it is linked to your salary level, which presumably will continue to rise, the size of the benefit will grow fastest in the final five to ten years on the job. That's why staying put can result in a significantly larger pension than changing jobs frequently and starting fresh in each new pension plan.

As noted earlier, an employee with a traditional defined-benefit plan, retiring at a salary level of $50,000 after 30 years of service, would typically receive a pension that replaces 37% of income, assuming he or she retires at an age that qualifies for full benefits under the plan. Someone with 20 years' service would replace about 24% of income, and someone with 15 years, about 18%.

An early retiree would probably see benefits reduced, depending on his or her age. For example, a 55-year-old retiring with 20 years of service is entitled to 90% of the full benefit earned. A 58-year-old with 26 years gets 96% of the full benefit.

DON'T FORGET INFLATION. One risk you do take in a defined-benefit pension plan is the risk that inflation will badly erode your benefit through your retirement years. Because fewer than one plan in ten adjusts future benefits for inflation, your worry-free plan must include inflationary protection elsewhere if you won't get it here.

It's crucial to factor postretirement inflation into your thinking about a defined-benefit pension. An amount that sounds large at the start won't seem nearly as large a few years after you have stopped working. For example, if inflation averages 4%, each $1,000 of benefits you receive at retirement will have the buying power of only $665 within ten years and a mere $542 after 15 years. The effect of inflation is to diminish the role that any fixed pension plays in your plan over the long term.

Social security benefits, which are indexed to rise with inflation, can help solve part of the inflation problem, as you'll see in Chapter 5. Social security might start out paying you less per month than your employer's pension. But as social security benefits get annual cost-of-living boosts, the size of your monthly checks

---

TRADITIONAL DEFINED-BENEFIT-PLAN PROFILE

Here's how a typical corporate defined-benefit pension would work for someone retiring with 32 years of service and a $50,000 income:

Final salary:	$50,000
Averaged earnings on which pension is based:	$42,440
Years on job:	32
Pension accrual rate per year:	1.35%
Accrued benefit (32 years x 1.35%):	43.2%
Annual pension (43.2% of $42,440):	$18,334
Annual pension as % of final salary:	37%

may overtake your company pension over time. (Possible threats to those cost-of-living adjustments are discussed in Chapter 5.)

The good news is that by planning ahead and inflation-proofing your nest egg, you can be prepared for this reality. That's why Chapter 2 shows how to make inflation expectation one of the many pieces that will make up your retirement-income puzzle.

HOW YOU'LL RECEIVE DEFINED-BENEFIT PAYMENTS IF YOU CHOOSE THE ANNUITY OPTION. Even companies that offer traditional defined-benefit plans may offer you a lump sum as an option, so you may be faced with the decision as to whether to take the lump sum or the annuity. If you take the annuity, the benefits accumulated in a defined-benefit pension plan determine only part of how your monthly payment will be set. Your marital status and the choices you and your spouse make at the brink of retirement will make a difference as well. Basically:

- **If you are single,** you get a fixed monthly benefit from the day you retire until you die.
- **If you are married,** half your benefit will continue to go to your spouse after you die, under a provision known as the joint and survivor (J&S) annuity. To pay for this, your beginning benefit will be lowered— usually by about 10% to 12%—for life. Basically, the younger you and your spouse are at retirement, the higher the percentage of reduction.
- **Under some plans,** in return for a larger reduction in your lifetime benefit, your spouse can continue to receive 66%, 75%, or 100% of the monthly payments after you're gone. In that case, expect benefits to be reduced about 20% for life.
- **Your spouse,** at the time of choosing options, can decline the right to continue receiving payments after your death, in which case your benefit will be the same as for a single individual.
- **Some employers** also offer a J&S "restore" option. If your spouse dies before you, this option lets you restore your benefit to the full amount it would have

been as a single individual. The catch is that in order to keep the right to make this switch, your benefit will be reduced by an additional 1% to 3% on top of the regular J&S reduction.

FITTING THE J&S DECISION INTO YOUR PLAN. For now, there's no need to sweat the J&S decision—the choice needn't be made until you're ready to retire. For planning purposes, figure your spouse will want the security of continued payments and that your pension will be lower as a result. Knowing that your benefit will be reduced will force you to save more in the other components of your retirement plan while you're in your 40s and 50s. Later on, if you and your spouse decide to go with higher benefits without the survivor protection, the benefit boost could help cement an early retirement by age 60 or sooner.

The choice later on will boil down to a couple of basics: If your spouse is younger than you are (and thus likely to outlive you) and doesn't have a pension of his or her own, the joint-and-survivor option makes the most financial sense. But if your spouse is older than you or has a pension or other financial resources of his or her own, you may needlessly sacrifice pension income by electing the J&S option.

GOVERNMENT PROTECTION FOR YOUR PENSION. In a defined-benefit pension, the employer is legally committed to making sure there's enough money in the plan to pay the guaranteed benefits. If the company fails to meet that obligation, the federal government steps in.

Defined-benefit plans—whether traditional or cash-balance—are the only type of pension insured by the Pension Benefit Guaranty Corp. (PBGC). The insurance works in much the same way that federal deposit insurance backs up your bank account. If your plan is covered (most are) and the sponsoring company goes bust, PBGC will take over benefit payments, but only up to a maximum (about $45,614 a year in 2005). The maximum is adjusted periodically for infla-

PENSION-PLAN CHANGES

Don't be surprised if your employer changes the rules of your retirement plan. Pension rules are often changed, and there is no law against doing so. However, any changes that have the effect of reducing benefits should generally apply only to the years following the change—not retroactively. Typically, changes affect the method of benefits calculation, rules for early retirement, benefit levels, and choices of payout options.

tion, but becomes fixed in the year in which your plan is terminated.

This insurance protection helps make your pension more secure, but it is not a full guarantee that you'll get what you expected if the company you work for gets into trouble. Former employees of such bankrupt companies as Pan Am and Eastern airlines, for example, saw their promised pensions reduced, and hundreds of other failed pension plans have been taken over by the PBGC.

Though the PBGC's own solvency could be threatened if other major pension plans fail, Uncle Sam would almost certainly step in with a bailout similar to that used to protect depositors in failed savings and loan institutions.

Defined-contribution plans (which are discussed in detail next) get no PBGC coverage. When Carter Hawley Hale Stores, a large retailer, filed for bankruptcy in 1990, employees saw the value of their 401(k) accounts plunge. Because the only investment choice in the Carter Hawley plan was the company's own stock, the shares' nosedive from a $70 peak in 1986 to $1.75 in 1992 virtually wiped out the 401(k) nest eggs of thousands of employees. Partly as a result of the Carter Hawley debacle, the rules now push employers into offering at least three distinctly different 401(k) investment options (not counting company stock).

In effect, this rule change is the government's way of saying that employers needn't take responsibility for how well your retirement dollars perform in the future as long as you are provided with enough choices to make sound investment decisions on your own. (We'll help on that score in Chapters 9 and 10.)

Defined-Contribution and Self-Directed Plans

The second basic type of retirement plan is a defined-contribution plan. These plans encompass several variations, including 401(k) salary-reduction plans, profit-sharing plans, and employee stock-ownership plans (ESOPs). Defined-contribution plans generally set aside (or allow you to set aside) a percentage of your salary or a portion of company profits into a retirement account controlled by you. The percentage that's set aside might be fixed, or it might fluctuate year to year. And the ultimate value of your nest egg will depend in part on what those retirement dollars earn. Money in the plan grows untaxed until you tap the account in retirement. If the investments do well, you win. If they don't, your nest egg will be smaller. In any case, you bear the risk. The most popular plan by far is the 401(k). Here's how it works.

401(K) PLANS: A SUPER DEAL FOR BUILDING RETIREMENT WEALTH. The 401(k) plan (named for the section of the tax code that created it) is, hands down, the hottest retirement-savings deal. For ease of use, tax-shelter power, and wealth-building potential, participation in a 401(k) may be the single most-important ingredient you can add to your retirement plan. The vast majority of all companies with more than 500 employees now offer this benefit.

This is a tremendous two-way tax shelter. Money you contribute to the plan, up to a yearly maximum, is subtracted from your taxable income. In 2005, maximums were raised to $14,000 and will rise to $15,000 in 2006. There's also a "catch-up" provision for older workers. If you're age 50 or older, you'll generally be able to contribute even more in a 401(k), 403(b), or 457 plan: an extra $4,000 per year in 2005, and $5,000 in

Money in a defined-contribution plan grows untaxed until you tap the account in retirement.

FOR EMPLOYEES OF PUBLIC INSTITUTIONS

If you work for a public institution, such as a university or some other type of nonprofit group, the retirement-savings plan equivalent to the 401(k) is called a 403(b) plan. The mechanics are mostly the same. Money diverted to the program is subtracted from your pay and is not immediately taxed.

2006. That's tax advantage number one. If you earn $60,000, for example, and put 8% of pay into a 401(k), that $4,800 isn't reported to the IRS as earnings. That lowers your taxable income to $55,200 and saves you $1,200 in taxes if you're in the 25% bracket. Thus, for an out-of-pocket cost of $3,600, you've poured $4,800 into a tax-sheltered account for your worry-free retirement.

Tax advantage number two is this: Once inside your account, funds grow tax-deferred until withdrawn. Because the IRS can't take a share of the earnings each year, you keep more in the plan to take advantage of long-term compounding. But the best is yet to come.

Many plans offer a special sweetener that you simply can't afford to pass up—an employer match of your 401(k) contribution. For each $1 an employee contributes, companies commonly kick in another 25 cents, 50 cents, or even $1, up to an established limit. That's an immediate 25%, 50%, or even 100% return on your money.

Cisco Systems, for example, provides a dollar for dollar match on employee contributions, up to $1,500 per calendar year. Hewlett-Packard (HP) matches employee contributions dollar for dollar up to 3% of salary. HP contributes 50 cents for every $1 on the next 2% the employee defers in the plan. As discussed earlier, IBM matches 50 cents on the dollar, up to 6% of salary. Matching employer contributions don't count toward your ceiling, but the total of both your contributions and your employer's cannot exceed $42,000.

How good is the matching deal? Say you make $60,000 and your employer matches 50 cents for each dollar you save, up to 10% of your salary. Each year you set aside $6,000 and the firm kicks in $3,000. Assuming your salary remains steady and the money grows at an annual rate of 8%, your 401(k) will be worth $57,000 in five years and $141,000 in ten years. That's a 90% gain over five years on your investment of $30,000 and a 135% gain over ten years on your $60,000 contribution.

Even if your employer doesn't match any portion of your 401(k) contribution, the tax advantages still make this a great deal for your retirement savings.

INVESTMENT CHOICES FOR YOUR SELF-DIRECTED MONEY. The trend since the 1990s has been toward offering employees a widening menu of options for investing retirement-plan money and more freedom to switch among those options. Options usually include a variety of stock-market mutual funds; a guaranteed investment contract (GIC), which is similar to a certificate of deposit; a money-market fund or short-term-bond fund; an income fund; employer stock; and a U.S. Treasury fund. Participants in IBM's tax-deferred savings plan, for example, have a choice of any combination of investment options, including the following types of investments:

- **Money-market fund**
- **Fixed-income fund**
- **Large-company stock-market index fund**
- **Small-company stock index fund**
- **Short-term U.S. government securities fund**
- **IBM stock**

Historically, the best-performing investment categories have been stocks, with large-company stocks returning an average of 10.4% annually since 1926, according to Ibbotson Associates, a Chicago-based firm that tracks historical investment returns. Small-company stocks have done even better, with an average annual return of 12.75% over the same period.

By comparison, long-term government bonds have produced an average annual total return of only 5.4% since 1926, while inflation has averaged 3.0%.

Because stocks hold a strong performance edge long term, that's where the bulk of your long-term retirement-plan money should be invested—probably 60% to 80% or more of your nest egg if you're ten years or more from retirement and progressively less as you near and enter retirement. Chapters 9 and 10 will explore investment allocations in more detail.

Just a few years ago, studies showed almost 47% of employee funds went into super conservative Guaranteed Investment Contracts (GICs) when the choice was available. Fortunately this is changing. In 2004, the Employee Benefits Research Institute (EBRI) reported that as of the end of 2003, almost 70% of 401(k)-plan balances were invested directly or indirectly in equity securities, 10% were invested in bonds, and 18% went into money-market or other stable-value investments.

It's tempting to play it safe with your retirement money, but you'll be much better off in the long run to weight your pension portfolio heavily toward the high-growth potential of the stock market. Yes, stocks are more risky. But with your eye fixed firmly on long-term results, you can afford to weather the inevitable ups and downs on Wall Street. The irony is that your retirement will be more secure, not less, if a bedrock portion of your money is invested in stocks over the long term.

Fitting a Profit-Sharing Plan or ESOP into Your Program

Your firm may offer a defined-contribution profit-sharing plan. Here the company takes the lead with annual contributions based on the firm's profitability. You may or may not have the option to contribute to the plan yourself.

Profit-sharing plans have several pluses. If the company does well, the profit-sharing arrangement lets you participate in that success. A company that's going gangbusters could net you a nifty nest egg over the years. And if a portion of the money in this plan is invested in stocks, you have another important tool for beating the corrosive effects of inflation.

A drawback is that the ultimate size of your nest egg is not entirely predictable with a profit-sharing plan, because the size of the contributions can change and future investment returns are always a question mark. Both uncertainties are minor, however, compared to the upside profit-sharing potential.

To get an idea of how much you can expect from company contributions, ask your benefits administrator what the average company contribution to the plan has been over the past ten or 20 years, and use that as a benchmark. Historical performance information on investment options should also be available from your plan administrator.

By plugging in those key indicators and using the money-growth table in Chapter 2, you can make a reasonable guess as to the size of this component come retirement, and the amount of money you can expect it to produce to help fill your retirement-income gap.

Employee stock-ownership plans (ESOPs) are one type of profit-sharing arrangement. Under these plans, the corporation contributes shares of company stock to your retirement account, or allows you to buy shares as a plan investment option.

This is a way to acquire stock in the firm you work for at little or no commission cost, or even at a share-price discount. The stock can appreciate tax-free as part of your retirement nest egg, and even if you leave and take the stock with you, you can continue the tax-favored treatment by rolling it over into an IRA.

Owning company stock can be a terrific deal. For example, employees at Cisco can contribute up to 10% of their compensation to purchase company stock at a 15% discount. But success isn't guaranteed. The risk is this: If the stock market slumps or your company's fortunes slip, the value of your nest egg could dip, as we mentioned earlier in the case of IBM. And Pan Am's ESOP plan was left holding a bag of large blocks of use-

With your eye fixed firmly on long-term results, you can afford to weather the inevitable ups and downs on Wall Street.

less stock when the company filed for bankruptcy. Still, if your firm has good prospects and offers an ESOP, it's a benefit you'll want to grab.

Gauging those prospects can be tricky, though, because 90% of today's active ESOPs are at small private firms, not the public giants. While federal law requires disclosure of the major provisions of the plan and values of the stock, you should also get an explanation from key company officers and assess the plan in light of your long-term retirement goals. To help determine whether the ESOP fits into your plan, take a critical look at any other retirement benefits your company offers. If, in addition to the ESOP, you also participate in a good defined-benefit plan or 401(k), there's less riding on company stock alone.

D-I-V-O-R-C-E

No matter what your age, the pension you've accumulated at work will probably be considered an asset to be divided with your spouse if you are later divorced. If you untie the knot at 50, for example, a portion of the benefit you stand to collect at retirement could belong to your ex-spouse under what's known in divorce lingo as a "qualified domestic relations order," or QDRO (pronounced kwa-dro). On the flip side, you may be able to collect a portion of your ex's pension from his or her employer.

Look at the ESOP in the broader perspective of your overall plan for a worry-free retirement. What you really have in an ESOP is an investment in the company you work for, not a traditional pension plan. That's how you should evaluate it. If you have any doubts about the firm's prospects, you can begin to move money out of the ESOP and into less-risky territory once you reach age 55 and have been in the ESOP for ten years. Federal law requires that, at that point, you be allowed to shift 25% of the assets in your ESOP account to other investments. At age 60 you have the right to shift 50% of your account elsewhere.

Your decision of whether to diversify should hinge on how positive you feel about the company's prospects and on the size of the ESOP holding in relation to the rest of your nest egg. If this one stock accounts for more than about 15% to 20% of the assets you're counting on for retirement by the time you're within five years of making the break, you're a strong candidate for shifting a portion of those assets elsewhere.

Vesting: Your Pension Plan's Golden Handcuffs

Employer retirement plans have a string attached: You have to stick around in order to earn full benefits. The process of acquiring a nonforfeitable right to the money that's being set aside for your retirement is called vesting. Think of vesting as a kind of golden handcuffs—a way for your employer to encourage you to stay on the job. To protect yourself against forfeiting benefits, it's important to know exactly how your plan works.

The law allows employers to make you wait a full five years before you have a right to any of the money that's been set aside for you. This is called cliff vesting—if you leave the job before putting in five years, you're pushed off the cliff and get nothing. An advantage to cliff vesting, though, is that once you've been in the plan for five years, you're fully vested: 100% of the money earmarked for you in the past—and in the future—is yours.

An alternative is graded or gradual vesting. The slowest pace allowed by law demands that you be 20% vested after three years and 100% vested after seven years.

In a defined-contribution plan, being fully vested means that if you leave the company you can take all the money in your account with you. (Any money you contribute to the plan is immediately considered fully vested; you can take it with you if you leave the company, no matter what your length of service is.) In a traditional defined-benefit plan, it means you've earned the right to receive a pension at retirement and the employer will probably make you wait until a specified retirement age to collect what you have coming.

There are exceptions to the basic vesting rules. When you reach age 65, for example, you are fully vested no matter how briefly you've been on the job. And if the company decides to terminate your plan, the law says you must also become fully vested automatically.

VESTING SCHEDULES COMPARED		
	Percent Vested	
Years Worked	**5-Year Cliff Vesting**	**Gradual Vesting**
1	**0%**	**0%**
2	0	0
3	0	20
4	0	40
5	100	60
6		80
7		100

When Two Pensions Are Not Better Than One

What does vesting mean to your plan? Mostly this: If you leave early, you'll leave some of your benefits behind. The more times you change jobs—even if you become fully vested in the traditional defined-benefit pension plan—the more pension potential you leave on the table as you head for the exit. That's because vesting gives you the right to only the money set aside in the plan up to that point. The really big money doesn't start to build until you've been in the plan for ten, 20, 25, or more years.

Even if you become fully vested in three or four different pension plans during your career, you'll get less total benefit from those pensions than if you stay at one job and get just one check (assuming all of the plans have similar pension formulas). In most cases, two pensions—or even five pensions—are not better than one. According to the benefits consulting firm Hewitt Associates, if you worked for four different firms for five years each (20 years) and one firm for ten years, the total amount of pension you would get will be almost 50% less than what you would get by working at the same firm for the entire 30 years.

Still, because faster pension-plan vesting was mandated in the 1980s, the consequences of job jumping are not as onerous as they once were. Faster vesting guarantees that if you do change jobs, you will at least take something with you if you've met the minimum-stay period.

Where to Find Details on Your Pension Plan

To locate the nitty-gritty details about your particular plan, start by reading the summary plan description (SPD) that your employer is required to provide. You probably received one and stuck it in a drawer somewhere.

The SPD is supposed to be a plain-English explanation of your plan, including details about the amount of the pension benefits, requirements for receiving those payments, and any conditions that might prevent someone from receiving them. While some SPDs are relatively clear, others are more an exercise in linguistic futility. In any case, your best bet is to skip the mumbo-jumbo about the legal form of your plan and head for the sections that show you specific examples of benefits that would be paid under the plan.

That, along with information from the annual statement of estimated benefits, will help you make your own estimate of what to expect and what you can plan on as a realistic future benefit. Most employers provide the benefit statement automatically each year.

Key Items to Look For

Here are five key items to look for in a summary plan description:

Eligibility and vesting. Employees typically become eligible if they're at least 21 years old, have been with the company for at least a year, and work at least 1,000 hours per year. The SPD will tell you when you become vested.

When you will receive benefits. This section of the SPD will spell out benefits for normal retirement, early retirement and late retirement. Normal retirement age for receiving full benefits is typically 62 or 65. Your plan may allow you to continue building benefits up to age 70 or so, or to retire as early as age 55.

How benefits are calculated. The formula used to calculate benefits will be stated here. This section of the SPD will also show you how benefits are reduced if you retire early or how they can be increased by working beyond normal retirement age.

How you will receive your benefits. Is there a choice of lump sum or annuity? For unmarried employees, the typical defined-benefit plan pays a "straight life annuity"—a monthly payment that starts when you retire and stops when you die. This section of the SPD will spell out the J&S option for married employees and any additional choices you have.

How breaks in service are handled. Here you'll find out what happens to your pension if you are transferred, laid off, take a leave of absence, are disabled, or undergo some other change in your employment status.

Discover the Real Deal from Social Security

First, stop worrying whether social security will be there when you're ready to start collecting benefits. It will play an important role in your worry-free retirement—perhaps even a major role. That's true despite all the gloom-and-doom talk about the system's future. (That doesn't mean that Congress won't tinker with the system. President Bush wants to privatize part of it; the democrats are resistant. That usually spells stalemate, but if there is a major change in the rules, you'll be able to find out how they might affect your retirement plans by going to our Web site—www.kiplinger.com— for an update.) For this chapter, we'll assume the system will continue to function as it has in the past.

As of now, the Social Security Administration (SSA) projects that today's average 46-year-old will receive slightly higher benefits (in today's dollars) than the average 65-year-old currently receives. Tomorrow's average retiree will get back what he or she paid into the system within about thirteen years, tops.

That's true even though higher tax rates (mitigated somewhat by the tax relief bill of 2001) and a steadily rising wage base (the maximum amount of income that is taxed each year) mean today's workers are paying far more into the system than today's retirees did. From a cost-benefit perspective, today's retirees—including, perhaps, your parents—are getting a better deal from social security than tomorrow's beneficiaries will. But that does not mean social security is a bad deal for you; nor does it diminish the key role it will play in your financially secure retirement. Yes, you'll pay in more than your parents did, but you'll get more in benefits, too.

It would be foolish to assume the system won't change between now and the time you collect your first benefit check. You can count on social security continuing to be the focus of hot political debate. Its very size makes that inevitable: In 2004, more than 47 million Americans received over $490 billion in social security benefits, and this figure is expected to continue rising. In addition to the possibility of privatizing part of social security payments, there continues to be talk of other changes, such as limiting cost-of-living adjustments, for example. But politically, social security is a sacred cow and changes won't come easily. The most profound changes of the past 15 years have been increased taxes on social security benefits. That's discussed later in this chapter.

As the huge baby-boom generation moves from paying taxes to collecting benefits, there's no doubt that the system will come under increasing strain. A sluggish economy—leading to fewer workers earning less on which to pay social security taxes—can add to the stress.

But you do yourself a disservice—and put unnecessary strain on your retirement planning—if you assume the system will go broke and the government renege on its promises. That will not happen. You can count on social security's filling an important part of your retirement-income need.

It won't replace all your income; it was never meant to. But if your preretirement income is at or below the social security wage base, a replacement of about one quarter to one half of it is a valuable piece in your retirement puzzle. Sure, you'll need other major retirement-income sources to make up the difference—that's what the other chapters in this book are all about.

What Will You Get?

How much can you realistically expect to receive from social security? You'll need an answer to plug into your financial plan for a worry-free retirement and the worksheet in Chapter 2. The news is probably better than you imagine. The key factor in setting your benefit is how much you make during your working career. The formula for calculating benefits is complicated, but in general it's based on your earnings over most of your working lifetime. You become eligible for social security when you've earned 40 work "credits." Basically, you pick up four credits for every year that your work, which means you qualify for retirement benefits after ten years of employment. Credits are based on earned income, which is income from a job or self-employment. The amount needed for each credit increases each year. (In 2005, you'd have earned one credit for each $920 of earned income.)

Earning more credits does not boost your benefit. Earning more money does. To figure your benefit, the SSA will start with your earnings for 35 years (up to each year's maximum, which is the top amount to which the social security tax applies), adjust them for inflation, then calculate a yearly average. Your benefit is a percentage of that average. The lower the income, the higher the percentage. Social security replaces about

WHO WILL GET MAXIMUM SOCIAL SECURITY BENEFITS?

Year	Earnings Max	Year	Earnings Max	Year	Earnings Max
1959–65	$ 4,800	1982	$ 32,400	1994	$ 60,600
1966–67	6,600	1983	35,700	1995	61,200
1968–71	7,800	1984	37,800	1996	62,700
1972	9,000	1985	39,600	1997	65,400
1973	10,800	1986	42,000	1998	68,400
1974	13,200	1987	43,800	1999	72,600
1975	14,100	1988	45,000	2000	76,200
1976	15,300	1989	48,000	2001	80,400
1977	16,500	1990	51,300	2002	84,900
1978	17,700	1991	53,400	2003	89,100
1979	22,900	1992	55,500	2004	87,900
1980	25,900	1993	57,600	2005	90,000
1981	29,700				

40% of income for the average wage earner (someone earning about $34,065 in 2005) and 24% for maximum earners ($90,000 in 2005). Because the top benefit is based on that maximum-earner figure, those who earn more will see a smaller portion of their earnings replaced by social security.

What does it take to qualify to receive the maximum benefit when you retire? You need to earn the maximum wage subject to the tax—so you pay in the maximum tax—for 35 years. But don't worry. If you're a little below the max for a few years it won't drop your benefit by much because the benefit amount is a long-term average. The table on page 75 shows you the wage maximums between 1959 and 2005 so you can get an idea of where you might stand. (After 2005, the SSA will calculate the maximum benefit using a formula based on the national average wage index from the previous year.

Here are two ways to track down your estimated benefit amount to plug into the Worry-Free Retirement Worksheet in Chapter 2.

Our Benefit Estimate Tables

The tables on the opposite page, based on SSA projections, give you some basic guidelines on what you can expect to receive from social security. For example, if your current earnings are at or above the social security maximum and you plan to retire at full retirement age in 2025, you can expect annual social security benefits of $24,900 calculated in today's dollars. The future inflation-adjusted annual social security benefit would be $49,572 in 2025 dollars.

Already, social security is starting to sound better than you thought, no?

Today's average wage earner (estimated by the SSA at $34,065 in 2005) who anticipates retirement at full retirement age in 2025 would receive social security benefits of $14,616 annually in today's dollars; that would be $28,932 in future inflation-adjusted dollars. A one-wage-earner couple will together collect 150% of these figures when both reach full retirement age because a husband or wife is entitled to a benefit equal to 50% of the working spouse's benefit. That's the case even if one spouse never paid a dime into social security. There's more on this point beginning on page 82.

The expanded tables on page 83, based on the Social Security Administration benefits calculator on its Web site, offer a larger range of incomes and retirement dates and include estimates of benefits payable to a wage earner and nonworking spouse. The figures show a monthly benefit for someone retiring at full retirement age. (Note that the tables use 2005 income levels.)

Select your income level in the left-hand column and find where that row intersects the column showing the year closest to when you expect to retire. That's your expected monthly social security benefit. The first table is in today's dollars and the second table in future, inflation-adjusted dollars.

The inflation assumption is 3% per year. If you want to use a different figure, go to the Money Growth and Inflation Factors table in Chapter 2 and find the multiplier for the inflation rate you wish to

EXPECTED ANNUAL SOCIAL SECURITY BENEFIT

FOR THE MAXIMUM EARNER*

Retirement Year	Today's $	Future $
2006	$ 21,552	$ 21,900
2015	23,112	32,028
2025	24,900	49,572

FOR THE AVERAGE EARNER**

Retirement Year	Today's $	Future $
2006	$ 11,976	$ 12,168
2015	13,236	18,276
2025	14,616	28,932

*$90,000 in 2005
** $34,065 in 2005

use. Multiplying the social security benefit in today's dollars by that figure will give you your approximate benefit at retirement.

Your Personalized Benefits Estimate

For a more precise estimate of your benefits based on your earnings history, use the Social Security Administration's "Personal Earnings and Benefit Statement," which the SSA has been sending annually to everyone age 25 and over since 2000.

The computerized SSA statement will show all the earnings that have been credited to your account up to a stated date, usually within two years or less. The statement will tell you whether you are a victim of the most common error—having zero earnings posted for a year that you were working. That can happen when an employer reports your wages under an incorrect social security number.

If you find errors in your records, call the toll-free number on the statement. A social security representative will tell you what documentation you need in order to fix the problem.

If you're under age 25 or want to check your records before you receive the statement, request an estimate form. Call 800-772-1213 and ask for Form SSA-7004, "Request for Social Security Statement" (there's a sample on pages 80 and 81). About four to six weeks after you return the completed form, you'll receive your estimate. You can also order a benefits estimate online at www.ssa.gov. (If you want more than one estimate—to see how retiring at different ages affects your benefits or those of other members of your household, photocopy the form or send in more than one request and vary the factors.)

The form is quite simple to complete, except where it asks you to provide an estimate of your future average yearly earnings.

WORRY-FREE TIP

Do you earn more than the social security maximum? If so, here's a painless way to give your retirement savings a boost each year. If you pass the social security ceiling ($90,000 in 2005) before the year is over and suddenly find your paycheck fatter, put that "bonus" aside for your worry-free retirement instead of spending it.

■ **If you already make more than the social security maximum** (see the list on page 75), don't sweat it. Put down what you earn now, and the SSA will assume you'll continue to earn above the maximum for the remainder of your career. This adjustment is automatic.

■ **If you're below the ceiling and expect your earnings to rise in line with the national average** (4% or so), again, all you need to do is put down what you make now. SSA automatically adjusts for average wage growth.

■ **If you expect future earnings to drop or to rise faster than 4% a year,** fill in an amount that most closely reflects the change you expect. For example, if you're making $45,000 now but expect a job change or promotion to boost your earnings to $60,000 in the next two to three years, use that figure instead.

Remember, these are just estimates; you don't need to be precise. Since you can request this free estimate as often as you like, you can try it different ways.

The report will show you how much you've paid in social security taxes and the monthly amount you can expect when you begin drawing benefits. Your projected benefits will be in today's dollars, not inflation-adjusted dollars. You can make that adjustment with the Money Growth and Inflation Factors table in Chapter 2.

The younger you are, however, the more likely that expected changes to the social security program will mean that your benefits will be squeezed by the time you retire—so the official statement you receive will probably overstate what you'll really get. There are plenty of ideas about how to "fix" social security for the long term. It's impossible to know exactly what will happen, but if you're under age 55, it's only prudent to crank probable cutbacks into your planning. Here's an easy way to do it: Instead of using the number you get from social security, reduce it by 15% if you're age 40 to 55, and by 30% if you're under 40.

continued on page 82

REQUEST FOR SOCIAL SECURITY STATEMENT

Request for *Social Security Statement*

☐ Please check this box if you want to get your *Statement* in Spanish instead of English.

Please print or type your answers. When you have completed the form, fold it and mail it to us. (If you prefer to send your request using the Internet, contact us at *www.socialsecurity.gov*)

1. Name shown on your Social Security card:

   _____ _____
   First Name   Middle Initial

   _____
   Last Name Only

2. Your Social Security number as shown on your card:

   ☐☐☐ - ☐☐ - ☐☐☐☐

3. Your date of birth (Mo.-Day-Yr.)

   ☐☐ - ☐☐ - ☐☐☐☐

4. Other Social Security numbers you have used:

   ☐☐☐ - ☐☐ - ☐☐☐☐

   ☐☐☐ - ☐☐ - ☐☐☐☐

5. Your Sex: ☐ Male   ☐ Female

For items 6 and 8 show only earnings covered by Social Security. Do NOT include wages from state, local or federal government employment that are NOT covered for Social Security or that are covered ONLY by Medicare.

6. Show your actual earnings (wages and/or net self-employment income) for last year and your estimated earnings for this year.

   A. Last year's actual earnings: *(Dollars Only)*

   $☐☐☐ , ☐☐☐ . 0 0

   B. This year's estimated earnings: *(Dollars Only)*

   $☐☐☐ , ☐☐☐ . 0 0

7. Show the age at which you plan to stop working.

   ☐☐ *(Show only one age)*

8. Below, show the average yearly amount (not your total future lifetime earnings) that you think you will earn between now and when you plan to stop working. Include performance or scheduled pay increases or bonuses, but not cost-of-living increases.

   If you expect to earn significantly more or less in the future due to promotions, job changes, part-time work, or an absence from the work force, enter the amount that most closely reflects your future average yearly earnings.

   If you don't expect any significant changes, show the same amount you are earning now (the amount in 6B).

   Future average yearly earnings: *(Dollars Only)*

   $☐☐☐ , ☐☐☐ . 0 0

Form **SSA-7004-SM** (1-2003)   EF (01-2003)
Destroy prior editions

Form Approved
OMB No. 0960-0466 SP

9. Do you want us to send the *Statement:*
   - To you? Enter your name and mailing address.
   - To someone else (your accountant, pension plan, etc.)? Enter your name with "c/o" and the name and address of that person or organization.

"C/O" or Street Address (Include Apt. No., P.O. Box, Rural Route)

Street Address

Street Address (If Foreign Address, enter City, Province, Postal Code)

U.S. City, State, Zip code (If Foreign Address, enter Name of Country only)

NOTICE:
I am asking for information about my own Social Security record or the record of a person I am authorized to represent. I declare under penalty of perjury that I have examined all the information on this form, and on any accompanying statements or forms, and it is true and correct to the best of my knowledge. I authorize you to use a contractor to send the *Social Security Statement* to the person and address in item 9.

▶

Please sign your name (Do Not Print)

Date   (Area Code)   Daytime Telephone No.

Unheralded Social Security Features

S ocial security offers a bevy of other, unheralded features that can make your retirement planning a little less stressful. For example, few people stop to consider the value of the life and disability insurance benefits that are included in social security. Yet, to the extent that this protection allows you to cut back on private insurance, the savings can go toward your nest egg. And, as noted above, a nonworking spouse of an eligible social security recipient gets benefits, too.

Couple's Bonus and Two-Earner Benefits

Once you begin receiving social security benefits, your husband or wife can also receive benefits based on your record, even if he or she never worked in a job covered by social security. A nonworking spouse is eligible to begin receiving benefits at age 62. Benefits at full retirement age will generally be about half what you are receiving—together you get 150% of what you'd receive on your own.

For example, if you were 56 years old in 2005, you will reach full-benefit retirement age (66 years, under current social security rules; see the chart on page 87) in 2015. If you have been earning above the social security maximum, the SSA says you can expect to receive $1,926 per month. But if you are married, you and your spouse would receive a minimum of $2,889 per month (150% of $1,926).

If your spouse does work, he or she will receive a benefit based on actual earnings *or* 50% of your benefit, whichever is more. If you and your spouse are both 56, and both of you work and will qualify for the maximum social security benefit when you retire at age 66 in 2015, you can expect to receive a combined $3,852 per month in benefits. If you're eligible for both your own retirement benefits and for benefits as a spouse, social security pays your own benefit first. If your benefit as a spouse is higher than your retirement benefit, you'll get a combination of bene-

WHAT TO EXPECT FROM SOCIAL SECURITY

These tables show your estimated monthly social security benefit at full retirement age in the years shown, in today's dollars and in future, inflation-adjusted dollars, given your 2005 income. (If you expect to retire early or late, see the tables on pages 90 and 91.)

Estimated Monthly Benefit in Today's Dollars

2005 Income	2006	2015	2025	2035	2045
Worker Only					
$ 40,000	$1,108	$ 1,232	$1,365	$ 1,440	$ 1,458
$ 50,000	1,294	1,449	1,609	1,653	1,663
$ 60,000	1,478	1,621	1,725	1,778	1,791
$ 70,000	1,624	1,723	1,842	1,903	1,918
$ 80,000	1,710	1,825	1,959	2,029	2,046
maximum*	1,796	1,926	2,075	2,154	2,173
Worker and Spouse					
$ 40,000	$1,662	$ 1,848	$2,048	$2,160	$ 2,187
$ 50,000	1,941	2,174	2,414	2,480	2,495
$ 60,000	2,217	2,432	2,588	2,667	2,687
$ 70,000	2,061	2,287	2,287	2,287	2,287
$ 80,000	2,565	2,738	2,939	3,044	3,069
maximum*	2,694	2,889	3,113	3,231	3,260

Estimated monthly benefit in Future, Inflation-Adjusted Dollars**

2005 Income	2006	2015	2025	2035	2045
Worker Only					
$ 40,000	$1,126	$ 1,699	$2,699	$4,036	$ 6,055
$ 50,000	1,314	1,996	3,187	4,777	7,036
$ 60,000	1,502	2,251	3,451	5,129	7,559
$ 70,000	1,649	2,390	3,679	5,481	8,081
$ 80,000	1,738	2,530	3,908	5,834	8,603
maximum*	1,825	2,669	4,131	6,173	9,101
Worker and Spouse					
$ 40,000	$1,689	$ 2,549	$4,049	$6,144	$ 9,083
$ 50,000	1,971	2,994	4,781	7,166	10,554
$ 60,000	2,253	3,377	5,177	7,694	11,339
$ 70,000	2,474	3,485	5,519	8,222	12,122
$ 80,000	2,607	3,795	5,862	8,751	12,905
maximum*	2,738	4,004	6,197	9,260	13,652

*Maximum wage subject to social security: $90,000 in 2005, to be adjusted annually using a formula based in part on the national average wage index.
NOTE: This table was created using the Social Security benefits calculator at www.ssa.gov and presumes that you and your spouse are the same age. Your spouse would qualify for benefits based on his or her work record. The figures assume no change in benefits other than cost-of-living adjustments.

fits equaling the higher spouse benefit. For example: A wife qualifies for a retirement benefit of $600 and a spouse's benefit of $963. At age 66 the wife collects her own $600 retirement benefit and social security adds $363 from the spouse's benefit, for a total of $963. If she takes her retirement benefit at any time before she turns 66, both amounts will be reduced.

Survivors' Benefits

"Life insurance" from social security? Yep. Part of the social security taxes you pay buys survivors insurance to provide monthly benefits for a surviving spouse, children, and dependent parents. In some circumstances, even a former spouse can collect. Right now, 98 out of every 100 American children could get benefits if a working parent died.

The number of work credits you need to qualify for benefits depends on your age. If you die at age 50, for example, you would need to have accumulated 28 credits for the survivor benefits to flow. Because you're likely to earn your credits for each year you work, you would need to have worked seven years. Most people have little trouble qualifying.

The amount of "life insurance" is based on your average lifetime earnings. The more you make, the higher the death benefit, up to a maximum level. The percentage of that amount your survivor will actually get depends on his or her age and situation; for example:

- **A widow or widower age 65-plus:** 100%
- **A widow or widower age 60 to 64:** 71% to 94%
- **A widow or widower any age with a child under age 16:** 75%
- **Children:** 75%

The maximum family benefit is generally about 150% to 180% of your benefit rate.

WORRY-FREE TIP

Few people think of it this way, but for most people, social security is a kind of matching employer-employee retirement savings program. You pay half of the total deduction and your employer pays the other half. Self-employed individuals pay the entire amount, but they get a special tax deduction that partially offsets the burden of paying both ends.

The benefit is also cut if a survivor's earnings top a certain level. Basically, a survivor under full retirement age loses $1 in benefits for each $2 earned above the threshold ($12,000 in 2005), and in the year a survivor reaches full retirement age he or she loses $1 for each $3 earned above a different threshold ($31,800 in 2005); thresholds change annually. Starting with the month in which you reach full retirement age, you will receive your full benefits with no limit on your earnings. The benefits for a child who does not work are not affected by a parent's earnings. For details on this, get the SSA leaflet, *How Work Affects Your Social Security Benefits* (Pub. No. 05-10069) from a local social security office, or look for it online (www.ssa.gov).

The benefits estimate you receive from the SSA will show an estimate of the benefits your family would qualify for if you die. Take this into account when determining how much life insurance you need to buy.

> **WORRY-FREE TIP**
>
> If you were married ten years or more, and you are not currently married, you may be eligible for benefits earned by your ex-spouse—if they are higher than you would collect on your own. You could even be eligible if your former spouse is deceased. If you collect on your former spouse's account (or vice versa), it will not affect the amount of benefits paid a current spouse and dependents. There are a number of eligibility requirements and restrictions. For more information call the Social Security Administration at 800-772-1213.

Disability Benefits

Social security also provides disability coverage—another useful piece in a retirement plan. It's tough to qualify for these payments, though. The SSA considers you disabled only if "you are unable to do any kind of substantial work for which you are suited and your inability to work is expected to last for at least a year or to result in death." That would include people with HIV infection or AIDS if their ability to work has been severely limited.

If you qualify, benefits continue for as long as you are disabled. A 45-year-old making about $49,000 who becomes disabled in 2005 is eligible to receive about $1,397 per month in social security disability; that individual plus a spouse and child would together receive about $2,529.

Inflation Adjustments

This is a biggie. Make that a BIGGIE! Social security benefits are indexed to inflation, which means they rise automatically in line with the consumer price index as long as you continue to collect. This may well be the only piece in your retirement puzzle that offers such a built-in advantage.

For example, say you retire 20 years from now, and your social security check at that point is $3,430 per month. If inflation averages 3%, your benefit would increase to $3,976 after five years, $4,610 after ten years and $5,343 after 15 years. Meanwhile, a company pension that started at $3,500 per month would probably still be $3,500 per month five, ten, or 15 years later.

The effect will be to increase the importance of social security relative to your other sources of retirement income over time. As noted earlier in this chapter, there is a possibility that Congress may trim, or even skip, the cost-of-living hikes temporarily if the federal debt becomes a problem again. Watch this issue carefully.

The Taxing Side of Social Security

Not so long ago, the tax rules for social security benefits were absolutely simple: Benefits were tax-free, period. Now beneficiaries fall into one of three categories:

1. **For most beneficiaries,** benefits remain totally tax-free.
2. **For some beneficiaries,** however, up to 50% of their benefits can be taxed.
3. **And, for a third group**—the most affluent retirees—up to 85% of the benefits fall victim to the IRS.

Basically, the higher your income in retirement, the more your benefits can be taxed. Knowing where you stand is important to retirement planning because tax-free benefits go a lot further than taxable ones will. One dollar of tax-free social security benefits replaces

WHEN FULL BENEFITS WILL BE AVAILABLE		
Year of Birth	**Age: Years**	**+ Months**
1940	65	6
1941	65	8
1942	65	10
1943–54	66	0
1955	66	2
1956	66	4
1957	66	6
1958	66	8
1959	66	10
1960 and later	67	0

$1.63 of wages nicked by federal, state, and social security taxes (assuming a 25% federal income-tax rate, a 7.65% social security tax, and a 6% state rate). But, alas, for more and more retirees, benefits are no longer totally tax free.

Your benefits are vulnerable if your "provisional income" exceeds a particular amount based on your filing status. Provisional income is a tricky creature. It's adjusted gross income as reported on your tax return (that's basically income before subtracting exemptions and deductions) plus 50% of your social security benefits plus 100% of any tax-free interest income.

If your provisional income is less than $25,000 on a single return or $32,000 on a married–filing jointly return, you're safe. None of your benefits are taxable. If provisional income is between $25,000 and $34,000 on a single return or between $32,000 and $44,000 on a joint return, up to 50% of your benefits can be taxed. The actual amount that is taxed is 50% of your benefits or—if less—50% of the amount by which your income exceeds the trigger point.

If your income is over $34,000 on a single return or over $44,000 on a joint return, a different formula kicks in and requires that between 50% and 85% of your benefits be taxed. Although complicated, the for-

WHO IS NOT COVERED BY SOCIAL SECURITY?

Most Americans are covered. The major exceptions are: police officers in most states because they have their own retirement systems, and federal government employees who have been continuously employed since before 1984. Federal government employees newly hired since 1984 are covered by social security. As of July 1, 1991, state and local government workers are automatically covered by social security and must pay social security taxes if they are not covered by a state retirement system.

mula generally produces the same result: When provisional income exceeds the $34,000 or $44,000 threshold, the full 85% of benefits is usually taxed.

If you are married and file a separate return, your threshold amount is $0, so it's almost certain that 85% of your benefits will be taxed. (The instructions you get with your income-tax forms include a worksheet for figuring what part of social security benefits should be reported as taxable income.)

Unlike many numbers in the tax law, these thresholds are not indexed for inflation. By leaving the thresholds fixed, Congress is relying on inflation to push more and more retirees into the group whose benefits are taxed. That means you have to look to your income in the future—which in 20 years could easily be double what it is today, if it simply keeps up with inflation—to predict what part of your benefits will be taxed.

Curious about what happens to the income-tax revenue collected on social security benefits that are taxed? The tax collected on up to 50% of the benefits goes to the social security trust fund and is used to pay future benefits. Money collected under the rule that taxes between 50% and 85% of benefits goes to help pay for medicare. If you choose to have federal taxes withheld from your social security payment, you may obtain a form W-4V from the IRS by calling their toll-free telephone number, 800-829-3676, or by visiting www.ssa.gov on the Internet. Complete and sign the form and return it to your local social security office by mail or in person.

When to Start Collecting: It's Your Choice

S ocial security offers another nifty feature that helps you fit this piece easily into your retirement puzzle. The choice of when to start collecting is yours. Basically, you have three options:

Going for Full Benefits

At your "full retirement age" (as defined by social security), you can begin collecting full benefits. Full retirement age is 65^1/$_2$ for persons born in 1940 and gradually increases to 67 for persons born in 1960 or later. The first retirees affected were those born in 1938, who had to be 65 years and two months old to qualify for full benefits. "Normal retirement age" will continue to rise (as shown in the table on page 87) until 2027, when workers born in 1960 or later will have to be 67 years old to qualify for full benefits. Be sure to factor this important change into your financial planning. If you were born in 1950, "normal" retirement age for receiving full social security benefits will be 66.

Tapping in Early

The earliest you can start collecting monthly checks is age 62, and that will not change as normal retirement age increases. If you start early, your benefits will be reduced—for life—by as much as 25% if your full retirement age is 66 or 30% if it's 67. The exact amount of the reduction depends on how early you begin collecting.

The table on the following page gives you the reduction figures to use if you want to calculate how collecting early will affect your benefits and thus how social security fits in your plan for an early exit. The benefits estimate you request from the SSA can take this into account if you show you plan to retire early. Or, if your estimate is based on applying for benefits at full retirement age, apply your own reduction percentage.

Although starting early means you'll get smaller checks, remember that you'll also get more of them. Even at reduced levels, benefits collected between ages

62 and full retirement age will give you a head start over someone who waits. It will take a dozen years of fatter checks to catch up with the total payments made to the early retiree. If you invest the early payments and count those earnings, the break-even point is further away.

Here's how the table works: Multiply your estimated benefit at full retirement age by the reduction percentage for the number of months early you plan to retire. For example, if you would receive $1,000 a month at 66 and you plan to retire 24 months early, you are entitled to 86.7% of that $1,000, or $867.

In considering when you'll want to start claiming social security, don't lose sight of the big picture. How will your benefits fit into your overall retirement plan? Money you would make by continuing to work past the first year you qualify for social security would far exceed the benefits you would receive over that period. And working longer would qualify you for higher social

HOW EARLIER RETIREMENT WILL REDUCE BENEFITS

Months Early	% of Full Benefits	Months Early	% of Full Benefit
2	98.9%	32	82.2%
4	97.8	34	81.1
6	96.7	36	80.0
8	95.6	38*	79.2
10	94.4	40*	78.3
12	93.3	42*	77.5
14	92.2	44*	76.7
16	91.1	46*	75.8
18	90.0	48*	75.0
20	88.9	50*	74.2
22	87.8	52*	73.3
24	86.7	54*	72.5
26	85.6	56*	71.7
28	84.4	58*	70.8
30	83.3	60*	70.0

*As full retirement age rises from 65 to 67, these early retirement percentages will apply.

security benefits and a bigger payout from a pension or profit-sharing plan from your employer.

Holding Out for More

Here's a little-known social security feature that, due to changes taking effect in coming years, could be a fantastic bonus for future retirees and an interesting twist in your planning for a worry-free retirement. If you delay applying for benefits beyond full retirement age, you'll receive significantly larger monthly checks when you ultimately decide to call it quits. This late-retirement feature can be quite a deal.

THE RETIREMENT BONUS	
Year You Were Born	Annual Bonus for Working Beyond Full Retirement Age
1939–40	7.0
1941–42	7.5
1943 or later	8.0

In order to encourage Americans to stay in the work force in years ahead, Uncle Sam will slowly boost the bonus offered to people who agree to hold off claiming their social security. Up to 1990, the bonus for delaying benefits beyond age 65 was a somewhat meager 3.5% increase for each year delayed.

That bonus is being raised in steps, all the way to an attractive 8% per year for anyone born in 1943 or later. And that's a compounded 8%—each year's 8% bonus is figured on the base benefit, plus any bonuses already earned. And that's on top of cost-of-living increases.

In effect, the government is offering you a guaranteed 8%, partially tax-free return if you agree to leave your social security money untouched for a few extra years. Even better, if you keep working, the wage base on which your benefit is calculated will also go up, leading to an even bigger sum.

By delaying for three years, for example, baby-boomers born in 1946 will be able to increase the size of their social security payments by a compounded 26%, for life, calculated on a higher wage base. Inflation adjustments would be additional. And the larger starting benefit ensures that those cost-of-living increases will be larger, too.

For example, a maximum-wage earner retiring in 21 years can expect a social security benefit of $2,092

WORRY-FREE TIP

Married women who keep their maiden names and are self-employed should watch for errors in their social security records.

If you and your husband own and operate a business together and expect to share in the profits and losses, you may be entitled to receive social security credits as a partner, even without a formal partnership agreement. However, to receive credit for your share, you must file a separate self-employment return showing your share of the income (Schedule SE, Computation of Social Security Self-Employment Tax) even if you and your husband file a joint income-tax return.

If you don't file a separate Schedule SE, earnings from the business will be reported under your husband's social security number. In that case, your social security record will not show your earnings, and you may not receive social security credits for them.

Also, make sure the name and social security number used on the tax return and Schedule SE exactly match what is in the Social Security Administration's records. Check regularly to be sure your earnings have been properly credited with Social Security (Request a SSA-7004: "Personal Earnings and Benefit Estimate Statement").

per month in today's dollars (adjusted for 3% annual inflation over the next 21 years, that would be about $3,892). A delay of three years would boost the benefit to $2,596 (an inflation-adjusted $4,829).

How does the late-retirement bonus figure into your plan? Two ways, mainly:

1. **As retirement nears,** if your nest egg and other post-retirement income sources aren't measuring up to your expectations, hanging in just a little longer could greatly boost your postretirement cash flow. Not only will your social security checks be a little bigger but you'll also have a bit more time to save and invest on your own. A matter of just another year or two could make all the difference.

2. **Or, you can retire as planned** but simply delay your application for social security. Your wage base will not rise, but you'll still get the bonus for each year you delay. And remember, the bonus becomes part of the benefits you receive for life. If your other income sources are adequate or investment returns elsewhere simply can't measure up to the partly tax-free 8% that social security is offering, this may be a good strategy. The trade-off: A short-term delay in exchange for more security long-term.

Pack an Insurance Parachute

Chapter 6

The keys to dealing most successfully with the insurance part of a worry-free retirement are simplicity and cost-control. Your goal is to establish the coverage you need to protect yourself, your family and your nest egg against financial disaster—but to spend as little as possible doing so. The savings can go toward your retirement stash.

Relax. The task is not as tough as you might think. Health, life, disability and long-term-care are four important types of insurance that fit different stages of your plan. Health coverage is always crucial. Life and disability insurance are important in your 40s and 50s, but the need often diminishes as you near retirement. Long-term-care coverage, while it probably won't be needed until well beyond retirement, is immensely cheaper if you buy it while you're still in your 50s. We'll show you how to make the best choices in all four areas to protect your retirement assets—and free up more cash for your nest egg at the same time.

While those four types of insurance have the most direct impact on your retirement-plan thinking, don't stop there. It's also wise to review your homeowners and auto coverage every two or three years to make certain the coverage will protect the assets you're counting on for retirement against the potential devastation of a fire, accident, or lawsuit. And only by taking the time to reshop your coverage can you protect yourself against overpaying.

Maximizing Your Health Benefits

Medical insurance is a must for a secure retirement. The cost of health care is so high, and has risen so rapidly, that the lack of health coverage jeopardizes your retirement nest egg if you fall victim to a serious illness or accident.

If you have employer-sponsored health coverage—either through your company or your spouse's—making the most of it now can free up resources for your worry-free retirement plan. Investigate the coverage you and your spouse have now. You may be able to save thousands of dollars a year by managing insurance benefits more effectively. Here are some things you can do:

Avoid double coverage for working couples. It's getting difficult to collect 100% of a medical claim, even when both spouses work and each has health insurance. In the past, one policy might have picked up where the other left off. But that's less common now, so it could be downright wasteful to keep funding the overlap. Take the time to study exactly what you get from each policy and what you'd lose by dropping either one. Before you cancel any insurance, however, find out the conditions under which you'll be allowed to rejoin the group if your other coverage is ever in jeopardy.

A PERK FOR SELF-EMPLOYEDS

Here's some good news about paying health insurance premiums on your own, if you're self-employed. Rather than treat the cost as a medical expense—meaning you get a tax deduction only to the extent the total of such costs exceeds 7.5% of your adjusted gross income—you may get to write off the premiums as an adjustment to income—meaning you're sure to get the tax benefit. There's a hitch, of course: Your business must show a net profit before you qualify to take the deduction. And you can't claim it if you are eligible for coverage under another employer-sponsored plan, including a plan that your spouse may have.

Select a balanced diet from the benefits "cafeteria." Many companies offer an insurance-benefits menu, allowing employees to choose among different types of coverage. Take advantage of the flexibility to select the coverage that best meets your needs. You and your spouse can make different choices to avoid overlapping coverage and free up funds for your 401(k) plan or other retirement savings.

Compare out-of-pocket costs. Suppose you're offered a choice between two policies. One carries a zero deductible—meaning you would never be required to pay out-of-pocket charges—and costs you $120 a month in premiums. The other option is paid for entirely by your employer but has a $300 deductible and requires you to pay 20% of any remaining charges. Which policy would you choose?

> **WORRY-FREE TIP**
>
> Insure.com Inc., of Darien, Illinois (800-556-9393), tracks rates, coverage, and safety ratings of over 200 insurance companies offering life and health coverage. Quotesmith provides instant quotes for coverage online at www.insure.com.

Most people are inclined to pick the first option to avoid unexpected, out-of-pocket expenses. Yet the second option is probably a better deal and would leave you with a nice chunk of immediate cash to sock away for your worry-free retirement. At $120 a month, you'd lay out $1,440 a year in premiums for the first policy. You'd have to incur medical expenses of $7,500 to spend that much in a year on the second policy.

Stash that $1,440 in a savings account and use it to pay any uncovered expenses. Or better yet, invest it or whatever's left over in a Roth IRA, from which you could withdraw your contributions without penalty, and where interest accumulates tax-free. Say you manage to hold on to only half that amount. By investing $720 a year in an IRA where it grows, untaxed, at a 10% annual rate, you'd add $12,600 to your nest egg after ten years, $45,000 after 20 years.

Individual Health Policies

If you and your spouse don't have health coverage through an employer, you'll need an individual (non-group) health policy. The cost of such coverage drops dramatically as the deductible amount you're willing to shoulder goes up and if you stay within an insurer's preferred-provider (PPO) network of doctors and hospitals. It makes sense for healthy families and individuals to go with a high deductible and stash the premium savings in a bank account, a Roth IRA, or a health savings account (HSA), which first became available in 2004.

To qualify for an HSA, you must be under age 65 and purchase a health policy with an annual deductible of at least $1,000 for an individual or $2,000 for a family. This policy must be your only health insurance. Once the policy is in place, you may set up an HSA and contribute up to the amount of your policy's deductible. If you are age 55 or older by the end of the year, you may contribute $500 beyond the deductible.

Money you put into the account can be deducted on your tax return—whether you itemize deductions or not. Earnings in the account grow untaxed, just as in a 401(k) or IRA. But unlike retirement plans, you can dip into an HSA at any age—tax-free—to pay for medical expenses, including your policy deductible and co-payments and many charges that are not typically covered by health insurance, such as over-the-counter drugs, vision and dental care, long-term-care insurance premiums, and future medigap premiums.

Unlike flexible-spending accounts used to pay for health-care expenses, HSAs allow unspent money to be rolled over from year to year. You will owe income tax on earnings if funds are used for non-health-care purposes, and a 10% penalty will be imposed on any non-qualified withdrawal before age 65.

HMO Alternative

Joining a health maintenance organization (HMO) or other type of prepaid medical plan is a money-saving way to secure complete health coverage for you and your family. These plans provide comprehensive health care for a set monthly fee, usually with no deductible. Charges for office visits are as low as $5 or $10.

The main drawback to HMOs is that your choice of doctors is limited to those who are on staff or under

---

MEDICARE AND MEDIGAP IN YOUR FUTURE

Once you reach age 65, Uncle Sam will step into the health insurance picture with medicare, which will pay a portion of your health costs in retirement—but *only* a portion.

You will also need medigap coverage— paid for either by your former employer or by you—to cover what medicare doesn't. The cost of medigap policies can vary astoundingly by insurer for exactly the same coverage, so it pays to shop. If you decide to delay retirement be sure to sign up for medicare three months before your 65th birthday.

---

contract with the HMO. But millions of HMO members are finding the savings to be worth the trade-off. Blue-Cross BlueShield, for example, is a major provider of both traditional fee-for-service insurance, called indemnity coverage, and HMOs. In California, the cost of monthly HMO "dues" (the premium) for an individual runs about 30% less than for an indemnity policy with a $250 deductible. Because the HMO has no deductible, the savings are even higher. For a family of three, the monthly premium savings are about 15%, but because a deductible applies to each family member the potential savings from that source are tripled.

Fitting Life Insurance into Your Retirement Plan

As long as your demise would cause economic hardship for your spouse, children, or other loved ones, you're a candidate for life insurance—or death protection, to put it more literally—as part of your plan for a worry-free retirement. The questions are: Which kind of life insurance? How can you get it without diverting any more than necessary from your savings goals?

The payoff from life insurance, invested at a reasonable rate, should be enough for your family to carry on without you, after accounting for amounts available from social security and all other assets that you've accumulated to date. The American Council of Life Insurers reports that the average insured household owns about $220,000 worth of coverage. That sounds substantial until you think of it this way: Take $220,000, invest it in Treasury securities paying 3.7%, and it will produce $8,140 a year. If that's enough to bridge the income gap your family would face following your demise, okay. If not, you need higher coverage.

The blizzard of life insurance products is confusing at first. But it really boils down to two basic choices:

1. **Do you want life insurance, pure and simple,** without any complicated investment or tax-deferred savings features attached? If so, your choice should be "term" life.

2. **Or do you want your life coverage to double** as a retirement-savings vehicle that offers the advantage of tax-deferred money growth over the long term? If so, and you have the money to spend on this higher-cost coverage, a "cash-value" or "whole-life" policy may be the direction to go.

Both routes have advantages and disadvantages, and financial-planning experts are forever debating which is better. The one you choose depends on the amount of money you have available, your age, the level of coverage you need, and the confidence level you have in your own investment abilities.

Here's one rule of thumb that may help you make a quick decision. If you already have trouble finding enough money to fund your 401(k) or IRA to the maximum each year, you should not shell out big money for cash-value coverage laden with high up-front costs, an uncertain investment return, and a large "early surrender" penalty if you try to cash in the policy before ten years or so. IRAs and 401(k)s match the key tax advantage of life insurance by generating tax-deferred earnings that the IRS doesn't get a crack at until you withdraw the money. (And, with the Roth IRA, the IRS doesn't get a crack at the earnings even then; qualified withdrawals are completely tax-free.)

If you have an existing whole-life policy that already has a built-up cash value, you'd probably be wise to hang on. By now, such a policy may be providing

> **WORRY-FREE TIP**
>
> Before issuing a life-insurance policy, the insurance company will want to know details of your medical history and require a physical exam and blood evaluation. They may investigate your medical records through the Medical Information Bureau (MIB), a credit-bureau-like firm based in Westwood, Mass. As with your credit file, if something negative turns up, you have the right to dispute the findings. In some cases, volunteering for further medical tests or treatments could result in a drastically reduced life-insurance premium.

coverage at a very reasonable cost compared with what you'd pay for a newly issued term policy.

Still, for most folks in the 40-to-55 age range with household incomes under $150,000 and life insurance needs of less than $750,000 or so, the old insurance adage applies: Buy term and invest the difference yourself in your own retirement-savings plan.

For example, a healthy, nonsmoking 45-year-old woman would pay a premium of about $263 in years one through ten of a ten-year level-term policy for $250,000 of coverage through State Farm Life Insurance. After ten years, that premium rises annually, starting at $4,058 in year 11 and hitting a whopping $8,178 in the 20th year, when she hits age 65. If she opted for 20-year term starting at 45, she would pay a level premium of $363 per year for 20 years. In year 21, payments would jump to $9,045. For a 30-year policy this 45-year-old woman would pay a premium of $613 each year.

The same 45-year-old would pay a fixed annual premium of $3,798 for a whole-life policy from State Farm with a beginning death benefit of $250,000. The difference goes toward building cash value in the whole-life policy but is subject to up-front commissions and fees. The death benefit might also go up each year when dividends are paid. (In these examples, State Farm quoted super preferred rates, which are not available to all customers.)

Here's help choosing the best plan at the lowest cost.

Term Life: Biggest Bang for Your Insurance Buck

Term is the simplest, cheapest form of life insurance, offering the most coverage for the lowest cost. You select whatever level of coverage you want—$50,000, $500,000 or any other number—and pay an annual premium. If you die while you own the policy, your beneficiaries will receive the money.

The premium is based on the amount of insurance, your general health and your age when you first buy the policy. It then rises as you grow older. A 40-year-old nonsmoking woman in good health, for example, can buy a $250,000 ten-year policy from State Farm for around $200 per year to start. A healthy nonsmoking 50-year-old woman buying the same policy would start at about $373 per year. (In these examples, State Farm again quoted its super preferred rates.)

Most policies sold today have premiums guaranteed for fixed time periods, most commonly ten and 20 years. The premium is fixed for the length of the guarantee period and then rises each year thereafter. Most plans are guaranteed renewable as long as you keep paying the premiums. To keep on track, be sure the policy you choose includes that feature.

You can also buy a level-premium, nonrenewable term policy for a fixed time period, say five or ten years, at a fixed premium. That's a sound choice for a plan that includes only temporary life insurance needs—say, until your children have finished college. When the period is up, the coverage disappears and you can channel the money into your retirement nest egg instead.

Remember that for most people, the need for life insurance diminishes as you reach retirement age. By then, the nest egg you've accumulated becomes your

> ### WORRY-FREE TIP
>
> If you already have trouble finding enough money to fund your 401(k) or IRA each year, "cash-value" coverage is probably not right for you. Instead, buy "term" for much less and invest the difference yourself in your retirement savings plan. One of the key advantages of life insurance as an investment is that there is no tax due on earnings as they build up in the policy. The same thing is true of earnings inside an IRA or 401(k).

> ## TERM LIFE IS SIMPLE INSURANCE
>
> This is death coverage, pure and simple, with no bells and whistles involving savings plans or complicated investments. For identical death benefits, term premiums are generally one-fourth to one-tenth the amount of cash-value premiums.

insurance, replacing a term policy that becomes prohibitively expensive beyond the age of 60.

While most people simply drop term coverage after age 60 or so, that may not be an option if you started a family in your forties or have a much-younger spouse. If you expect to need life insurance after age 60, make sure that you buy a term policy that is renewable beyond that age or a policy that can be converted (guaranteed, with no medical exam) to whole-life coverage. The right to convert should be yours at least until age 60. You'll probably pay more for the whole-life coverage. But because some term policies can't be renewed after age 65, you have no choice if you want to continue coverage.

The Case for Cash-Value Coverage

For most retirement plans, term life is terrific. But cash-value (whole-life) coverage can be a sound addition if:

- **You need lots of insurance**—say, more than $750,000.
- **You are already contributing the maximum** to IRAs for you and your spouse, a 401(k) plan at work if you have one, a Keogh plan if you qualify, or any other tax-sheltered retirement-savings plan that's available to you.
- **You can afford it**—which is to say, you're probably earning more than $150,000 per year.

If you meet these criteria, cash-value coverage may be your best life insurance parachute. The main reason: Cash-value life doubles as a tax shelter for retirement savings. The shelter aspect works much the same as an IRA or 401(k): Cash inside the policy is granted the advantage of tax-deferred growth. A portion of what you pay out in premiums every year goes to pay for the life insurance coverage, but the bulk of the money is devoted to the savings and investment features that are intended to build cash value for your nest egg over time.

Because insurance policies are complicated and involve various fees, commissions, and other charges, the best place to capture the benefits of tax-free money growth is in an IRA, 401(k), Keogh, or similar plan. That's why it makes sense to fund those plans fully before considering cash-value insurance.

SHOPPING FOR THE BEST INSURANCE DEAL

Pay attention to ratings of insurers. It's crucial for your plan to pick an insurer that won't die before you do. That means buying only from companies that earn the highest ratings from independent evaluators. Ask your insurance agent to provide the latest ratings for any company you're considering.

A.M. Best Co. has been rating insurers about half a century longer than anyone else, and Best's ratings are the industry standard. Buy only from insurance companies that have achieved an A rating or better from Best. You can check a Best rating yourself by calling the company (908-439-2200, ext. 5742). You can sign up for free daily news via e-mail by going to www.bestreview.com. You can have individual company reports mailed to you for $75 each for each rating and $35 for each accompanying report. Ratings and reports can also be ordered from Best's Web site (www.ambest.com).

Weiss Research, Inc. also rates insurance companies. You can obtain an oral report over the phone (800-289-9222) for $19 per company, or you may obtain a one-page company rating report online for $14.95 at www.weissratings.com. Three other companies that follow the insurance industry—Moody's Investors Service (212-553-0377; www.moodys.com), Standard & Poor's (212-438-7187; www.standardandpoors.com) and Fitch Ratings (212-908-0800; www.fitchratings.com)—will each give you a single rating over the phone at no cost, or you may check out companies at their Web sites.

For help in evaluating cash-value policies, you can tap a service offered by the Consumer Federation of America (CFA) Insurance Group. A detailed evaluation costs $55 for the first policy, then $40 for each additional policy sent at the same time. For information, log onto www.consumerfed.org, call 202-387-6121 or send a stamped, self-addressed business envelope to CFA, 1424 16th St., N.W., Suite 604, Washington, DC 20036.

Unlike term policies that will eventually expire, whole-life policies—also called permanent policies—remain in place for as long as you live. With most policies, the annual premium remains fixed and the insurance company agrees to pay a specified benefit when you die. But this type of policy has a value that increases over time and that you can tap for retirement income. It's a bit like a forced savings plan with life insurance attached. Part of your premium pays for insurance, part goes toward your savings, and investment earnings are allowed to accumulate tax-free.

If you use whole-life as a tax shelter for retirement savings, there two basic ways you can get your money out:

1. **Borrowing:** You can borrow against the policy's cash value while keeping the insurance in force. Because it's a loan, the money is not taxed. (Any loan outstanding when you die is automatically paid by the proceeds of the policy, reducing the amount paid to your beneficiaries.)

2. **Surrendering:** You can collect the entire cash value by surrendering the policy and terminating your insurance coverage. The payment is tax-free, up to the amount that you paid in premiums over the years. Any excess is taxable.

Because commissions and fees take a large bite out of your cash value in the first couple of years, you'll need to keep funding a policy for at least ten years for your investment to pay off.

Comparison shopping is a must. Not all cash-value policies are created equal—not by a long shot. Different types of policies offer different combinations of investment choices, life insurance levels, and premiums. A. M. Best Co. rates the financial health of insurance companies. You may check a company's rating at its Web site. (See the box on the previous page.)

Variable life is a whole-life hybrid that offers the most flexibility and probably the most potential for building the investment portion of your life insurance nest egg. Variable-life plans let you invest part of your

Comparison shopping is a must. Not all cash-value policies are created equal—not by a long shot.

cash value in stocks and other securities offering the possibility of higher returns than other whole-life policies in which yields are fixed. You'll have the flexibility to shift your investments among the options offered within the plan. Most life insurance companies offer you a choice of mutual funds. Both the total death benefit and the cash value of a variable policy rise and fall with the results of the investment accounts.

Don't Overlook Disability Coverage

Most people are quick to acknowledge the need for life insurance to protect a spouse and children, yet for anyone under age 60 the risk of becoming disabled is far greater than the risk of death. The American Council of Life Insurers reports that nearly one-third of all Americans ages 35 to 65 will become disabled for more than 90 days, while the National Safety Council reported that about two-thirds of all disabling injuries suffered by American workers in 2002 occurred off the job and were not covered by workers' compensation. An injury or illness that slams the door on your income would devastate your plans for a worry-free retirement.

Disability or "income protection" insurance provides the perfect parachute to protect your retirement

---

IF YOUR INSURANCE COMPANY GETS IN TROUBLE

If you own a term policy and the company goes bust, your best move will be to buy a new policy from a healthy carrier. Because there's no cash value to worry about, your main concerns are keeping coverage in force without gaps and paying no more than you did before.

If you own a cash-value policy at a crippled or failed carrier, your best source of information on what to do will be your state insurance department. All states have programs that guarantee the value of your policy if the insurance company goes under.

Basically, healthy insurance companies assume the burden of covering policyholders of a failed company.

nest egg. If you become disabled, this insurance will pay a portion of your regular income. While life insurance is necessary only for those with dependents to protect, disability insurance is recommended for almost anyone who relies on earned income.

You may already have some type of disability coverage through a benefit plan at work. Paid sick leave is one possible source. Find out how much you've accumulated and how much you stand to add in the future.

If your employer provides disability coverage, pinpoint how much you would receive and for how long. Almost all employers in California, Hawaii, New Jersey, New York, Rhode Island, and Puerto Rico pay benefits for up to 26 weeks on nonoccupational disability. Elsewhere, nearly 90% of medium-size and large firms offer some form of salary continuation during periods of incapacity, but benefits are often limited or short-lived. Benefits from an employer's policy may be taxable, unlike benefits under a policy you pay for yourself.

Social security also includes benefits for long-term disabilities, so count that, too. But keep in mind that social security pays only a limited benefit for severe disabilities that are expected to last at least a year or result in death. If social security is your nest egg's only disability safety net, a solid strategy calls for added coverage.

Disability insurance isn't cheap. A policy from UnumProvident Life Insurance that kicks in after you've been disabled for 180 days, pays $2,500 per month without an inflation adjustment provision would cost a 45-year-old male earning $50,000 about $975 per year. The premium jumps to about $1,415 if you want coverage to start after a 90-day waiting period and you want the monthly benefit to be adjusted for inflation.

A 55-year-old male office worker earning $80,000 with a base benefit of $5,000 would pay about $2,335 per year for the policy without inflation protection and with a 180-day waiting period; the cost would be $3,067 for a policy that includes an inflation adjustment and the shorter wait of 90 days.

Those figures are for nonsmokers in jobs that insurance companies consider safe. If you smoke or are

Buying a policy without inflation protection can also save money, but it's a move you probably do not want to make.

employed in a more hazardous field, such as construction, your premiums will probably be higher.

Keeping Disability Costs Down

Fortunately, there are several factors that can hold down the cost of disability insurance and help you channel the savings into your retirement nest egg. The waiting or "elimination" period is one. The longer you agree to wait before coverage starts, the lower the cost. For example, going with a 180-day period instead of 60 or 90 days trims 25% to 30% from the premium.

The examples above are for "total and residual" policies that pay off for partial as well as total disability. You can cut the premium another 20% to 25% by buying coverage that pays off only for total disability. That shifts more risk to you but still gives your retirement nest egg catastrophic protection.

The amount of income you choose to replace also affects the premium. Because disability insurance benefits under a policy you pay for yourself are tax-free, you needn't replace 100% of your current income. In fact, most disability policies will replace a maximum of about 60% to 80%. If you buy a social security rider, you can further reduce your premium by 15% to 30%. This rider will allow the insurance company to deduct your social security benefits from your monthly benefit payment, but you'll end up with the same amount to live on.

How long do you want the payments to continue? The policies described above provide coverage to age 65. But you can elect a shorter time period that would lower the premium even more. Choosing the shorter period is a calculated gamble that you'll have other assets or income sources—a pension, perhaps—to carry you through once disability payments stop.

Buying a policy without inflation protection can also save money, but it's a move you probably do not want to make. This feature, which automatically boosts benefits for inflation, can raise your premiums by 15% to 25%. But the protection is worth it when you consider that over ten years the current purchasing power of a

---

WHAT TO LOOK FOR IN A POLICY

If you opt for long-term-care insurance, there are several features you should get in the policy.

A prior stay in a hospital should not be required before you collect benefits, and coverage for Alzheimer's disease or related disorders should be guaranteed.

Home care should be included as a regular benefit or available with an extra premium. A policy that allows beneficiaries to alternate between home and nursing home is best.

Look for at least a partial inflation-adjustment provision.

The policy should be guaranteed renewable for life.

The policy should have a "waiver of premium" clause that allows you to make no payments after receiving benefits for a specified time.

The policy should have a "free look" period. This period allows you to change your mind and cancel the policy at no cost within the first 30 days.

$2,300 monthly benefit would dwindle to just $1,500 if inflation averages 4%.

Your Long-Term-Care Insurance Choices

Chronic illness requiring long-term care is one of the most dire events we worry about facing—and having to pay for—in retirement. For many people, this is a key motivator in building as large a retirement nest egg as possible. Little wonder. Nursing-home costs average over $70,000 annually per person. In some regions the bill tops $120,000 in today's dollars. Without insurance, an extended stay could wipe out your retirement nest egg.

Although the concept of long-term-care insurance is appealing—benefits cover the cost of nursing-home care or of care that allows you to stay in your own home—most of us are understandably reluctant to buy any kind of insurance coverage that probably

GUIDE TO LONG-TERM-CARE INSURANCE

To obtain a free copy of *AHIP's Guide To Long-Term Care Insurance,* call the Federal Citizen Information Center toll free at 888-878-3256. Or view and download a copy online at America's Health Insurance Plans Web site, www.ahip.org.

won't pay off for 20 years or more, if ever. But if you wait until retirement age to buy this coverage, the cost will be high.

As with whole-life insurance, however, the earlier you start paying for this insurance, the less you have to pay each year. A 55-year-old couple would pay about 60% less in annual premiums than a 65-year-old couple for the same long-term-care coverage.

How much does this coverage cost? Consider these two policies: The premium for a 55-year-old would be $1,787 a year for long-term-care insurance that pays $150 a day for three years of assistance in the home or community, or that pays the same benefit for three years of care in an assisted-living or nursing-home facility. (It also includes 5% inflation protection, compounded annually.) A 65-year-old would pay $2,749 a year for the same coverage.

Part of the premiums you pay can be considered a medical expense, so you could get a tax break for buying this insurance. But there are restrictions. First, the amount you can deduct is limited based on your age. If you're under age 40, the deduction is capped at a measly $260—regardless of how much you actually pay for your policy. The annual limit rises with your age, to a maximum of $3,250 for purchasers over age 70. As with other medical expenses, you get a tax benefit only if the total of your qualifying costs exceeds 7.5% of your adjusted gross income.

Should You Bite?

Given the high cost, should long-term-care coverage be part of your worry-free retirement parachute? The answer depends on your present circumstances. To see whether long-term-care insurance fits your retirement planning needs, answer these questions. "Yes" answers to the first two questions, then to several others, mean you should seriously consider adding it. Otherwise, one of the alternatives discussed next may be a better bet.

Is your net worth, excluding your house, between $100,000 and $1.5 million? With more than that, you can self-insure. With less, you may merely be delaying the onset of government assistance by purchasing long-term-care insurance.

Can you pay the monthly premium with no more than 5% of your income? Use this benchmark because premiums will make up a larger portion of your budget in the future if they increase faster than your income. If premiums outstrip your budget, you might have to cancel the policy or dip into your savings to pay the premiums, which defeats the purpose of the insurance.

Do you need to preserve assets for a spouse, child, or relative who is financially dependent on you? Income and asset protection are the best features of long-term-care insurance.

Would you rather pay premiums than risk the high cost of an extended nursing-home stay? Here are the odds: A 65-year-old has a 40% chance of spending at least a day in a nursing home, a 20% chance of spending at least a year there, and less than a 10% chance of spending five or more years there, according to the *New England Journal of Medicine*. Almost half of nursing-home residents live there for three months or less.

What's your family's health history? Does your family tend to live to ripe old ages or have a history of conditions that increase the likelihood of needing long-term care? Those conditions argue in favor of buying long-term-care coverage. But if there has been a lot of cancer in your family, you can better protect your nest egg by purchasing top-flight Medicare supplement insurance after age 65.

Are you a woman? Women have longer life expectancies and tend to enter nursing homes sooner and stay longer than men. Three out of four nursing-home residents over age 85 are women.

Is your family too far-flung to provide you at-home care indefinitely? Also, consider that single people are more likely to need nursing-home policies and less likely to need home health care benefits. The latter are designed to relieve the primary caregiver (usually a spouse), not to provide round-the-clock care at home.

Consider Some Alternatives

If your answers to the above questions were mostly no, there may be more cost-efficient ways for you to protect your retirement nest egg. Consider the following long-term-care insurance alternatives:

- **Self-insure.** Instead of shelling out money for premiums, invest that money in your own "self-insurance" account. Unlike a policy you'd buy, your self-insurance has no restrictions or loopholes. You can spend the money on any kind of care, and there are no eligibility requirements. You run the risk of needing nursing-home care before you've saved enough. But most nursing-home stays by single retirees end up depleting savings by less than $20,000, according to a recent study.
- **Tap your home equity.** If you are house-rich, you may want to plan on tapping home equity, if necessary, to pay for long-term care. You can do that with a home-equity line of credit (Chapter 3) or a reverse mortgage (Chapter 12).
- **Wait.** Pressure from consumers and regulators is spawning a new generation of long-term-care policies with better benefits and fewer loopholes. While existing policyowners may be offered the option to upgrade to these new-and-improved policies, that's not guaranteed.

Get a Turbocharged Earnings Edge with IRAs

Hooray for the IRA—the individual retirement account. It's a perpetual-motion money machine with a single goal—encouraging you to sock away retirement money that will grow unfettered by any taxes. The turbocharged power of tax-deferred or tax-free growth inside this tax shelter makes this simple tool a potent financial force over the long term. And part of the genius behind how it accomplishes its goal is the way it keeps you at arm's length from the money until you get close to retirement. With one exception—taking your own already-taxed contributions to a Roth IRA—there's no raiding the piggy bank for expensive toys along the way without incurring both tax on the withdrawal and a stiff penalty as well.

IRAs have had their ups and downs in the public's eye. They burst on the scene as "everybody's tax shelter" in 1981; then they suffered the indignity of losing tax-deductibility for higher-income individuals in 1986. They began reclaiming popularity in 1998 with the introduction of the Roth IRA and its promise of tax-free, not just tax-deferred, earnings. They became even more enticing with the passage of the Economic Growth and Tax Relief Reconciliation Act of 2001, with rules that increase the amount you can stash away yearly—$4,000 in 2005 and $5,000 in 2008. And workers age 50 or older may make a "catch up" contribution of an extra $500 in 2005; in 2006, they may raise the catch up contribution to $1,000.

Using the 2005 maximum contribution as a base, if you put $4,000 into an IRA each year, that seemingly

THE POWER OF TAX-FREE GROWTH INSIDE AN IRA

YEARS	TOTAL OF YOUR DEPOSITS	VALUE AT THIS RATE OF RETURN		
		8%	10%	12%
5	$15,000	$ 19,000	$ 20,100	$ 21,300
10	30,000	46,900	52,600	59,000
15	45,000	88,000	105,000	125,200
20	60,000	148,300	189,000	242,000
25	75,000	236,900	324,500	448,000

modest amount can grow into a powerful part of your worry-free retirement. Imagine that you begin depositing $4,000 a year into an IRA starting in the year you are 35 and keep it up until you're 65. If the account earns an average of 10% a year, the account will hold nearly $724,000. If your spouse kicks in $4,000 a year, too, your combined IRAs will hold more than $1.4 million after 30 years. Assuming you use the Roth IRA, every dime will be tax-free when withdrawn in retirement. If you and your spouse increase your contribution to keep pace as the maximum rises, by 2008 you'll be contributing $10,000 a year. To keep things simple we will use $4,000 for most of the calculations in this chapter.

Traditional versus Roth: The New Rules of IRAs

Okay, you know an IRA should be an integral part of your worry-free retirement plan. But, which variety is best for you—traditional or Roth? And should you take Congress up on its offer to let you convert an old-style IRA to a Roth? We'll get to that, but first, a review of the rules:

Compensation Is Required
To have any kind of IRA, you must have "compensation." That's basically income from a job, self-employment, or alimony. Investment income doesn't

count, nor does income from pensions or annuities. The most you can put into an IRA each year is $4,000, rising to $5,000 by 2008, or 100% of your compensation, whichever is less. Thus, if you earn just $1,000, your maximum IRA contribution for the year is $1,000. The government is serious about the annual limit. Excess contributions are hit with a 6% penalty tax every year until the extra money is removed from the account.

Spousal Accounts

There is an important exception to the rule that you must have compensation to have an IRA. If you have a job but your spouse does not, you can also contribute as much as $4,000 to $5,000 (depending on the year) of your income to a spousal IRA—either traditional or Roth—for him or her. If you choose a traditional IRA and are permitted to deduct contributions to your own account, you may write off deposits to the spousal IRA, too. In fact, even if you can't deduct traditional IRA contributions—due to the restrictions explained below—you can probably still write off spousal IRA contributions.

You're Never Too Young . . .

There is no minimum age for IRA participation. If your 10-year-old has compensation—from a paper route, say, or from working in a family business—he or she can stash as much as $4,000 to $5,000 (depending on the year) of that pay in an IRA.

. . . But You Can Be Too Old

Although you're never too young to have an IRA, the law forbids contributions to traditional IRAs starting with the year you reach age 70$^{1}/_{2}$. There is no age limit for deposits to Roth IRAs, though.

Who Gets the Deduction?

What made the original IRA a "no brainer" investment was a simple, indisputable fact: Contributions were deductible. Put $2,000 into an IRA (the original maximum amount); write off $2,000 on your tax return. In the then-existing 28% bracket, that saved $560 and delivered instant gratification. That was too simple, though, so Congress introduced restrictions to prevent some higher-income earners from getting that deduction. There are two tests that determine whether you can deduct deposits to a traditional IRA, and tens of millions of taxpayers still qualify for the write-off. If you do qualify, when the new IRA maximum contribution of $5,000 is reached, if you're in the 25% bracket, you'll save $1,250.

COMPANY-PLAN TEST. First, are you an "active participant" in a company retirement plan? You are, as far as the law is concerned, if you are eligible during any part of the year to participate in a pension, profit-sharing, 401(k), or similar plan. (If you are in a profit-sharing plan but no contribution is made to your account for the year, however, you are not considered covered for that year.) The Form W-2 you receive from your employer should indicate to you—and the IRS—whether you're covered.

If you are not tripped up by the company-plan test, you can deduct IRA contributions regardless of how high your income is.

INCOME TEST. If you are covered by a plan, you may lose your right to the deduction. The write-off is phased out for active participants in company plans whose "modified" adjusted gross income (AGI)—which is basically AGI before subtracting IRA contributions—exceeds certain levels. Those phaseout zones are climbing, as shown in the table on the opposite page, so as time goes on, more taxpayers will get to deduct contributions.

However, if you are covered by a company plan, the IRA maximum deduction is reduced by $20 for each $50 of AGI over the trigger point. AGI of $5,000 over the threshold, then, would cut the maximum annual deduction by $2,000 ($5,000 ÷ $50 × $20). You could still contribute up to $4,000, but whether you

PHASEOUT ZONES FOR REGULAR IRA DEDUCTIONS

YEAR	SINGLE RETURNS	JOINT RETURNS
2004	45,000–55,000	65,000–75,000
2005	50,000–60,000	70,000–80,000
2006	50,000–60,000	75,000–85,000
2007	50,000–60,000	80,000–100,000

deposited $2,000, $4,000 or any amount in between, only $2,000 would be deductible. On a joint return reporting AGI of $75,000 for 2005, each spouse could write off up to $2,000 of IRA contributions.

A higher trigger point is used to figure whether spousal IRA contributions for the nonworking husband or wife of someone who is covered by a retirement plan are deductible. In that case, the right to the deduction is phased out as AGI rises between $150,000 and $160,000.

INCOME TESTS FOR ROTH IRAs. Although no one gets to deduct contributions to Roth IRAs, there is an income test to determine whether you can use this tax shelter at all. The right to stash retirement cash in a Roth disappears as AGI rises between $150,000 and $160,000 on a joint return and between $95,000 and $110,000 on the return of a single person, whether filing as an individual, a head of household, or a surviving spouse. Married taxpayers who file separate returns may not contribute to Roth IRAs, regardless of their income.

If your AGI on a joint return is $155,000, for example, that's halfway through the phaseout zone, so your maximum contribution would be cut in half: to $2,000. If you report $105,000 AGI on a single return—two-thirds of the way through the phaseout zone—your top Roth pay-in for the year would be $1,333, one-third of the $4,000 maximum. When AGI passes the top of the phaseout zone, you may not contribute to a Roth at all.

Note that the Roth phaseout zones apply regardless of whether you are covered by a retirement plan at work.

> **WORRY-FREE TIP**
>
> If you qualify to deduct IRA deposits, here's a way to get double-barreled action. First, make your $4,000 contribution (or $5,000 in 2006), then take the money you save in taxes ($1,000 on $4,000 in the 25% bracket) and squirrel that away for retirement, too. Over 20 years, those extra $1,000 investments will grow to more than $36,700 even if after-tax earnings average a skimpy 5.5%. Alternatively, skip the deduction and stash your $4,000 in a Roth IRA. Assuming you're not in a lower tax bracket when you retire, tax-free withdrawals from a Roth will give you more spendable income than the combination of taxable withdrawals from the IRA and cash from the side account.

Do Nondeductible Contributions Make Sense?

Before Congress created the Roth IRA, nondeductible contributions to a regular IRA still made good financial sense, because—deductible or not—the money inside the IRA grew without annual interruption from the IRS; interest accumulated tax-deferred. Now, however, it would be a serious blunder for anyone who qualifies to use a Roth—and that's almost everyone—to make nondeductible contributions to a regular IRA. Sure, Roth contributions are also nondeductible, but the Roth has many advantages over the regular, nondeductible variety. In rejecting the traditional nondeductible IRA, you need to consider just one major advantage: Earnings inside a regular nondeductible IRA will be taxed when withdrawn; earnings inside a Roth can be completely tax-free.

Deadlines

Regardless of what kind of IRA you use, the deadline for making your IRA contribution each year is the day your tax return is due for that year. That's usually April 15, of course, but it can be a day or two later if the 15th falls on a weekend. The deadline for making 2005 contributions, then, is April 17, 2006. Although you may be tempted to hold off as long as possible to make your deposit, making it sooner rather than later can be an important contribution to your worry-free retirement. The earlier you make your contribution, the sooner your money goes to work in the supercharged environment of the tax shelter, as the table below indicates. In each case, an annual deposit of $4,000 and a yield of 10% are assumed.

Getting Your Money Out

This book is about building up your retirement nest egg, not spending it, but to make the right choice between a traditional and a Roth IRA, you need to know how the rules differ when it comes to getting at your money. There are big differences on this point, and in nearly every case the advantage goes to the Roth.

Early-Withdrawal Penalties

First, consider the rules if you want to get at your money before retirement. If the tax breaks are the carrots Congress uses to encourage you to save for retirement, penalties for early withdrawal are the sticks that make sure you keep at it. That's not necessarily bad, either, since your goal is a worry-free retirement.

	MAKE YOUR DEPOSIT SOONER THAN LATER	
	IF ANNUAL $4,000 DEPOSIT MADE AT	
TOTAL AT END OF YEAR	**END OF YEAR**	**BEGINNING OF YEAR**
5	$ 24,420	$ 26,862
10	63,750	70,125
15	127,090	139,799
20	229,100	252,010
25	393,388	432,727
30	657,976	723,774
35	1,984,097	1,192,507
40	1,770,370	1,947,407

A TRADITIONAL IRA. With a traditional IRA, if you dip into the account early—as far as the law is concerned, generally anytime before you're 59½ is early—you may be hit with a 10% penalty for premature distribution. Take $5,000 out at age 50, for example, and you probably will be slapped with a $500 penalty. In addition, the full $5,000 will be included in your income for the year and taxed in your top tax bracket. (If you've ever made nondeductible contributions, part of the withdrawal would be both tax- and penalty-free.)

We say you may be hit with a penalty because there's an ever-growing list of exceptions to the penalty: It's waived if you become permanently disabled, for example, or if you use the IRA money to pay medical bills that exceed 7.5% of your adjusted gross income. Also penalty-free is money you withdraw to pay for medical insurance during an extensive period of unemployment. Even though qualifying withdrawals escape the 10% penalty, they would still be taxed.

Two additional exceptions apply:

One allows you to withdraw up to $10,000 penalty-free from your traditional IRAs at any age to help pay to buy or build a first home for yourself, your spouse,

---

ESCAPE-HATCH WITHDRAWALS

You may withdraw money from a traditional IRA before age 59½ if you do so as part of a series of equal annual amounts based on your life expectancy. This table shows the amount of annual penalty-free withdrawal for each $10,000 in a traditional IRA, given these annual rates of return.

AGE AT WHICH WITHDRAWAL BEGINS	6%	8%	10%	12%
49	$660	$800	$945	$1,095
51	710	810	950	1,100
53	725	820	960	1,105
55	740	835	975	1,115
57	760	850	985	1,125

your kids, your grandchildren, or even your parents. That $10,000 is a lifetime limit, not an annual one. Sounds great, but there's a serious downside. Although the 10% penalty is waived, the money would still be taxed in your top bracket (except to the extent it was attributable to nondeductible contributions). That means as much as 35% or more of the $10,000 would go to federal and state tax collectors rather than toward a down payment.

The other exception: Penalty-free withdrawals (with no dollar limit) of money used to pay higher-education expenses for yourself, your spouse, a child, or grandchild. Qualified expenses include tuition, fees, and room and board for post-secondary education, including graduate work. This break has the same drawback as the one for first-time home buyers. Although the 10% penalty doesn't apply, the regular federal and state tax bills do. So, a big chunk of your IRA money will wind up at the IRS and state tax department rather than at the bursar's office. Another way to get at a traditional IRA early without penalty—that doesn't turn on how you spend the money—is discussed on page 130.

EARLY OUT OF A ROTH. At first blush, Roth IRAs also threaten you with a 10% penalty if you cash in before age 59½. And, any withdrawal that is penalized loses tax-free status, too, to deliver a painful double whammy.

To understand the early-withdrawal penalty, you must begin with the definition of a "qualified distribution" from a Roth, which is what the law calls a withdrawal that is tax- and penalty-free.

First, there's the five-year rule. It holds that a Roth must be open for at least four calendar years after the year of your first contribution to it for you to qualify for tax- and penalty-free withdrawals. Say, for example, that you made your first contribution to a Roth sometime in 2005. The earliest you could make a tax- or penalty-free withdrawal would be in 2010. Note that a Roth doesn't have to be opened for five full years to pass this five-year test. Say that you opened a Roth for

2005 on April 17, 2006, under the rule that allows you to make contributions up to the due date of the tax return for the year involved (see page 118). That would start the clock ticking in 2006, so once four calendar years passed (2006, 2007, 2008, and 2009) payouts beginning in 2009—less than 45 months after the account was opened—could be tax- and penalty-free.

They could be, that is, if the payout also meets one of the following conditions:

■ **It is made after you reach age 59 1/2;**
■ **It is made after your death;**
■ **It is made after you become disabled; or**
■ **It is used to help buy a first home for you, your spouse, your kids, your grandchildren, or your parents.**

So, it looks like your money is locked up tighter in a Roth than in a regular IRA, since tapping the account before age 59 1/2 generally means not only a 10% penalty, but also triggers a tax bill on earnings that would otherwise be avoided. But not necessarily. . . .

Roth IRA investors can reclaim contributions at any time and at any age, without tax or penalty. And the first money coming out of Roth IRAs will be considered contributions. Only after you have withdrawn an amount equal to all of your contributions tax- and penalty-free do you have to begin to worry about the early-withdrawal penalty.

Say, for example, that you contribute $4,000 a year for five years and, at the end of the fifth year, the account is worth $26,862. Regardless of your age, you could withdraw $20,000 tax- and penalty-free.

Note this: The exception to the early-withdrawal penalty for traditional IRA money used for college bills applies to Roth IRAs, too, but because such withdrawals wouldn't be "qualified distributions," any amount that represents earnings would not be tax-free.

Tapping Your IRA in Retirement

This is the point, right? With a traditional IRA, once you reach age 59 1/2, the threat of the 10% penalty disappears. You can withdraw as much from your regular IRAs as you want, penalty-free. Cash coming out of the account is taxable in your top tax bracket, except to the extent that it represents a return of nondeductible contributions to the account.

You can cash in your IRA all at once, but doing so could subject you to an enormous tax bill. You'll probably do better tax-wise by taking out as little as necessary each year. Not only does that hold down your tax bill, but it also leaves more money in the tax shelter to enjoy continued tax-deferred (or with a Roth, tax-free) growth. But this tax shelter does not last forever.

Regular IRAs were created to help you accumulate money for your retirement—not build up a pile of money for your heirs to inherit. So the law demands that you begin pulling money out when you reach age $70^{1}/_{2}$. The minimum withdrawal schedule is designed to get all your money out—and taxed—by the time you die, or at least by the time your designated IRA beneficiary dies. If you don't take out the minimum

---

WORRY-FREE RETIREMENT... FOR YOUR CHILDREN

The Roth IRA gives parents an exciting opportunity to set their children on course for their own worry-free retirements. As soon as your children have jobs—flipping burgers, baby-sitting, mowing lawns, whatever—they can have IRAs. Rare indeed, of course, is the teen who would sock summer earnings into a retirement plan. But his or her money doesn't have to go into the account. Mom and Dad (or grandparents or any other generous soul) can fund the IRA with a gift.

Consider this: Claiming your child as a dependent on your tax return saves you money. For the 2005 tax year, that's $1,067 if you're in the current 25% tax bracket. Assume that for four years starting when the child is 15, you put that $1,067 in an IRA in the child's name—assuming he or she earned that much from jobs (investments don't count).

Guess what that $4,268 of deposits will grow to by the time the child is 65, assuming the account earns an average annual rate of 10%. More than $436,000!

That assumes that not a single additional dime is contributed to the IRA. And, because this is a Roth IRA, the entire $436,000 will be tax-free when withdrawn.

required each year, the IRS will claim 50% of the amount you fail to withdraw.

ROTH IRAs. Things are a lot easier with Roth IRAs, thank goodness. Once you reach age 59½ and the account has been opened for at least five years, you can take as much or as little from your account as you need—all tax- and penalty-free.

What if you open a Roth in 2005 and you're already older than 59½? You need to wait until at least 2010 to take tax- and penalty-free withdrawals of earnings. Remember, you have to wait until four calendar years have passed after the year in which you made your first contribution.

You don't have to worry about a minimum distribution schedule, either. You never have to take a dime out of your Roth IRA, at age 70½ or any other age. Unlike regular IRAs, a Roth IRA can be used to build up a stash of cash to leave to your heirs.

Death and the IRA

What if the IRA owner dies while there's still money in the tax shelter? This is another area where the Roth comes out head and shoulders ahead of the traditional IRA.

First of all, with either type of account, there's no early-withdrawal penalty for your beneficiary, regardless of your age when you die or the beneficiary's age when he or she withdraws the money.

The potential problem, however, is that the money pulled out of a traditional IRA is taxable to the beneficiary (except to the extent that it represents nondeductible contributions) in his or her top tax bracket. That could create a substantial tax bill if the IRA is cashed in all at once. The heir may be better off leaving the money in the IRA to continue taking advantage of the tax shelter. Of course, the IRS has something to say about that. The rules set a minimum pace at which the money must be withdrawn and taxes paid.

With a Roth IRA, money goes to your beneficiary tax-free. Still, even though the government has no stake in the account, Congress doesn't want the heir to perpetuate the tax shelter forever. There is a minimum withdrawal schedule for heirs—but again, withdrawals are tax-free.

With both traditional and Roth IRAs, there's a special rule if a widow or widower is the beneficiary. In that case, the surviving spouse can claim the account as his or her own. If it's a traditional IRA, no withdrawals would be required until the new owner is $70^{1}/_{2}$; if it's a Roth, the heir would never have to tap the account.

Choosing Between a Roth and a Regular IRA

So, how on earth do you decide whether a traditional or a Roth IRA belongs in your worry-free retirement plan? Which set of tax advantages is best for you? Which tax shelter will help you build the biggest nest egg? Does it make sense to convert an old IRA to a Roth? Good questions, and tough to answer.

First, if your income is too high to deduct regular IRA contributions, the Roth IRA is a great addition to your retirement-savings arsenal. Fund it to the annual max—between $4,000 and $5,000 (depending on the year)—if you can afford to. The table on page 114 shows how your contributions will grow. Smile when you reflect that withdrawals will be tax-free.

But what if you can deduct your regular IRA contributions, as more taxpayers can, thanks to the new, higher-income limits? The Roth has clear advantages, primarily the fact that there's no mandatory withdrawal schedule to worry about and that money in a Roth can go to an heir tax-free. Another plus is that there is no way tax-free withdrawals will trigger extra tax on your social security benefits. (As taxable income—including regular IRA withdrawals—rises above certain levels, up to 85% of otherwise tax-free social security benefits can be taxed.)

What about the financial advantage of getting tax-free versus taxable withdrawals? Believe it or not,

ROTH OR 401(K)?

Q. *Because money coming out of a Roth IRA is tax-free, should I contribute to a Roth before I put money in my company 401(k)?*
A. Not if your company matches part or all of your 401(k) contribution or there's a real possibility that you'll need to borrow from the 401(k). There's no matching money with a Roth and you can't borrow from an IRA. But if your employer doesn't make matching contributions—or if you've contributed enough to capture the maximum match—put the first (or next) $4,000 (or $5,000 starting in 2006) of your retirement money in a Roth. Tax-free earnings inside the Roth will mean more to your worry-free retirement than what you lose by passing up the chance to put pre-tax money into the 401(k). An even better idea: Fund both your 401(k) and your Roth to the max.

there's no guarantee that—when all else is equal—the Roth will beat the regular IRA. You need a crystal ball as much as a financial calculator to know whether it makes sense to give up tax deductions today in exchange for tax-free income tomorrow. It really depends on what your tax bracket will be when you retire. If you'll be in a lower tax bracket, the regular IRA will prove to have been a better choice; if you'll be in a higher tax bracket, the Roth will shine. Again, that assumes that all things are equal, but there's a good chance you'll be able to give the Roth a leg up.

For an apples-to-apples comparison, assume that you deposit $4,000 a year in a regular IRA and just $3,000 in a Roth—because that's all the regular IRA really costs you if you're deducting contributions in the 25% bracket. Assuming the money in the accounts earns at the same rate, at the end of any period, the "spendable" amount in the accounts will be identical. Sure, the traditional, deductible IRA will hold more money. But you'll owe tax on withdrawals. Assuming a 25% rate, the after-tax amount will be the same as the tax-free amount coming out of the Roth IRA.

As noted, however, there is a way to give the Roth a big advantage. Put a full $4,000 into the account each year rather than a stunted $3,000. That costs you more than a regular IRA contribution now, but you'll come out way ahead in the end.

So, if you can afford a $4,000 contribution without the help of a tax deduction, the Roth will help you grow a bigger nest egg.

But what if you find yourself in a lower tax bracket in retirement, perhaps because Congress enacts a flat tax or abolishes the income tax altogether? Then you might be kicking yourself for passing up regular IRA deductions in the bad old days of high income-tax rates.

Assuming there will still be an income tax when you retire (a pretty good bet), how can you know whether you'll be in a higher or lower bracket? You can't. In the past, it was generally assumed that retirees would fall into a lower tax bracket because they'd have less taxable income. Now, however, it's increasingly likely that retirees will maintain their income levels. Ironically, because opting for a Roth will reduce taxable income in retirement, it's more likely that you'll be in a lower bracket (which is a minus for the Roth); conversely, using a regular IRA will boost taxable income in retirement, possibly pushing you into a higher bracket (which is a minus for the regular IRA).

Convert an Old-Style IRA to a Roth?

If your AGI is $100,000 or less, you can convert your old-style IRA to a Roth, so that all future earnings inside the account would be tax-free. That $100,000 trigger point applies to all kinds of returns, except married filing separately. If you are married and file a separate return, you are forbidden to convert an old IRA to a Roth.

Although rolling old IRA money into a Roth sounds great, there's a catch: To do so, you have to pay tax on the amount rolled over—except to the extent that you have made nondeductible contributions to the old IRA. Say, for example, that your IRA holds $100,000, all of it from deductible contributions and tax-deferred earnings. To convert that IRA to a Roth, you'd have to report and pay tax on that $100,000 in your top bracket. Ouch!

Converting to a Roth is not an all-or-nothing deal. If you have several old traditional IRAs, you may convert one or more to Roths and maintain the others; in other words, you can reduce the tax bite by converting smaller sums each year and paying the tax on those sums.

But does it make sense to pay a tax bill now to avoid taxes in retirement? The dollars-and-cents answer turns on your tax bracket now and what it will be when you retire.

- **If you'll be in a higher bracket in retirement,** switching to a Roth will pay off. You'll be paying tax at today's rate to avoid tomorrow's higher rate. (When figuring today's rate, remember that adding the IRA amount to your income could push you into a higher bracket.)
- **If you stay in the same tax bracket,** paying tax now or later makes no difference. Although the stunted Roth IRA would have a lower balance when you retire, it would produce the same spendable income as a regular IRA.
- **If you wind up in a lower tax bracket in retirement,** paying tax at today's rates to avoid tomorrow's more lenient rates would be a blunder.

That win-lose analysis assumes you pay the tax on the conversion with money that's inside the regular IRA now. If you can pay the tax bill without tapping your IRA, switching to a Roth account can put you far ahead because it lets you keep more money in the tax shelter, where it will grow faster than it would on the outside. This could be a real boost to your worry-free plan.

There's a big catch to using IRA money to pay the tax on a Roth conversion. If you're under age 59½, you'll have to pay a 10% penalty on the amount that's not rolled over into the Roth or rolled into a Roth and then pulled out to pay the tax. (Adding 10% to your tax rate makes it more likely that you'll face a lower rate in retirement—and therefore you'd be better off skipping the conversion.)

The Power of the IRA— Traditional or Roth

Don't let the choice in IRAs distract you from the real beauty of this tax shelter. Whether you choose a traditional IRA or a Roth, remember that earnings inside the account grow minus the drag of taxes.

Consider a 45-year-old, shooting for retirement at 65, who contributes the $4,000 maximum to an IRA for 20 years. She will have kicked in $80,000 to the IRA over that time. If the money grows at an average rate of 8% per year, the total value of the account will be more than $197,600—an extra $117,600 on top of what she's contributed to the account.

But if she invested her $4,000 a year where the 8% interest earned would be taxed each year—that is, outside an IRA—her $80,000 in savings would grow to only $155,900 over 20 years, assuming earnings were taxed in the 25% bracket. That's $41,700 shy of where her nest egg would be with the power of tax-free compounding on its side. (She'd have even less if state income taxes were taking a bite out of each year's earnings.)

Now look what happens if the rate of return is higher, at say, 10%. A $4,000 annual retirement set-aside would skyrocket to over $252,000—more than three times the $80,000 invested over those 20 years. The $172,000 of earnings generated inside the IRA is the result of tax-free compounding.

If the earnings were taxed every year at 25%, the account would reach just $186,200 after 20 years, trailing the untaxed sum by over $65,800.

A two-income couple can supplement their retirement savings to an even greater extent with dual IRAs. Even for late starters, if each spouse puts $4,000 into an IRA annually starting at age 50 and the money earns an average 10% per year, their combined IRA retirement pool will be almost $279,600 in 15 years—the $120,000 they contributed plus $159,600 generated by tax-free growth.

That's the power of tax-deferred growth. The opportunity for completely tax-free withdrawals offered by the new Roth IRA is icing on the cake.

Extra IRA Blessings

An IRA, whether it's a traditional one or a Roth, can give your financial plans for retirement a boost in other ways as well:

HELP IN ESTABLISHING THE SAVINGS HABIT. Putting aside even a small amount regularly in your IRA is a handy way to build your nest egg. Unlike other portions of your savings, which may be diverted to pay for college, a house, a car, or other expenses, your IRA represents a pool of funds earmarked specifically for retirement (although with the Roth, you can withdraw your contributions tax-free if you need to to help pay the bill).

A PLACE TO PUT YOUR PENSION. If you switch jobs and depart your previous employer with a pension payout in tow, an IRA could be the best way to protect that money from the tax man and continue receiving the benefits of tax-free or deferred growth. (Important IRA rollover procedures are spelled out in Chapter 11.)

KEEPING YOU FOCUSED. An IRA enforces savings discipline with the threat of a 10% penalty if you try to take this money early—generally, that's before age 59½ (except as noted above for the contributions you make to a Roth).

AN ESCAPE HATCH, IF YOU NEED IT. Still, some folks are uncomfortable locking up their money long term. And financial emergencies can arise. If you're the financially claustrophobic type, you should be encouraged by the growing number of loopholes that provide a penalty-free escape hatch if you need to take your IRA money out. Several exceptions to the regular 10% early-withdrawal penalty have been discussed earlier—including the chance to tap an account to pay for a first home, for college for the kids or for a medical emergency. Another option could be just what your doctor ordered if your worry-free plan calls for retiring earlier than age 59½.

Let's say you launched your traditional IRA when you were 30. Now you've hit 40 and plan to retire at age 55. The contributions you've been making every year have built the account to almost $45,000. Looking ahead, you'll need a key source of income to help carry you from age 55 until social security benefits begin at age 62. An IRA can be your ticket to an early exit. Here's how to put this opportunity to work in your strategy:

While the early-out penalty generally claims 10% of any funds withdrawn from a traditional IRA before age 59½, you can avoid all penalties if you withdraw the money in approximately equal annual amounts designed to exhaust the account during the course of your life expectancy. Because you would be expected to live another 25 to 30 years, the allowable distribution per year would seem to be tiny.

But there's good news here. The IRS says that you can take "reasonable" future IRA investment earnings into account when figuring the size of the penalty-free payouts. That can easily double or triple the size of your withdrawal. By counting future earnings for years to come, the penalty-free payout allowable at age 55, or some other age you choose to start, could be the key to making your strategy for a worry-free early retirement work. The payouts can begin whenever you want—even if you are still employed.

Assume, for example, that when you reach age 55 you've accumulated $150,000 in your IRA. If your annual withdrawals from the IRA had to be spread evenly over your life expectancy of almost 29 years (the exact figure is found in IRS life expectancy tables), you'd be able to withdraw only about $5,200 annually. But assuming your IRA investments will continue to build at a compound annual return of 10%, that $150,000 can get you annual penalty-free payments of about $15,000—a handy bridge to help carry you to age 62 when social security can kick in. (Although you'd avoid the penalty, you'd pay taxes on the withdrawals, except any part that represents nondeductible contributions.)

If you set up a payment schedule to dodge the 10% penalty, you must stick with it for the longer of five consecutive years, or until you turn 59½.

For example, a 56-year-old who elects to start withdrawing her money by this penalty-free method wouldn't be allowed to modify the schedule until age 61. If she fails to comply with those conditions, her withdrawal is subject to the 10% penalty.

The table on page 120 gives you a rough idea of how large a penalty-free withdrawal you'd be able to get from an IRA starting at various ages and with different rates of return. The dollar figures in the chart represent the approximate amount of withdrawal for each $10,000 of assets in the IRA. Thus, a 55-year-old with $100,000 in an IRA could withdraw about $8,350 per year if the presumed annual return was 8%. Getting these calculations exactly right can be tricky, so you may wish to consult a professional for assistance.

The Roth IRA is even more vulnerable to early raids, because you can withdraw the total of your contributions tax- and penalty-free at any time. That troubles some retirement advisers, who fear that easily accessible retirement accounts will be depleted long before retirement. But it can be a plus if it encourages folks who are skittish about tying up their money to use the Roth.

Consider, for example, a young couple, just starting a family and strapped for cash. They might feel that feeding a college fund for their progeny must take precedence over funding an IRA for themselves. The Roth lets them have it both ways.

Assume that Mom and Dad each make $4,000 contributions to Roth accounts for the 18 years before their firstborn heads off to college. At that time, their combined accounts will hold more than $401,000, assuming 10% annual returns inside the accounts. $144,000 of that amount—the total of the parents' contributions—will be available tax- and penalty-free to pay tuition and other costs. If they need to tap the earnings, too, taxes will be due, but there will be no penalty.

And if funds are available from other sources to pay the college bills, the twin Roth IRAs will give the folks a huge head start toward their worry-free retirement.

Get Maximum Action from Your IRA

Most retirement savers fall into one of three categories when it comes to IRAs:

THE PROCRASTINATORS. These folks have never gotten around to opening an IRA but are probably familiar with some of the benefits. Money for savings has been scarce. And, hey, didn't they eliminate some of the advantages? If you fall into this group, the creation of the Roth IRA should get your attention, and your goal now is to get an IRA going immediately, even if you put away only a few hundred dollars to start. If you're married, open IRAs for both of you.

THE INACTIVE ONES. You and your spouse have IRAs but you haven't made any deposits in several years, nor have you paid much attention to where the money is and how the account has performed. Your strategy now is to resurrect your IRA habit—dust it off and get it running again. Plan to resume annual contributions immediately, probably to a Roth IRA, and take a closer look at where the funds are invested. If the money is mired in low-paying money-market funds, bank accounts, or CDs you've been rolling over every year, it's time to move it somewhere with greater growth potential. For example, the bulk of the money should be invested in the stock market, where historical returns have topped 10% annually. If you're in stocks or stock mutual funds that have been disappointing, remember that inside this tax shelter you can switch investments without tax consequence.

If switching investments means changing the place you keep your IRA account, the section later in this chapter on moving your IRA money will show you how to go about it. Chapters 9 and 10 will explore the range of investment options and specific strategies for retirement investing at different ages.

THE DYNAMOS. Folks in this category have regularly funded their IRAs and are well on their way toward a worry-free retirement. Here the strategy is simple: Decide whether future contributions should go into a traditional or a Roth IRA.

Take a Total-Plan Approach

You have almost unlimited choices of how and where to invest your IRA money—and this is the same whether you stick with a traditional IRA or use a Roth IRA. You can use a bank, savings and loan, or credit union. Branch into the multitudinous world of mutual funds. Or take the reins yourself through a self-directed account, managed by you and run through a brokerage firm.

Once you've decided on a sponsor or sponsors (you can have as many separate IRA accounts as you want as long as your total contribution doesn't exceed the yearly maximum allowed), you'll need to decide specifically where to deploy your money. Blue-chip stocks? Small-company stocks? Foreign stocks? Corporate bonds? Treasury bonds? Certificates of deposit?

The deployment strategy you select for your IRA will depend on your age, the size of your portfolio, your tolerance for risk, and the investments you hold in other components of your plan, among other factors.

For example, a 42-year-old couple with more than 20 years to go until retirement should probably have at least 70% to 80% of their retirement savings

---

KEEP AN EYE ON COSTS

You know all about the tax benefits of the IRA. But how much do you pay in fees to keep this tax shelter up and running? Most IRAs carry maintenance fees—generally $10 to $50 a year—and if you trade stocks and bonds inside the account, you'll pay brokerage fees, too.

The long-term nature of retirement investments makes IRAs attractive to sponsors, and that means there's hot competition for your business. Discount broker Charles Schwab waives annual fees for any IRA holding $50,000 or more. Schwab also offers no-transaction-cost trading of hundreds of no-load mutual funds. The Fidelity-fund family has no sales charge for most stock mutual funds purchased inside an IRA and waives the account-maintenance fee for IRAs worth $30,000 or more.

Periodically, check what you're paying and make a few phone calls to see if you can do better. Switching to a lower-cost sponsor could save you a tidy sum over the long-term life of your IRAs. And, since your money is inside an IRA, there's no tax consequence of switching from one investment to another.

---

invested in stocks. But if their 401(k) plans are 100% in stock mutual funds already, the route they choose for their IRA will be to diversify their holdings among different investments.

To make wise investment choices, you'll want to consider all of your retirement-plan pieces in unison. That's where Chapters 9 and 10 come in. There you'll find specifics on investment choices and strategies for your IRAs and other retirement-plan parts.

Put Your IRA on Autopilot

You may find it easier to stash between $4,000 and $5,000 (depending on the year) annually in your IRA if you make the deposits in smaller pieces throughout the year. For example, setting aside one-fourth of your IRA target every three months avoids the crunch of trying to fund the entire amount at once—especially for a dual-income couple setting aside the maximum (between $8,000 and 10,000).

A helpful tactic is an automatic-investment program. Most of the major mutual fund families offer these plans, which transfer deposits automatically to your IRA from a checking account at your bank, credit union, or savings and loan on a regular basis. You get the benefits of convenience, instant self-discipline, and access to a broad range of investments. For example, the Automatic Account Builder plan from Fidelity Investments, a giant mutual fund group, offers these services (similar features are available at other fund families):

- **A $500 minimum investment for IRAs.** After that initial investment, deposits can be as little as $100. (Some firms offer minimum initial investments as low as $100 and no minimum on subsequent deposits.)
- **Convenience.** You have the ability to customize the strategy by choosing both the timing and amount of deposits to your IRA.
- **Control.** You can stop the program anytime with a simple phone call or arrange to skip a payment—during the holidays, for example. Or, as your income rises, you can arrange to have your annual contributions increased, up to the annual maximum, between $4,000 and $5,000, depending the year.
- **A savings discipline.** Since the money is transferred directly from your checking account, you aren't tempted to spend it somewhere else. There are no checks to write, and your assets accumulate steadily.

Moving Your IRA Money

Another important IRA feature is flexibility. With a vast array of sponsorship and investment choices available, it's comforting to know that you have the ability to exploit new opportunities as they arise by moving your IRA money. The ability to react to changing conditions is a key weapon in your worry-free retirement arsenal. Not only does your own situation change as you and your family grow older, but market conditions will change, too.

You might, for example, decide to add a type of mutual fund to your IRA that isn't offered by your current sponsor. You could switch your account to a different sponsor with a wider selection or simply shift a portion of your IRA money elsewhere by setting up an additional account.

What if it turns out that the IRA investment you thought would soar like an eagle flails like a turkey? The ability to adapt is built right into an IRA, letting you move your money to friendlier skies.

Another reason to make a move would be to bring some or all of your IRA into a self-directed IRA account at a brokerage firm. This becomes an option if you want to invest in individual stocks or real estate and have enough money in the account to justify the move—say, $40,000 or so—because commissions and fees will be involved in a self-directed IRA.

Two Ways to Do It

No matter why you want to move your IRA money, you have two ways to do it—a direct transfer or a rollover. Note this: Unless you are converting a traditional IRA to a Roth IRA—which, as noted earlier, triggers a tax bill on the amount converted—you can't move money between the two varieties of accounts. The discussion here assumes you are moving from traditional to traditional or from Roth to Roth.

DIRECT TRANSFER. In most cases, a direct transfer will be the best way to move your IRA money. It's simple: You instruct your current IRA sponsor to pass the money directly to another sponsor of your choosing—from a bank to a mutual fund, for example. The money in the account never actually passes through your hands. All you need to do is issue the orders, usually relayed through the new sponsor once you've set up your account there.

You can transfer all the funds in your IRA or only a portion. And you can make as many moves as you

> If the IRA investment you thought would soar like an eagle flails like a turkey, move your money to friendlier skies.

want. You could, for example, order $30,000 in a bank IRA transferred in $10,000 chunks to three separate mutual funds.

While this method is the easiest, it's not necessarily the fastest. The new sponsor you are switching to should be willing and able to offer tips on how to expedite the move. Sponsors giving up an account are sometimes less than swift.

First, open an account with the new sponsor you've selected. You needn't deposit any money right away. Instead, you'll fill out a form with instructions to the old sponsor for transferring your funds to the new account.

Unfortunately, things don't always run smoothly. Some transfers take weeks or, in the most horrific cases, months. Snags can occur for several reasons. The paperwork might be forgotten, misinterpreted, misdirected, or buried on someone's desk. The information it contains could be incomplete or incorrect, causing further delay.

Barring any hitches, though, three weeks should be ample time to complete a direct transfer. If you haven't gotten confirmation within that time, call both the new and old IRA sponsors and make it clear that you're concerned. Request a definite answer about what is causing the delay and when it will be resolved. Ask whether you can do anything to expedite the process. If nothing happens, talk to a supervisor and follow up in writing.

ROLLOVER. The second way to move your IRA is with a rollover. In this case you're the go-between. The current sponsor closes the account and sends you the money. You're then responsible for sending it on (rolling it over) to a new IRA sponsor. For example, you close an IRA bank account, receive a check, and send the money on to a newly opened mutual fund IRA account.

WORRY-FREE TIP

Delays in IRA transfers are most likely in the weeks just before or after the April tax deadline, when the volume is heaviest. So if you can, avoid ordering a transfer during tax season.

This method has two advantages that can be useful strategic moves. One is speed: Because you take control, you can personally push things along. Thus, if you spot an investment opportunity—an attractive stock you want to buy through a self-directed IRA brokerage account, for example—you could quickly shift money where needed by using this rollover method.

The other advantage is flexibility. Because the rules grant you 60 days to complete your rollover, you can, in effect, tap this money for a 60-day loan to meet a short-term financial emergency.

But it's crucial not to breach the 60-day limit. If you miss the deadline, the IRA tax shelter dissolves, the money withdrawn from a traditional account is taxed (except for already-taxed contributions), and, if you're under age 59½, you'll be hit with a 10% early-withdrawal penalty as well. If you miss the deadline on a Roth rollover, you can be taxed and penalized on any amount that exceeds your contribution to your Roth accounts.

To make sure you're not penalized, you must get the assets into the new account by the 60th day. Also, make sure the old sponsor knows you're rolling over your IRA so that no money will be withheld for taxes. Otherwise the sponsor may nab 10% of the amount involved and send it to the IRS. Ask whether any documents must be signed to prevent the 10% withholding. (Note that rollovers are permitted just once every 12 months for each IRA that you have.)

Set Up
Your Own
Pension Plan

Chapter 8

Welcome to the wonderful world of the special retirement deals for small-business owners and self-employed individuals. Your business—whether it's full- or part-time, with or without any employees in addition to yourself—can speed your way to a worry-free retirement. When you work for yourself, you instantly qualify to design your own tax-favored retirement plan in which you call the shots. The premise is this: Because you are self-employed or operate a small business, you have no pension plan from the likes of an IBM or General Motors to cover your retirement needs. Uncle Sam lets you substitute your own custom-designed pension plan.

No matter how small your business—even if you alone make up the entire staff—it has the same basic rights the giants have to install and fund an attractive pension plan for you and employees. For example, you can:

- **Choose from a trio of plans** that let you set aside as much as 25% of earnings—or $42,000 in 2005, whichever is less—per year. Every dollar that you contribute is tax-deductible.

- **Write your own retirement ticket** with a plan that lets you set a personal retirement-income target, then put aside—and deduct—whatever is necessary to meet it.

- **Select a "business IRA"** with simple paperwork and a contribution limit that goes as high as $42,000 in 2005, compared with the traditional IRA's $4,000 (in 2005 and $5,000 by 2008) ceiling.

■ **Use a "simple" plan** to set aside up to $10,000 (for 2005) of your earnings for your retirement, even if that's 100% of your business income. And if you are age 50 or older you can make additional catch-up contributions to your SIMPLE plan—$2,000 in 2005 rising to an additional contribution of $2,500 in 2006.

Wait. There's more. While most pension plans require that you set aside the same percentage for your employees that you do for yourself, there's a twist that permits some small-business owners to tip their plans in their own favor if their employees are younger than they are.

In this chapter, we'll tell you what you need to know about each of these plans in order to choose the best fit for your circumstances.

Pension-plan basics are remarkably similar whether you're Microsoft or Jane Entrepreneur generating $5,000 of self-employment income from a business in your garage.

With a "defined contribution" retirement plan, your business (even a one-person business) can set aside a percentage of earnings each year. A "defined benefit" plan works in reverse. As in the TV game show *Jeopardy!*, you begin with the answer—an annual retirement-income target of your choosing—then provide the question. How much must I contribute annually to reach that goal? This plan lets you put away whatever amount is necessary to meet your income target.

As with company-provided plans and IRAs, the tax breaks offered by plans for small businesses and the self-employed come with a catch: Because this is supposed to be retirement savings, you have to agree not to dip into the money early. There's a 10% penalty (possibly 25% for SIMPLE IRAs) if you tap the account too soon, and as far as the law is concerned that's generally anytime before you reach age 59½ or, if you leave or close the business that's generating the income, age 55.

The Keogh Plan: A Sweet Deal

The basic retirement program for self-employed individuals is often called a Keogh plan, named after Donald Keogh, the congressman whose legislation authorized the tax breaks that make the plan work. An alias for Keogh is the H.R. 10 plan, a reference to the legislation itself. Some plan sponsors don't use either label, though, and instead refer to the plan simply as either a defined-contribution plan or a defined-benefit plan.

By whatever name you call it, this is a sweet deal. Contributions are fully tax-deductible, and the plan serves as a tax shelter—there's no tax on earnings until you withdraw the money, presumably in retirement. This gives the Keogh the same supercharged earning capacity as an IRA.

Who Qualifies?

You qualify for a Keogh plan if you earn any self-employment income:

- **as owner or sole proprietor in a full-time or part-time small business,** whether incorporated or unincorporated;
- **as part owner in a business partnership;**
- **as a self-employed professional;**
- **from a sideline or "moonlighting" business** you operate from your home or elsewhere; or
- **as a self-employed freelancer,** speaker, instructor, or consultant.

As long as you have income from any of these sources, you can set up a Keogh, even if you also have a full-time job and participate in your employer's retirement plan at work.

How a Plan Might Work

Say that you're a self-employed 40-year-old making $52,000 per year and figure that your income will rise an average of 5% annually. You establish your own pension plan and stash 20% of your earnings (all tax-deductible) into the account annually. Here's what happens if the money earns an average return of 10% per year:

- **In ten years:** You'll have invested a fully tax-deductible $130,800 in your retirement account and it will be worth about $220,700.
- **In 15 years:** Your deductible contributions total $224,400 and the value of your nest egg has hit $480,000.
- **In 20 years:** You've now contributed, and written off, $343,800. But your nest egg has zoomed to $1,055,700.
- **In 25 years:** You're now 65, and the $496,300 you've contributed to your profit-sharing retirement plan has grown to $1.7 million.

Saving the same amounts outside the Keogh—in the cold, cruel world where after-tax dollars are invested and the tax man claims a share of each year's earnings—would leave you far behind. Make that FAR behind. Because you're saving after-tax money, there's less to set aside each year, and the annual tax bill inhibits growth of your nest egg:

- **In ten years:** Since taxes are paid on the 20% of your earnings before the money is saved, you have invested only about $98,000, and the value of the account (with taxes paid annually on the earnings) will be about $165,500.
- **In 15 years:** You've invested $168,300 and your nest egg is $360,071.
- **In 20 years:** The value of your taxable nest egg is about $699,100—around two thirds as much as the $1,055,700 in the Keogh.
- **In 25 years:** The value of nondeductible investments is about $1.2 million, compared with the $1.7 million in the Keogh.

Yes, the Keogh money is taxed when you take it. But you'll still be smiling.

Or consider a 44-year-old self-employed couple shooting for a $1-million nest egg and retirement at age 62. Their combined income of $85,000 is also rising 5%

WORRY-FREE TIP

You may have to pay a trustee fee for maintaining your Keogh account. Charges typically run less than $100 per year for each individual in the plan. But this fee is tax-deductible as a business expense. Simply pay the expense separately, out of your business checking account, rather than having the trustee deduct it from your Keogh.

---

annually, but they opt for a different type of pension plan that fixes their annual set-aside at 20% of their self-employment earnings each year—up to a yearly maximum of $42,000 each. They take a tax deduction for the full amount. If the money earns an average return of 10% inside the plan, here are the results:

- **In five years:** The couple's $94,000 in contributions has grown to $125,000.
- **In ten years:** The nest egg hits $361,000.
- **In 15 years:** The couple's retirement pot has swelled to $777,000.
- **In 18 years:** The couple has invested $451,000 in tax-deductible dollars and at age 62 has more than $1 million in their account.

The Blessings of a Keogh

As noted above, contributions to your personal pension plan are always fully tax-deductible, no matter how high your income and regardless of whether you or your spouse is covered by another retirement plan. There's no such thing as a nondeductible contribution, as there is with an IRA. And you can have an IRA—traditional or Roth—in addition to your Keogh. (Whether traditional IRA contributions would be deductible depends on your income, because the Keogh is considered an employer-provided plan for purposes of the IRA deductibility tests.)

How much can you contribute? That depends on how much self-employment income you have and what kind of Keogh you choose. The limit is generally 25% of your self-employment earnings, to a maximum of $42,000 per year.

The major drawback to having your own small-business pension plan is this: If you have employees, they must be included in the plan and you must basically contribute the same percentage of income to their accounts as you contribute to your own. There's an important exception to that rule, called an age-weighted plan, discussed later in this chapter.

Different Kinds of Keoghs

There are three kinds of defined-contribution pension plans that let you set aside a fixed or fluctuating percentage of your self-employment profits each year. Here's how they work.

PROFIT-SHARING PLANS FOR MAXIMUM FLEXIBILITY.

You can put as much as 25% of your net self-employment earnings, up to a maximum of $42,000, into a profit-sharing defined-contribution plan. Figuring those earnings gets a bit tricky, to say the least. Business earnings for a self-employed person means your net business income minus the amount you contribute to your Keogh, minus one-half of any social security tax you pay on your self-employed earnings. If you have another job where social security is deducted and you earn above the annual social security maximum, there won't be any additional social security tax on your self-employment income. Otherwise, this offset has the effect of slightly reducing your Keogh contribution.

To cut through the math, and to keep things simple, we've used 20% of income as the applicable lid on profit-sharing Keogh contributions. That's 20% of net self-employment earnings, ignoring the Keogh contribution itself and the social security tax offset.

The key advantage to a profit-sharing plan is flexibility. You don't have to contribute the same percentage of earnings every year—you can put in 20% one year, 6% another year, even skip a year if your finances

KEOGH PAPERWORK

Paperwork to establish your pension plan will vary from sponsor to sponsor. Some have a simple one-page application. Others hit you with ten pages or more. If you have no employees, annual Keogh paperwork is rather simple. The general rule is that you must file a Form 5500 with the IRS each year. But if the plan covers only you or just you and your spouse and the balance is $100,000 or less, you don't have to file this form.

absolutely force you to cut back. If you are uncertain about your ability to contribute to the plan each year or if you don't want to lock yourself into a set percentage contribution, this is your best choice.

Say, for example, you have your own photography studio but your income is highly erratic. Some years you feel flush—plenty of extra dough to sock away for retirement. Other years you're hard-pressed to make the mortgage. A profit-sharing plan lets you roll with the self-employment punches, putting in more money in good years and less money in bad ones. In return for that flexibility, the amount you are allowed to contribute is lower than in other plans.

MONEY-PURCHASE PLANS FOR HIGHER LIMITS. In a money-purchase defined-contribution plan, you can make a deductible contribution of up to 25% of your net self-employment earnings. Again, net is defined as the amount that's left after you subtract your contribution. To take a shortcut through the math, use 20% of self-employment earnings instead. The social security tax offset may lower this a bit. The top annual contribution in this case is $42,000 for 2005.

The big plus with a money-purchase plan is that you can put away more money toward your worry-free retirement. This is a terrific choice if you meet three criteria: you have self-employment income on top of other employment wages, you can afford to devote a large portion of the self-employment income to retirement savings, and you expect to be able to continue funding your plan at the same level year after year.

A drawback of money-purchase plans is that once you decide what percentage of income you want to contribute, you must contribute that percentage each year no matter how high or low your self-employment income. If you elect to make a 20% contribution, say, you're required to contribute 20% each year. Basically, you trade the flexibility of profit sharing for the ability to contribute a greater amount.

Money-purchase plans will work best for you if you have a fairly steady, predictable income from your small business or other self-employment.

HAVE IT BOTH WAYS. A superb strategy to capture both the flexibility of a profit-sharing plan and the higher limits of a money-purchase pension is to have both types of plans. That's perfectly legal, and it's an easy way to extract the optimum nest-egg-building potential from your self-employment income. Here's how to tap the maximum tax-deductible benefit for your plan:

First, set up a money-purchase plan and commit a fixed 7% of your self-employment earnings to this pension every year. That's now your minimum annual pension-funding obligation, but at that modest level it shouldn't be too tough to meet.

Then, set up a profit-sharing plan that can be separately funded for up to 13% more of your self-employment income. As long as your contributions to the two plans together total no more than 20% of your earnings (up to the $42,000 annual cap), you're within the established limits. You have the flexibility to alter your contribution year to year but also the ability to put in as much as the law allows, if you can afford it.

This approach has another advantage in that it imposes some discipline on you, requiring you to put aside at least 7% of your income annually. But it also allows you to nearly triple your contribution, to a maximum 20%. Even if you can't afford that high a contribution at this point, building the higher limit into your program while limiting your commitment to 7% of earnings is a great way to give yourself room to grow and accelerate your retirement plan in the future.

The Age-Weighted Plan Opportunity

The "age weighted" or age-based profit-sharing pension plan works much like a Keogh plan, but if you have employees and the age differential between you and them is large, this could be a super deal for building your retirement nest egg. This plan is especially well-suited to business owners in their 50s whose employees are younger by an average of about ten years or more. You still have to include employees in the plan. But you can accelerate your own retirement savings while putting less away for your employees.

To see the potential, consider a 55-year-old small-business owner whose three employees are 45, 35, and 25 years old. Under a standard profit-sharing plan, if the owner contributes 13% of income (equaling about 15% of net income after the contribution is made) to her own plan, she must also put aside 15% of the net earnings for her three employees. Say the owner's net income is $75,000 and her employees' are $30,000, $25,000, and $20,000, respectively. At 15% of net income, the owner's annual pension contribution would be about $11,250 and the employees would receive $11,250 divided among the three of them (15% of their combined net income of $75,000).

The age-weighted formula dramatically changes all that and allows the owner to put far more of the total retirement-money contribution ($22,500 in this example) into her own account. Using a table that assigns a specific discount factor to each individual based on age and years to retirement, this 55-year-old business owner can boost her own contribution to $17,780, while reducing employee contributions to a total of $4,720. If you think this kind of plan may work well for you,

Whether you earn a few bucks selling crafts on weekends or you're a founding partner in a high-powered consulting firm, you qualify for a SEP.

get in touch with an accountant or financial planner who has experience in retirement planning.

The Simplicity of a Business IRA

There is an alternative to the Keogh, a super-low-cost, low-maintenance plan: the "business IRA," which permits fully tax-deductible contributions far above the $4,000-to-$5,000 limit for individual IRAs.

This plan, called a simplified employee pension (SEP), or SEP-IRA, is easier to set up and requires less ongoing paperwork than a Keogh or other small-business pension plan. Just like the complex pension programs offered by big corporations, SEPs deliver important tax savings to both you and your employees. Your business or self-employment taxable income is reduced by the amount of money you put into the SEP. And the money in your plan, including earnings on investments, grows untaxed until you withdraw it.

Just about anyone who has income from self-employment—sole proprietors, partners, owners of corporations or S corporations, even freelancers and moonlighters—is eligible to open a SEP. Whether you earn a few bucks selling crafts on weekends or you're a founding partner in a high-powered consulting firm, you qualify for a SEP.

A SEP is a cross between a profit-sharing Keogh plan and a traditional IRA. Your contributions go into a special SEP-IRA. You can contribute as much as 25% of your net self-employment earnings, up to a maximum of $42,000 in 2005. Again, net means the amount that's left after you subtract your contribution and the offset for any social security taxes paid on self-employment income. For simplicity's sake, figure 20% of net income—not counting those two factors—is the limit.

You are free to vary your contributions each year or even skip a year, as conditions warrant. If you have eligible employees, you must contribute to their SEP-IRAs each year you contribute to your own.

There's just one form for the business to fill out to open a SEP, and all the money you contribute for yourself and your employees is deductible as a business expense. Employees—not you—choose how their money is invested, so you're relieved of that worry.

Another advantage: You can open and fund a SEP up until your tax-filing deadline—usually April 15—including any extensions. By contrast, you must open a Keogh plan by December 31, although you have until April 15 to fund it. Also, there are no SEP reports to file with the IRS.

The SIMPLE Plan for Small Business

This tax break is yet another plan designed to encourage self-employeds to save for retirement. SIMPLE stands for "savings incentive match plans for employees." These plans were really created by Congress as a simplified retirement plan for small companies—only firms with fewer than 100 employees can use a SIMPLE, and if you have employees, you must include them in your plan. But the door to SIMPLEs is also open to self-employed workers with no employees. Whether your business is full-time or you do freelance or consulting work in addition to a full-time job, you can have a SIMPLE. And you can have one even if you have a job that offers a pension plan. You may not, however, have both a SIMPLE and a Keogh.

There are actually two kinds of SIMPLE plans—a SIMPLE IRA and a SIMPLE 401(k). It's likely that the IRA version will be best for a self-employed person with no employees, so that's what's discussed here.

The advantage of a SIMPLE IRA is that you can stash up to $10,000 a year (for 2005) into the plan—even if that's 100% of your self-employment income. With the 20%-of-income cap that applies to Keogh plans, you need net income from your business of at least $50,000 to make a $10,000 contribution. So if your business income is under those levels—and you can afford to set aside $10,000 a year for your retirement—a SIMPLE is especially alluring. (Actually, the SIMPLE can be a winner even if your business income is higher because you may be able to boost the amount contributed to the plan with an employer "match" to the plan. The match can be 2% or 3% of your income.)

Contributions to a SIMPLE IRA can be deducted on your return, and earnings inside the account are tax-deferred. As with traditional IRAs, there's usually a 10% penalty if you withdraw funds before age 59½— but the penalty is a whopping 25% if you pull money out before 59½ and you've been in the plan for less than two years.

You have until the filing deadline for your tax return to make your SIMPLE contribution for the previous year, but there is a catch: The plan must have been opened by October 1 of the year for which the contribution is being made. Thus, to make a 2005 contribution, your plan must be opened by October 1, 2005. As with Keoghs, SEPs, and IRAs, SIMPLEs are offered by banks, brokerage firms, and mutual funds.

Write Your Own Retirement-Income Ticket

Typically, a small-business owner sets up a pension plan when the business is stable and profitable enough to afford it. By that time, you may be in your mid-40s to 50 or older, and the $42,000 limits in other plans may not be adequate to bridge the retirement-income gap that looms ahead.

In that case, you have another option: the defined-benefit plan. It lets you flip-flop your approach. You may make contributions of the amount needed to provide an annual benefit no larger than the smaller of $170,000 (for 2005) or 100% of your average earnings for your highest three consecutive calendar years. Within this rule, you decide how much income you want to receive in retirement and the law lets you set aside enough current income to reach that goal—and deduct every dime. This type of plan can be attractive if:

- **You want to build a big retirement fund as fast as possible.** This probably means you've procrastinated on your plan and are now playing catch-up;
- **You are within 15 years or so of your targeted retirement date.**
- **You can afford to sink a big chunk of your annual income into the plan.** That means you are prosperous and have a fairly predictable income; and
- **You have no employees.**

The major drawbacks to defined-benefit plans are their expense and Rube Goldberg–like complexity. Each plan is unique, depending on your age, life expectancy, and financial circumstances, and will involve some complicated math. You'll need a lawyer, accountant, actuary, or other financial pro to help you set it all up and figure out the required annual contribution each year. The IRS is strict about following the rules on calculating contributions to avoid overfunding your plan.

A 50-year-old earning $80,000 who wants to retire at 62 and receive a pension of $4,500 per month would initially contribute about $25,000 per year to the plan, assuming the money will grow at an 8% annual rate, according to Sam Gilbert, president of the pension consulting firm United Plan Administrators, in Westlake Village, Cal. In general, the older you are, the more you'll need to put into the plan, because the money has less time to grow on its own. The contribution is adjusted yearly and could rise substantially in future years.

That makes defined-benefit plans a highly demanding choice. You must come up with enough yearly funding to eventually reach the income level you've selected. If you fail to meet your targets, the plan could be penalized or dissolved. And if you have employees near your own age who would also qualify for pension coverage, the same math that translates into hefty pension contributions for you translates into hefty pension contributions for them, too.

The Right Plan for You

Making the right choice among do-it-yourself pension plans will depend on the type of business you operate, your age, how much money you can afford to set aside, and whether or not you have employees. These scenarios can help you choose what's best for you:

■ **Employee with a sideline business or moonlighting; self-employment income under $25,000.** The SIMPLE IRA allows you to sock away $10,000 of your self-employment income each year—that's 40% of $25,000, a larger share than a SEP or Keogh plan would accept.

■ **Self-employed consultant; no employees; uncertain income.** If you work for yourself and by yourself, and are fairly certain you'll never go above the 20% ($42,000 maximum in 2005) contribution limit on a profit-sharing plan, a basic SEP is the best way to go. You get the tax benefits, keep the right to vary your contributions year to year, and have the simplest paperwork possible.

■ **Self-employed professional; no employees; high, stable income.** A money-purchase Keogh plan is your ticket to boosting annual contributions to 20% ($42,000 maximum in 2005). If you don't mind a little extra paperwork, twin plans—a profit-sharing and a money-purchase—get you the 20% lid along with flexibility to vary contributions. If you're already in your 50s and have little set aside for retirement, a defined-benefit Keogh may be your best choice for rapidly building your nest egg.

■ **Self-employed professional with few employees.** An age-weighted profit-sharing plan may be the best way to go if your employees are younger than you by an average of about ten years or more. Your contributions can fluctuate year to year and you can set aside more for yourself than for your younger employees.

■ **Owner of a small restaurant with mostly low-paid, high-turnover employees.** A SEP is a good choice here. The trick? Structure the plan so that only employees who have been with your business for three of the preceding five years are eligible to participate. That lets you maximize contributions for yourself and minimize the cost of contributions for employees.

■ **Owner of a small retail store with many seasonal but long-time employees.** A SEP will probably not be a good choice if you employ a large number of part-time or seasonal workers. SEP rules say you must also contribute to their retirement plans, even if they make as little as $450 or so in a year. A profit-sharing Keogh is a better choice because employees must work for you at least 1,000 hours in a year to qualify for inclusion in the plan.

Make the Best Investment Choices

Next to putting money aside for retirement in the first place, deciding where to invest that money is the most important step. Because the bulk of your nest egg's ultimate value will come from investment growth, rather than from dollars you invest, making the best investment choices is critical to your success.

Just look at the table on page 158. If you put aside $10,000 today where it will earn an average annual rate of 4%, you'll have $26,700 in 25 years. But if you invest the $10,000 where it earns 10%, you'll have $108,300 at the end of 25 years—quite a difference!

But how do you achieve the return you want? A cacophony of financial voices—Aunt Mildred's latest stock tip, a brochure blizzard from banks, an advertising avalanche from brokers and mutual funds—makes your decisions seem more complicated than they really are.

To put your retirement investments on track and keep them there, you need only master a few financial fundamentals that will influence each retirement investment decision you make from now on. Think of it as operating your own at-home business—Joan & Jim's Worry-Free Retirement, Inc. The purpose is to build as big a nest egg as possible without taking outlandish risks.

First you'll need to start thinking about investing your retirement money, not simply saving it. By itself, saving isn't enough—it's only part one of a two-part process. Investing is what you do with the money you save. That means learning about the investment choices, deciding where they fit in your "business plan," weighing the risks, and taking action. Some of the terms you'll hear from brokers and other financial pros are listed beginning on page 160 in "Investment Speak: 66 Key Investment Terms You Should Know." Check there for anything you don't understand.

Three Fundamental Truths

While there are countless books that espouse one philosophy of investing or another, there's also a simpler approach, one that boils down to three fundamental truths.

TRUTH #1: Your goal—money for retirement—brings investment choices into focus. Every investor should have a goal—say, buying a house, sending the kids to college, or starting a business. Your goal is retirement, and it influences each decision you make with your nest egg.

It means that your time frame is long-term—stretching not just to the day you retire, but for the rest of your life. You'll want to keep money for other goals, such as vacations, cars, or tuition, tucked away outside your retirement nest egg where it will be more accessible. Accumulating money for retirement is a unique goal, and there are distinctive means for reaching it.

For one thing, you can be certain that time is on your side. Whether you're five years from cutting your employment bonds or still have 25 years to go, one of your key investment allies is the ability of compound growth to build retirement capital automatically. For example, $10,000 invested at 8% grows to $14,700 after

---

THE IMPORTANCE OF CHOOSING RIGHT

What a $10,000 investment today will be worth in 25 years if the annual return is:

4%	6%	8%	10%	12%
$26,700	$42,900	$68,500	$108,300	$170,000

five years, $31,700 after 15 years, and $68,500 after 25 years, even if you never add another dime to the pot.

With retirement as your goal, you needn't concern yourself with short-term investment swings, such as the ups and downs of the stock market. You're not an investment dabbler or someone who tries to precisely time each investment move; you're a long-term player who stands to benefit from putting time to work. This chapter and Chapter 10 will show you how to do that.

TRUTH #2: Investing successfully for retirement requires taking some risks, but not unnecessary risks. Investing for retirement—which is to say, investing for the long term—highlights a conundrum about risk. The more time you have to reach your retirement goal, the more risk you can afford to take in pursuit of it. But the longer you have to go until retirement, the less risk you actually need to take, since your nest egg has longer to reap the benefits of compound growth. (See Chapter 2 for more on the power of compounding.)

While no investor wants to lose money, investment categories with the best long-term performance records don't produce their standout results in a straight line. They inevitably experience ups (gains) and downs (losses) along the way. If you're caught in a "down," you'll lose money—at least on paper and at least for a while. But it isn't a real loss until you sell, and as a long-term player you aren't selling. Thus, there is really much less risk than it might first appear. History testifies that in the long run, wisely selected investments will brush off those occasional short-term dips to deliver stellar gains for your retirement nest egg.

If you were close to retirement and your nest egg wasn't growing as fast as it should to meet your anticipated retirement-income needs, you might need to increase your risk in hopes of achieving a higher return that would boost your nest egg more rapidly. But that's exactly the time you should be starting to reduce risk to conserve the capital you have. The best approach is to start out with higher-risk investments (we'll tell you where to look in this chapter and in Chapter 10), then

continued on page 166

With retirement as your goal, you're not an investment dabbler trying to time the market. You're a long-term player who'll benefit from putting time to work.

INVESTMENT SPEAK

66 KEY INVESTMENT TERMS YOU SHOULD KNOW

Here are some terms you'll hear when you talk to financial planners, brokers, and other financial types. Don't let the lingo intimidate you. Check here for answers, and don't be shy about demanding straight talk from anyone trying to get you to invest your retirement money.

Accrued interest. Interest that is due (on a bond, for example) but hasn't yet been paid. If you buy a bond halfway between interest-payment dates, for example, you must pay the seller for the interest accrued but not yet received. You get the money back—tax-free—when you receive the interest payment for the entire period.

American depositary receipt (ADR). Certificates traded in the U.S. stock market that represent ownership of a specific number of shares of a foreign company. ADRs are an easy way to add foreign stocks to your worry-free portfolio.

Annuity. A tax-favored investment that generates a series of regular payments guaranteed to continue for a specific time (usually the recipient's lifetime) in exchange for a single payment or a series of payments. With a deferred annuity, payments begin sometime in the future. With an immediate annuity, payments begin immediately. A fixed annuity pays a fixed income stream for the life of the contract. With a variable annuity, the payments may change according to how successfully the money is invested.

ARM fund. A mutual fund that invests in adjustable-rate mortgages (ARMs).

At-the-market. A term used when trading a stock or bond. When you buy or sell at-the-market, the broker will execute your trade at the next available price. Your alternative is to name a specific price, called a limit order.

Beta. A measure of how volatile the price of an individual stock or mutual fund is compared with the market as a whole. A stock or fund with a beta higher than one will likely move up or down more rapidly than the market average. A beta below one indicates below-average volatility.

Bid/asked. "Bid" is the price a buyer is willing to pay for a security; "asked" is the price the seller will take. The difference, known as the spread, is the broker's share of the transaction. Expect larger spreads for small, thinly traded stocks.

Blue chip. A stock that is issued by a well-known, respected company, has a good record of earnings and dividend payments, and is widely held by investors.

Bond. An interest-bearing security that obligates the issuer to pay a specified amount of interest for a specified time, usually several years, and then repay the bondholder the face amount of the bond. Bonds issued by corporations are backed by corporate assets; in case of default, the bondholders have a legal claim on those assets. Bonds issued by government agencies may or may not be collateralized.

Bond rating. An analysis by an independent firm (such as Standard & Poor's Corp. or Moody's Investors Service) of a bond issuer's ability to honor its promise to pay interest on schedule and repay the bond principal when due.

Book value. The value of a company's net assets (total assets minus all liabilities). That number divided by total outstanding shares gives you the stock's book value per share. If a stock is selling at a low book value relative to similar companies, it may be a bargain.

Capital gain or loss. The profit or loss from the sale of investments such as stocks, bonds, mutual funds, and real estate—in short, the difference between the price paid and the selling price. When the asset has been held for more than 12 months, the gain or loss is said to be long-term; assets owned a year or less produce short-term gain or loss. The distinctions don't matter if your investments are in a tax-favored retirement plan like an IRA, Keogh, or 401(k). But in a taxable account, long-term gains face a maximum tax rate of 20%, and short-term gains are taxed in your regular tax bracket, perhaps as high as 35%

Certificate of deposit (CD). A savings instrument issued by a commercial bank, savings and loan, savings bank, or credit union. CDs are issued for a specified period of time, usually for a fixed interest rate in line with general market interest rates. Terms generally range from one to five years, and there is usually a penalty for early withdrawal.

Closed-end fund. A type of mutual fund or investment company that issues a set number of shares, then no more. Shares of the fund trade like other stocks on one of the stock exchanges.

Cold calling. The practice of brokers' making unsolicited telephone calls to people on lists they buy or borrow in an attempt to drum up business. Never make investment decisions based on cold calls.

Common stock. The most basic type of share ownership in a U.S. corporation. Owners of common stock are entitled to all the risks and rewards that go with owning a piece of the company. Also see preferred stock.

Convertible bond. A special type of bond that can be exchanged, or converted, into a set number of common stock shares of the issuing company. The choice of when to convert is up to the bond owner. The appeal of a convertible is that it gives you a chance to cash in if the stock price of the company soars.

Discount broker. A cut-rate brokerage firm that executes orders to buy and sell stocks, bonds, and mutual funds but offers

continued on next page

INVESTMENT SPEAK (continued)

little if anything in the way of research or other investment assistance.

Dividend. A share of company earnings paid out quarterly to stockholders, usually in cash, but sometimes in the form of additional shares of stock.

Dividend reinvestment plan. Also called DRIPs, these are great nest-egg-building programs under which the company automatically reinvests a shareholder's cash dividends in additional shares of common stock, often with no brokerage charge to the shareholder.

Dollar-cost averaging. A strategy for investing a set amount of money on a regular schedule, regardless of the share price at the time. In the long run, dollar-cost averaging results in your buying more shares at low prices than at high prices.

Earnings per share. A company's profits after taxes, bond interest, and preferred-stock payments have been subtracted, divided by the number of shares of common stock outstanding.

Ex-dividend. The period between the declaration of a dividend by a company or a mutual fund and the actual payment of the dividend. On the ex-dividend date, the price of the stock or fund will fall by the amount of the dividend, so new investors don't get the benefit of it. Companies and funds that have "gone ex-dividend" are marked by an X in the newspaper listings.

Fixed-income investment. A catchall description for investments in bonds, certificates of deposit (CDs), and similar instruments that pay a fixed amount of interest.

Foreign stock. Shares of companies based outside the U.S. Stocks of many British, German, and Japanese companies trade in the form of American depositary receipts on the U.S. stock exchanges and can make good additions to a diversified investment portfolio. Foreign stocks can also be conveniently bought through international mutual funds.

401(k) plan. An employer-sponsored retirement plan that permits employees to divert part of their pay into the plan and avoid current taxes on that income. Money directed to the plan may be partially matched by the employer, and investment earnings within the plan will accumulate tax-free until they are withdrawn, presumably at retirement. The 401(k) is named for the section of the federal tax code that authorizes it.

403(b) plan. Similar to a 401(k) plan, but set up for public employees and employees of nonprofit organizations.

Full-service broker. A brokerage firm that maintains a research staff and other services designed to supply its individual and institutional customers with investment advice. Commission rates are higher than those of discount brokers.

Ginnie Mae. A dual-purpose acronym that stands for both the Government National Mortgage Association (GNMA) and the mortgage-backed securities that this government agency packages, guarantees, and sells to investors.

Good-til-canceled order. An order to buy or sell a stock or bond at a specified price, which stays in effect until it is executed by the broker because that price was reached, or until it is canceled.

Guaranteed investment contract (GIC). An investment product—issued by an insurance company—that works like a giant CD, but without federal deposit insurance. The contracts generally run one to seven years. Managers of 401(k) plans often put many GICs together into a fund and offer this investment to plan participants.

Individual retirement account (IRA). A tax-sheltered account ideal for retirement investing. It allows contributions of up to $4,000 in 2005 (rising to $5,000 by 2008) each year. In a traditional IRA, contributions may be deductible, earnings grow tax-deferred, and withdrawals are taxed. With Roth IRAs, contributions may not be deducted, but all withdrawals in retirement can be tax-free. For both types, penalties usually apply for withdrawals before age 59 1/2.

Initial public offering (IPO). The first public sale of stock by a company to investors. They're generally high-risk investments unsuitable for most retirement portfolios.

Institutional investors. Pension plans, mutual funds, banks, insurance companies, and other institutions that buy and sell large quantities of stocks and bonds. Institutional investors account for 70% or more of market volume on an average day.

Junk bond. A high-risk, high-yield bond rated BB or lower by Standard & Poor's, Ba or lower by Moody's, or not rated at all by any agency. Junk bonds are generally issued by relatively unknown or financially weak companies.

Keogh plan. A tax-sheltered retirement plan for the self-employed. Up to 20% of self-employment income can be diverted into a Keogh, and contributions can be deducted from taxable income. Earnings in the account grow tax-free until the money is withdrawn, and there are restrictions on tapping the account before age 59 1/2.

Limit order. An order to buy or sell a stock or bond if it reaches a specified price. A stop-loss order—a standing order to sell if a stock's price drops to a predetermined level—is a common variation.

Liquidity. The ability to quickly convert an investment to cash without suffering a noticeable loss in value. Stocks and bonds of widely traded companies are considered highly liquid. Real estate and limited partnerships are illiquid.

continued on next page

INVESTMENT SPEAK (continued)

Load. There are two basic types: front-end and back-end. A front-end load is a fee (sales commission) charged when you purchase a mutual fund, insurance policy, or other investment product. A back-end load is a commission charged to mutual fund investors who sell their shares before owning them for a specified time, often five years. True "no-load" mutual funds charge neither fee.

Margin buying. Financing the purchase of securities partly with money borrowed from the brokerage firm. Regulations permit buying up to 50% "on margin," meaning an investor can borrow up to half the purchase price of an investment.

Money-market fund. A mutual fund that invests in short-term corporate and government debt and passes the interest payments on to shareholders. A key feature of money-market funds is that share value doesn't change, making them an ideal place to earn current market interest with a high degree of liquidity.

Mutual fund. A professionally managed pool of stocks, bonds, or other investments divided into shares and sold to investors. Minimum purchase is often $2,000 or less. An "open end" mutual fund continues issuing shares as investors send more money and stands ready to buy back shares at any time. The market price of the fund's shares, called the net-asset value, fluctuates daily with the market price of the securities in its portfolio. A "closed end" fund issues

a specified number of shares, and those shares then trade in the stock market just like other stocks. The price may be higher (called selling at a "premium") or lower (called selling at a "discount") than the net-asset value of the stocks or bonds in the fund's portfolio.

Nasdaq (pronounced Naz-dak). Formerly the acronym for the National Association of Securities Dealers Automated Quotations System, a computerized price-reporting system used by brokers to track over-the-counter securities as well as some exchange-listed issues. Now the term refers to the computerized "stock market" on which hundreds of millions of shares trade every day.

Odd lot. A purchase or sale of stock involving fewer than 100 shares (also see round lot).

Opportunity cost. The cost of passing up one investment in favor of another. If the investment you choose outperforms the one you passed up, your opportunity cost is zero. If the one you passed up does better, however, your opportunity cost is the difference between the two choices.

Over-the-counter (OTC) market. Where stocks and bonds that aren't listed on any exchange—such as the New York Stock Exchange (NYSE) or American Stock Exchange (ASE)—are bought and sold. The OTC market is a high-speed computerized network called Nasdaq, which is run by the National Association of Securities Dealers.

Par (also called par value). The face value of a stock or bond.

Penny stocks (also known as microcap stocks). Generally, stocks selling at low prices—often for less than $5 a share—and traded over the counter. Penny stocks are usually issued by tiny, unknown companies and lightly traded, making them more prone to price manipulation than larger, better-established issues. They are very high-risk and not appropriate for a retirement nest egg.

Preferred stock. A class of stock that pays a specified dividend, set when it is issued. Preferreds generally pay less income than bonds of the same company and don't have the price-appreciation potential of common stock. They appeal mainly to corporations, which get a tax break on their dividend income.

Price–earnings ratio (P/E). The price of a stock divided by either its latest annual earnings per share (a "trailing" P/E) or its predicted earnings (an "anticipated" or "forward" P/E). The P/E is an important indicator of investor sentiment about a stock because it shows how much investors are willing to pay for a dollar of earnings. Listings in the *Wall Street Journal* include the P/E. A P/E above the market average indicates a stock that investors feel has strong growth potential—sentiment that has already pushed the price of the stock up.

Price-sales ratio (PSR). The stock's price divided by its company's latest annual sales per share. It is favored by some investors as a measure of a stock's relative value. The lower the PSR, according to this school of thought, the better the value.

Prospectus. A detailed document that describes the operations of a mutual fund, a stock offering, insurance annuity, limited partnership, or other investment. The prospectus reveals financial data about the company, background of its officers, and other information needed by investors to make an informed decision. It is required by federal securities laws.

Real estate investment trust (REIT). A closed-end investment company that buys properties or mortgages and passes all of the profits on to its shareholders. REIT shares trade like stock on the NYSE and other stock exchanges and offer a convenient way for small investors to add a real estate component to their investment portfolio.

Registered representative. The formal name for a stockbroker, so called because he or she must be registered with the National Association of Securities Dealers as qualified to handle securities trades.

Return on equity (ROE). A key measure of a corporation's investment results. ROE is calculated by dividing the total value of shareholders' equity—that is, the market value of common and preferred stock—into the company's net income after taxes.

continued on next page

INVESTMENT SPEAK (continued)

Return on investment (ROI).
A company's net profit after taxes, divided by its total assets.

Roth IRAs. See Individual Retirement Account.

Round lot. The counterpoint to odd lot. A round lot is 100 shares of stock, the preferred number for buying and selling and the most economical unit when commissions are calculated.

Spread. Basically, a stockbroker's markup on a stock or bond. It is the difference between the bid and asked prices of a security.

Stop-loss order. Standing instructions to a broker to sell a particular stock or bond if its price ever dips to a specified level.

Street name. The term used to describe securities that are held in the name of your brokerage firm but that still belong to you. Holding stocks in street name makes trading simple because there is no need for you to pick up or deliver the stock certificates in person.

10-K. A detailed financial report that must be filed with the Securities and Exchange Commission (SEC) each year by all companies whose shares are publicly traded. It is much more detailed than a typical annual report and can be obtained from the company or from the SEC.

Total return. An investment performance measurement that combines two components: any change in the price of the shares and any dividends or other

begin reducing the risk level of your investments once you're within five years or so of retirement.

A willingness to take some risk with your money is what provides the chance for you to earn an increased return—something a great deal better than you would get in "riskless" bank certificates of deposit, U.S. Treasury securities, or money-market funds. The hidden risk of retirement investing comes from taking no risks. With only supersafe investments, you forfeit your chance at bigger gains—and a more secure retirement. You swap one kind of risk (investment volatility) for another: the risk that your nest-egg performance will badly lag what it could have earned.

TRUTH #3: Diversification works. Deploying your retirement money among many investments is both a distributions paid to shareholders over the period being measured. For example, the total return on a utility stock that rose 4% over a year and that paid a dividend of 6% (calculated as a percentage of your original investment) would be 10%.

12b-1 fees. Fees charged by some mutual funds to cover the costs of promotion and marketing. Such fees reduce a fund's overall return to investors.

Yield. In general, the annual cash return earned by a stock, bond, mutual fund, real estate investment trust, or other investment. A stock yield is its annual dividend calculated as a percentage of the share price. For example, a stock priced at $50 per share and paying an annual dividend of $3 per share would have a yield of 6%. Bond yields can take several forms: "Coupon yield" is the interest rate paid on the face value of the bond (usually $1,000). "Current yield" is the interest rate based on the actual purchase price of the bond, which may be higher or lower. "Yield to maturity" is the rate that takes into account the current yield and the difference between the purchase price and the face value, with the difference assumed to be amortized over the remaining life of the bond.

Zero-coupon bond (zero). A type of bond that pays interest only when the bond matures. Zeros sell at a deep discount to face value. For example, a $10,000 zero yielding 7.5% and maturing in 20 years would sell initially for about $2,350, with the investor receiving the full $10,000 20 years later.

safe approach and a way to increase your opportunity for higher returns. Because no investment performs well all the time, when one is down, something else will be up. And best of all, because a well-diversified portfolio can include some higher-risk, go-for-broke choices, sensible diversification can also increase your return.

Stocks Promise the Best Long-Term Gains

Where's the single best place to invest a long-term retirement nest egg? Simple: stocks. In the long-term performance derby, stocks are winners by a big margin over almost any time period you choose. Since 1926, a basket of large-company stocks has shown an average annual gain of 10.4%. Small-company stocks, which tend to grow faster but with more risk, have produced an average annual gain 12.7% since the 1920s.

Since 1926, stocks have pummeled long-term corporate bonds, which averaged a mere 5.9%. Over the same period, long-term government bonds produced annualized returns of 5.4%. Meanwhile, inflation has averaged 3.0%.

During the 1970s, '80s, and '90s, stocks remained the clear winners, though bonds narrowed the performance gap. Since 1970, large-company stocks have returned an average of 11.28% annually. Small-company stocks have posted average annual gains of 14.15%, and long-term corporate bonds have returned an average of 9.39% yearly.

In short, if it's retirement wealth you want, look to the stock market! No other choice delivers as much. Not gold, bonds, real estate, or any of the other major investment categories. You can see for yourself on the "Long-Term Investment Scorecard," located on page 170.

Even the outstanding investment returns you see for stocks on that table tend to understate what investors could actually have earned. That's because these figures track a broad stock index that includes many bad stocks as well as the good ones. If you can pick better-than-average stocks—possible, though not easy—you can probably do better than the figures above. Chapter 10 has tips on picking the right stocks for your portfolio.

Since even a small difference in annual return can mean a big difference in the accumulation of wealth over time, the advantage stocks have enjoyed gives them a gigantic edge in an investment nest egg. Consider this scenario:

It's 1986 and a 45-year-old aiming to retire at the end of 2004 at age 63 invests his $60,000 savings three

---

WORRY-FREE TIP

The hidden risk of retirement investing comes from taking no risks. With only supersafe investments you forfeit your chance at bigger gains—and a more secure retirement. You swap one kind of risk (investment volatility) for another: the risk that your nest-egg performance will badly lag what it could have earned.

ways: $20,000 in government bonds, $20,000 in large-company stocks, and $20,000 in small-company stocks. At retirement, the three investments looked like this:

Government bonds: $109,214
Large-company stocks: $161,645
Small-company stocks: $184,553

Need we say more? The difference will depend on the time period selected and is sometimes much more dramatic. During the time covered in this example, small-company stocks posted a higher average return rate than large-company stocks did. But if this same 45-year-old had invested the same way just three years earlier, large-company stocks would have vastly out-performed small-company stocks. There's truth in the old investment adage: Past results are no guarantee of future performance. But the basic message is clear: Stocks have been long-term winners and should be the focal point for your retirement-plan money.

Stock Basics You Should Know

The term "stock" usually refers to common stock, which represents an ownership share in the company that issued it. If you own stock in Wal-Mart Stores, Inc., for example, you own a proportionate share (tiny though it may be) of Wal-Mart's empire—and you will share in its profits or, possibly, help shoulder its losses. Common stock may or may not pay dividends, which are profits the company distributes to its owner/stock-

---

WHERE SMALL STOCKS FIT

The message for retirement investors is basically this: Small stocks deserve a place in your portfolio, but you have to hold on for the long term to have the best chance of capturing their performance advantage. Small-stock mutual funds, which we'll explain in Chapter 10, are the best way for most people to buy.

---

holders. Divide the current annual dividend rate by the share price and you get the stock's yield. For example, with Wal-Mart selling at $53.08 in January 2005, and paying $0.52 per share for the fourth quarter, the stock's yield was 0.98%. Both the dividend and yield are often included in newspaper stock listings, so you won't need to do the math yourself.

Many companies also issue a special class of shares called preferred stock. These shares generally pay a higher dividend than common stock but don't have the same price-appreciation potential of common stock. They appeal mainly to corporations, which get a tax break on their dividend income. Individuals don't get that break, so there's no good reason to include this more esoteric stock investment in your retirement portfolio.

There are six basic, sometimes overlapping common-stock categories to consider for your retirement portfolio: Growth stocks, blue-chip stocks, income stocks, cyclical stocks, small-company stocks, and international stocks. You can buy them directly through a

LONG-TERM INVESTMENT SCORECARD

This table compares historical investment total returns to January 1, 2005.

Investment Category	% Average Annual Rate of Return Since							
	1926	1950	1960	1970	1980	1990	2000	2004
Large-Company Stocks	10.4	12.06	10.5	11.28	13.53	10.93	−2.3	10.9
Small-Company Stocks	12.75	14.9	14.46	14.15	15.23	14.83	14.32	18.4
International Stocks*	NA	NA	NA	11.09	11.49	4.55	−0.8	20.7
Long-Term Gov't. Bonds	5.4	6.0	7.39	9.16	10.65	9.35	10.49	8.5
Long-Term Corp. Bonds	5.9	6.39	7.62	9.39	10.67	9.13	10.7	8.7
Intermediate-Term Gov't. Bonds	5.4	6.26	7.39	8.53	9.15	7.35	7.65	2.3
U.S. Treasury Bills	3.7	4.92	5.61	6.11	6.04	4.18	2.7	1.2
Inflation	3.0	3.88	4.25	4.75	3.73	2.83	2.62	3.9

Sources: Ibbotson Associates, Chicago. Used with permission. All rights reserved.
*Courtesy of T. Rowe Price.

broker or gain instant diversification and the advantage of professional management by selecting mutual funds instead. Discount brokers can save you money on commissions, but they won't offer any advice on which stocks to buy. Chapter 10 will explain the advantages of mutual funds in detail and will also list strategies for selecting good stocks.

Growth stocks. These are so named because they have good prospects for growing faster than the economy or the stock market in general. Investors like them for their consistent earnings growth and the likelihood that share prices will go up significantly over the long term.

Blue-chip stocks. This is another loosely defined group; you won't find an official "Blue Chip Stock" list. Blue-chip stocks are generally industry-leading companies with top-shelf financial credentials. They include such names as Coca-Cola, General Electric, Procter & Gamble, and Xerox. Kellogg, Merck, and some other large growth stocks are also considered blue chips. They tend to pay decent, steadily rising dividends (many blue-chip companies, including the first five above, have paid an unbroken string of dividends for 50 years or more), generate some growth, and offer safety and reliability. These stocks can form your retirement portfolio's core holdings—a grouping of stocks you plan to hold "forever," while adding to your position as your portfolio grows.

Income stocks. These securities pay out a much larger portion of their profits (often 50% to 80%) to investors in the form of quarterly dividends than do other stocks. These tend to be more mature, slower-growth companies, and the dividends paid to investors make these shares generally less risky to own than shares of growth or small-company stocks. Though share prices of income stocks aren't expected to grow rapidly, the dividend acts as a kind of cushion beneath the share price. Even if the market in general falls, income stocks are usually less affected because investors will still receive the dividend.

Historically, utilities have been one type of dividend-paying stocks to consider for a retirement portfolio—especially if you were within ten years of retirement. As earnings rose, the best of the utility companies raised their dividends regularly, usually every year, and they brought investors steady, low-risk returns. In recent years, however, competition between utility companies and the specter of further deregulation have led to cutbacks, reduced dividend yields, and greater volatility. The utility sector is still considered safer than other industry sectors by many analysts, but investors will need to follow these stocks more closely than in past years.

One measure of any income stock is its yield, which is the annual dividend calculated as a percentage of its share price at the moment. And the yields on utility shares over the past two decades have been double, sometimes triple, the yield of the average blue-chip stock. Analysts expect that you may see a decline in dividend yields, but this should occur slowly. This once staid industry is in for a shakeout, with mergers, acquisitions, and companies going out of business, but the changes won't occur overnight.

But dividends are only one way that income stocks make money for your retirement nest egg. The key is their total return—the combination of dividends plus growth in the price of the shares. In other words, if a utility stock priced at $20 and yielding 6% rises to $21 in a year (a 5% gain) and the dividend remains steady, your total return on the stock is 11%.

Small-company stocks. These are typically newer, fast-growing companies. Shares in these companies are riskier than blue-chip or income stocks, but as a group historically their long-term average returns have been higher. Since 1926, small-company stocks have gained an average of 12.75% per year versus 10.4% for a 500-stock basket of the market's largest issues. (But as seen in the example given earlier, during some periods large-company stocks have outperformed small-company stocks.)

The price of that historic advantage has been greater short-term volatility. The best year for large stocks was 1933, with a gain of 54%; the worst year was in 1931, with a loss of 43%. But the biggest-ever one-year gain for small-company stocks was 143% in 1933, and they suffered a 58% drop in 1937.

Foreign stocks. These investments also have a place in your retirement nest egg, and they are easily available through a wide array of foreign-stock mutual funds. We'll give you some top names in Chapter 10. The two key benefits of adding an international flavor to your nest egg are diversification and performance.

Looking beyond the U.S. market broadens your investment universe. And that's essential in this era of global interdependency when your personal prosperity is ever more closely linked to the prosperity of the world's economies. While most investors still think only in terms of owning U.S. shares, the American market represents less than half of all stock-market opportunities worldwide. Why ignore the other half?

Foreign shares help diversify your nest egg because international markets generally perform differently than the U.S. market does. When stocks in the U.S. are down, those in other countries may be rising. The reverse is also true, of course, but by investing in a mutual fund that owns stocks in many different countries, you can reduce the effects of a downturn in any one foreign market.

Investing in foreign shares does present an additional risk involving the relationship between foreign currency values. A portion of your gain or loss on foreign stocks will come from the fluctuating value of the U.S. dollar overseas. When the dollar drops against other currencies, the value of your foreign stocks will rise, independent of what happens to the price of the foreign shares themselves. For example, if you own stock in a German company and the dollar drops 5% in relation to the German mark, the value of the stock

> Foreign shares help diversify your nest egg because international markets generally perform differently than the U.S. market does.

The net effect of holding a small portion of your nest egg in bonds is to cushion the entire basket.

to you as a U.S. investor rises roughly the same 5%. A rising dollar would reverse the situation. Adding the currency movement to any change in the price of the stock itself produces your total gain or loss.

Because of the currency risk in owning foreign stocks, most small investors are better off in an international mutual fund that spreads the risk among many different countries and currencies.

The Role of Bonds and GICs

Some financial planners maintain that investors with ten or more years to go until retirement should have their money in the stock market—period. That view isn't universally held, and not all individuals feel comfortable enough with stocks—despite their winning long-term performance—to put an entire nest egg in that basket. Adding modest amounts of bonds or other fixed-income vehicles, such as a guaranteed investment contract (GIC), to your retirement portfolio can reduce the overall risk level. The price may be a slightly lower return, but the additional diversification and safety of bonds and GICs will make for a steadier ride toward retirement.

The Basics

A bond is an IOU issued by a corporation or, in the case of Treasuries, by Uncle Sam. When you buy a bond, you are making a loan to the bond issuer. In return, the company or the federal government agrees to pay a specified interest rate known as the coupon rate. You will be paid a fixed amount of interest, usually twice yearly, until the bond matures, at which time you are paid the bond's face value. For example, if the face value of the bond is $1,000, you get back $1,000. If you wish, you can also sell the bond to another investor before it matures.

Why might you want to own bonds in your retirement portfolio? As you saw in the "Long-Term Investment Scorecard" on page 170, both corporate and government bonds have lagged the stock market over

WHERE TO BUY NOTES AND BONDS

You can buy Treasury notes and bonds through banks and brokers, or from the government through a program called Treasury Direct. There is no service charge, but there is an annual maintenance fee on all Treasury Direct accounts exceeding $100,000. For details on setting up a Treasury Direct account at the Federal Reserve bank nearest you, call the Bureau of Public Debt in Washington, D.C. (800-722-2678), or check its Web site at www.publicdebt.treas.gov.

the very long term. Since 1926, long-term government bonds have shown an average annual return of just 5.4%, compared with large-company stock's 10.4%.

However, bonds have mostly performed better than their historical average. Long-term corporate bonds scored average annual returns of 10.67% between 1980 and 2004, but that's still considerably below the 13.53% and 15.23% showing for both large- and small-company stocks respectively during the same period.

Given that performance gap, why even consider bonds? If you are ten, 15, 20, or more years from retirement and won't be spooked into selling stocks if the market swoons, there's probably little reason. Go for the bigger gains that stocks are likely to offer over the long haul.

But if stocks are just too unsettling to you personally, or if you have less than ten years until retirement, bonds' lower volatility is important. The net effect of holding a small portion of your nest egg here is to cushion the entire basket.

Still, bonds entail several kinds of risk. Chief among them is interest-rate risk. The bond market thrives when interest rates fall. The reason is fairly simple. A bond paying 8% that was issued last year will be worth more this year if new bonds are paying only 6%. So if you paid $1,000 for your bond, you could probably sell it for around $1,300.

But the reverse is also true. When interest rates rise, bond values drop, and if you happen to be holding some of those bonds, you could lose money if you had to sell. (In 1994, for example, interest rates rose rapidly and bonds had a terrible year, with many bond investments showing a net loss for the year.) If you bought an 8% bond for $1,000 and the going rate for new bonds jumped to 9%, your bond would be worth only about $890. But you'd still be earning 8%, and if you hold the bond to maturity, price swings don't matter. You still receive full value when it comes due.

Different Types of Bonds

As with stocks, there are several major categories of bonds and bond cousins for you to consider: U.S. Treasuries, corporate bonds, zero-coupon bonds, foreign bonds, and bondlike animals known as mortgage-backed securities. One kind of bond you don't want for your IRA, Keogh, or other tax-deferred retirement account is the municipal variety. Because interest on those bonds is tax-free, there's no advantage to putting it in a tax shelter, and there's a big disadvantage: When the interest comes out of the shelter, it will be taxed.

You can buy bonds through a broker or, in the case of U.S. Treasuries, directly from the government. Discount brokers can save you money on commissions but won't provide advice on which bonds to buy. For most investors, bond mutual funds are the way to go. They offer instant diversification and professional management. Chapter 10 explains the advantage of mutual funds and offers tips and strategies for investing in bonds.

U.S. Treasuries. These are the safest bonds to buy. In maturities of two to ten years they're known as Treasury notes; the longer maturities of ten to 30 years are called Treasury bonds. They are backed by the full faith and credit of the federal government, and interest is paid semiannually. Notes start with a $1,000 minimum, then sell in $1,000 steps. Longer-term notes and bonds also sell in minimum $1,000 increments. Interest is free from state income taxes, which slightly boosts the in-your-pocket return.

Corporate bonds. These bonds, which are backed by the companies that issue them, are riskier than Treasuries, so they pay higher rates to compensate investors. The safest bonds are those given the highest ratings from agencies such as Standard & Poor's (S&P) Corp. (www.standardandpoors.com) and Moody's Investors Service (www.moodys.com). For example, bonds issued by the very strongest corporations receive AAA ratings from S&P. Corporate bonds with low ratings or no ratings at all pay the highest rates and are more commonly known as junk bonds. They are generally not appropriate investments for a worry-free retirement portfolio. Typically, corporate bonds are sold in increments of $1,000, or sometimes $5,000, with interest paid twice yearly.

Zero-coupon bonds. These bonds, known as zeros, pay interest only when they mature. At that point, they pay all the accumulated interest at once. You pay a relatively small sum for the bond when you buy it and receive a giant payback at maturity. Zeros come in face values as low as $1,000 and are sold at large discounts of 50% to 80% from that face value, depending on how long you have to wait to collect the interest at maturity. For example, a $10,000 zero yielding 7.5% and maturing in 20 years would sell initially for about $2,350.

Because zeros sell for such huge face-value discounts, they're a good choice if you want to know precisely how much money will be available on a set date—at retirement, for example. The longer the term of the zero, the less you have to pay now to buy one.

Taxes are a potential drawback. Even though you don't actually receive interest on the zero each year, the IRS annually taxes the interest that accrues each year. This is why zeros work best inside an IRA, Keogh, or other type of retirement account that allows investment earnings to build tax-free.

There is a bright side to the fact that zeros don't pay interest semiannually. You don't have to worry about reinvesting that income in your retirement nest egg. In

> **Zeros are much more sensitive to interest-rate changes than regular bonds.**

effect, as interest accrues it is automatically reinvested at the yield promised when you bought the zero.

One final point: Zeros are much more sensitive to interest-rate changes than regular bonds. If market rates fall after you buy zeros, you could score a significant profit by selling before maturity. But if rates rise and you have to sell before maturity, you could face a steep loss.

Foreign bonds. Just as foreign stocks offer opportunities beyond U.S. borders, so do foreign bonds. If you own bonds, most of them should be issued by Uncle Sam or U.S. corporations. But bonds issued by foreign governments or corporations can pay higher yields—sometimes much higher—than their U.S. counterparts. The early '90s provided a good example. While shorter-term Treasuries yielded in the 5% range, similar bonds issued by the French, German, and British governments were paying 9% to 10%. As with foreign stocks, there's currency risk. If the value of the U.S. dollar goes up while you own foreign bonds, the value of your investment will drop. The best way to buy is through foreign-bond mutual funds.

Mortgage-backed securities. These are not really bonds, but they have some similar characteristics. Briefly, these securities represent pools of home mortgages that have been made by lenders around the country. Owners of the securities receive "pass-through" payments of both interest and principal on those mortgages.

There are many types of mortgage-backed securities. Perhaps the best known are those guaranteed by a federal agency called the Government National Mortgage Association (GNMA, or Ginnie Mae). The guarantee means that if a homeowner defaults on a mortgage, the government will make good on all payments. Securities issued by two quasi-government organizations, the Federal National Mortgage Association (FNMA, or Fannie Mae) and Federal Home Loan Mortgage Corp. (FHLMC, or Freddie Mac) are backed by the assets of those agencies but not directly by Uncle

Sam. In all cases, the guarantee does not mean that the market price of the securities is guaranteed—this will fluctuate in response to changes in interest rates. In fact, mortgage-securities prices tend to fluctuate more than Treasury or corporate bonds.

Because a mortgage-backed security pays back both principal and interest throughout its life—unlike a bond, which pays only interest and returns principal at maturity—mortgage-backed securities behave differently than bonds and carry a higher risk. The good news is that they usually pay higher returns than corporate bonds or U.S. Treasuries. The bad news is that when interest rates drop, homeowners rush to refinance their mortgages at lower rates, thus eating into the returns that investors receive on mortgage-backed securities.

> ## NEW ARM TWIST
>
> The latest in mortgage funds invests in packages of adjustable-rate mortgages (ARMs) as opposed to fixed-rate loans. The attraction is greater price stability, with less risk, because homeowners with this type of mortgage presumably will not rush to refinance when rates are low. When rates in general rise, the interest rate on an adjustable-rate mortgage increases, and so does the return to the investor.

The yield edge can make this investment category a worthwhile diversification for larger retirement portfolios, in modest proportions. While it's possible to buy mortgage-backed securities directly through a broker (minimums can be as high as $25,000), the best way to add them to a portfolio is through mutual funds. Nearly every major fund group now offers a Ginnie Mae fund.

CDs: A cash consideration. In the early '80s, when interest rates soared well into double digits, certificates of deposit were an investment favorite. Since then, recession, then low inflation, and most recently global economic problems have brought CD interest rates way down. You can expect low single-digit rates on one- to five-year CDs; most are paying under 4%, which offers little incentive to the long-term retirement investor unless you are seeking the safety of federal deposit insurance on deposits up to $100,000.

But rates change, so you should never say never to CDs. If rates push near or above the 10.4% historical average return for large-company stocks, CDs could again have a place in your portfolio. The sleep-at-night safety of government insurance is certainly one benefit. The other is that when CD rates jump, stocks sometimes run the other direction.

Based on historical interest-rate swings, a good approach is this: If five-year CD rates reach 10%, stock up for your portfolio. By staggering the maturities of CDs you buy, you can protect yourself against rapid rate changes. If rates rise, the shorter-term CDs in your portfolio will mature in time for you to roll the money into new CDs at higher rates. If rates fall, your longer-term CDs will continue earning you top CD dollar for up to five years.

Guaranteed investment contracts. If you participate in a 401(k) plan at work, a guaranteed investment contract (GIC), also sometimes called a stable value fund, may be one of your investment choices—nearly three-fourths of all 401(k) plans offer GICs as an investment option, and 13% of employee contributions are put into GICs when the option is available.

GICs are kind of like a giant certificate of deposit issued by an insurance company or bank, but without any federal deposit insurance. The contracts generally run three to five years. As with a CD, your interest rate is fixed. Rates in early 2005 averaged about 4% for five-year GICs, while five-year CDs hovered around 3.9%.

Managers of 401(k) plans often buy many GICs and put them together into a GIC fund. The money you designate for a GIC in your 401(k) then goes into that fund. The fund approach is good because it spreads the risk over as many as 20 issuers. The different rates of return are blended to arrive at the yield you receive on your investment. When the term of any individual GIC contract is up, your pension fund recoups the principal and either reinvests it in another GIC or returns it to employees who are retiring or cashing out of the plan.

GICs have delivered what their name implies—a guaranteed return. The major risk is that a GIC is only as good as the company that issues it. And some of these companies, burdened with junk-bond investments and sour real estate loans, have seen their creditworthiness dwindle.

Are you endangered? There is risk in any investment, but the chance that big insurance companies will tumble and cost you your money is remote for a number of reasons. Because GICs in an individual company's plan are most likely drawn from a number of insurance companies, the failure of one insurer would not necessarily cause a significant drop in your 401(k) assets. And GIC contract holders are covered by insurance plans in most states under the same terms as holders of life insurance policies.

Many major GIC sellers hold only small amounts in junk bonds, so that's probably not a major concern. But such reassurance shouldn't tempt you to ignore your own 401(k) plan. Your money and your worry-free retirement are at stake.

With supposedly safe and secure GICs, it's also easy to be recklessly cautious. The perception of safety is seductive. But on a $10,000 investment, the difference over 20 years of a 10% return from stocks (roughly the long-term average) and a 4% return from a GIC is more than $45,000.

While most of your money should be in stocks, don't dismiss GICs out of hand. They can be a better choice than bonds for the fixed-income portion of your retirement portfolio, and GICs tend to pay higher rates than Treasuries.

Variable Annuities

Variable annuities are retirement investments sold primarily by life insurance companies and occasionally by mutual fund companies. The life insurance component doesn't offer much—no more than a guarantee that if you die before taking out your

> **While most of your money should be in stocks, GICs can be a better choice than bonds for the fixed-income portion of your retirement portfolio.**

money, your heirs will get back at least as much as you put in.

But variable annuities can shine as a component in your portfolio if you have exhausted your other tax-deferred retirement options. Actually, the annuity itself is not what counts—it's the mutual fund investments offered inside the annuity that tell the performance story. The annuity is the wrapping that allows these investments to double as a retirement tax shelter. You can invest as much money as you like in one or several funds within the annuity and let that money compound without immediate taxation. Chapter 10 has more details on how to fit variable annuities into a retirement-investment strategy and some suggestions of top choices.

Your House as a Retirement Piggy Bank

For most people, the first and only piece of real estate they'll ever own is the roof over their heads. While home prices in the next ten to 20 years won't generally outrun inflation as dramatically as they did in the '70s and '80s, they'll stay a step or two ahead in most areas.

The home you buy can be much more than a place to live. It can be a key element in your retirement plan as well. Because the down payment you make is only a fraction of the home's value, you get a degree of financial leverage that is hard to find elsewhere. The long-term mortgage you use to finance your home permits you tap into a great retirement wealth builder. Your mortgage payments buy increasing equity each month (even more if you follow the early-payoff scenario described in Chapter 3). That's like a forced savings plan that builds value rapidly over the years.

What's more, a home remains one of the few major tax shelters still available to the average individual: In almost every case, the profit from the sale of a home

---

REAL ESTATE FUNDS

Another way to invest in real estate is through a group of relatively new specialty mutual funds that buy the stocks of developers, builders and REITs. Two that have been around the longest and invest heavily in REITs are Fidelity Real Estate Investment Portfolio(800-343-3548; www.fidelity.com) and Cohen & Steers Realty (800-330-7348; www.cohenandsteers.com).

---

will be tax-free. Tax-free profit comes on top of the fact that mortgage interest you pay is tax-deductible. If you're in the 25% tax bracket, for every $1,000 of interest you pay on your principal residence, you get a $250 tax subsidy for homeownership. State tax deductions can give you a hand, too.

If you don't want to sell your home to help finance retirement, you can tap its value through a reverse mortgage, covered in Chapter 12.

A Break for Homeowners: Tax-Free Profit
In the past, homeowners could postpone the tax bill on profit when they sold one home by buying a more expensive home. And once the owner turned 55, up to $125,000 of home-sale profit could be tax-free.

Things are a lot better now. First of all, the tax law won't force you to buy a more expensive house than you need, a change that, in and of itself, may make it easier for you to save for retirement. Now, regardless of your age, up to $250,000 of home-sale profit is tax-free if you file a single return. The tax-free amount for joint-return filers is a cool half-million dollars. And unlike the old $125,000 break that could be used only once in your lifetime, the new break is available once every two years. Basically, to qualify for tax-free profit, you must own and live in the house as your principal residence for at least two of the five years before the sale.

Imagine the possibilities: When you retire, you can sell the family homestead, add up to $500,000 of tax-free profit to your worry-free retirement nest egg, and move into what has been a vacation home. After two years, you could sell that place and, again, pocket up to half-a-million dollars in profit tax-free—including profit that built up while it was your vacation home. Be sure to crank potential home-sale profits into your plans.

The REIT Way to Invest in Real Estate

Investing directly in real estate beyond the confines of your own home is a move best left to deep-pocket investors with specialized knowledge of real estate markets. Even the pros have had a tough time of things in the 1990s.

But for larger nest eggs, those that have moved into six-figure territory, real estate does offer the twin advantages of further diversification and a hedge against inflation. The simplest way to add a real estate component is through real estate investment trusts. A REIT (rhymes with street) is a bit like a mutual fund that owns apartments, office buildings, shopping centers, or other types of real estate instead of stocks or bonds. It offers a convenient way to add real estate to your investment portfolio without the headaches of direct ownership. You can buy shares in approximately 180 publicly traded REITs the same way that you'd buy any stock: through a broker.

REITs can be high-yielding investments, paying dividends that are often four times the dividend on Standard & Poor's 500-stock index stocks. Near the end of 2004, for example, with the dividend yield on Standard & Poor's 500-stock index at 1.8%, most equity REITs (see description below) yielded 5% on average, and some yielded as much as 7.6%.

REITs fall into three general categories, based on their investment focus:

1. **Equity REITs** are at least 75% invested in classic brick-and-mortar real estate, such as shopping centers,

offices, hotels, and apartments. You earn dividend income from rents. Capital gains are possible when properties are sold. You are definitely in the real estate business, but you don't have to fix screen doors.

2. **Mortgage REITs** are like banks in that they hold a portfolio of real estate mortgage loans. Mortgage REIT shares typically pay higher yields and entail higher risks than equity REITs.

3. **Hybrid REITs** invest in both property and mortgages.

Of the three, concentrate on equity REITs for your retirement portfolio. Neither the mortgage nor hybrid variety give you as pure a real estate play. The best equity REITs can plausibly produce annual total returns in the range of 10% over the next decade as the commercial real estate industry recovers from deeply depressed levels of the early 1990s. These REITs will usually have a straightforward specialty—a particular geographic area, a specific type of real estate project, or both. For example, Health Care Property Investors owns health care properties in 44 states throughout the country. New Plan Excel Realty Trust specializes in shopping centers and garden apartment communities in 35 states. And Washington Real Estate Investment Trust owns commercial and residential property, primarily around Washington, D.C.

A Place for Gold?

Gold has an ancient reputation as the ultimate way to hedge against disaster and inflation. But there are serious chinks in gold's inflation-fighting armor. Since gold prices peaked at $850 per ounce in 1980, the metal has failed miserably to live up to its billing. Gold prices have continued to drop since that time.

Profits from owning gold have eluded investors. Not only that, but the opportunities lost by not investing the money in stocks or other investments have been costly for stubborn gold bugs.

In the aftermath of a decade or more of disappointments for gold owners, should you conclude that

OVERSEAS GROWTH

In spite of the turmoil in many foreign economies, Kiplinger believes that the economies of many nations will grow more rapidly than the U.S. economy over the next ten to 20 years, offering enticing investment opportunities for those willing to look beyond U.S. borders. Morgan Stanley's index of developed countries (the benchmark for international stock performance) gained 39% in 2003, ten percentage points better than Standard and Poor's 500 stock index.

Despite that impressive performance, the most compelling reason for owning foreign stock isn't that kind of run-up: Adding these stocks to your portfolio can dampen volatility and may even boost long-term performance.

gold's claim of protection against disaster and inflation no longer rings true? Or should you keep the faith, anticipating that the day will come again when gold outshines all other investments? For most people looking to build a long-term retirement nest egg, the best answer is to forget gold and invest the money elsewhere. Even the most fervent believers in gold don't recommend making it more than 5% to 10% of your assets.

Most long-term investors who buy this metal are likely to consider gold as a kind of insurance policy against some huge future financial disaster—a measure of protection in your portfolio, even though you hope that you never need it. This is probably the best reason to even consider a small gold allotment for your retirement nest egg.

Ways to Invest

To add such an insurance policy, you could buy gold bullion in the form of bars or coins, or gold-mining stocks, either directly or through mutual funds. American Eagle gold bullion coins and Canadian Maple Leaf coins sell for at least 3% to 5% above the spot price of gold. You'd need to store the gold securely—say, in a safe-deposit box—and you'd earn no interest on your investment.

Gold stocks and gold-oriented mutual funds also qualify as gold surrogates. But the stocks are affected by overall trends on Wall Street and by corporate decisions good and bad that have nothing to do with gold itself. Still, a company that institutes low-cost mining methods, strikes a rich lode, or hedges its sales through the futures market can see its earnings rise smartly. Mutual funds that invest in gold-mining stocks have done poorly in recent years, reflecting the overall market in precious metals. But for convenience and low costs, a gold mutual fund is probably the best way to add this insurance policy to your portfolio. AIM, American Century, Evergreen, Fidelity, and Vanguard are a few of the major investment companies that offer gold funds.

Use These Money-Wise Strategies

Pssssst! Do you want to know the single most important strategy for successful retirement investing? It's this: Stick to your plan. That's pretty basic, simple stuff. But then, basics and simplicity are what it takes to succeed.

Your plan, of course, is for long-term growth of capital to finance your worry-free retirement. No exotic investment gambles or complex systems. No quick ins and outs. No panic dumping of stocks when the market goes down.

Instead, we'll show you some sample portfolio allocations, by stages, in the retirement-planning process. Your plan will almost certainly include mutual funds, so we'll tell you about key mutual fund advantages for retirement investors. We'll help you figure where different types of funds fit into your retirement-plan puzzle, and when buying into mutual funds through variable annuities can be a wise move. Your strategy may involve some individual stock and bond selections, so we've included techniques that will help you make the best choices for long-term growth.

A simple, no-cost strategy called dollar-cost averaging can put your investment plan on the fast track—this chapter shows you how. And we'll tell you about some useful programs that can put your nest egg on autopilot. Because success also depends on sidestepping mistakes, we've listed some common pitfalls that are critical to avoid.

Together, the super strategies presented on the following pages will help put your investment plan on the right track—and keep it there.

Strategy #1: Set the Stage

Investing your nest egg during each stage is largely a matter of allocating the money among different investment categories. How you do that will depend on how much risk you are willing to take—whether you consider yourself a super-conservative investor or an aggressive one, more willing to go for broke—and how near you are to retirement. Think about investing for retirement in three basic stages:

1. **Getting started** (20 or more years to go)
2. **Full speed ahead** (ten to 20 years)
3. **Closing in** (less than ten years)

Deciding where you stand on the risk continuum is your first strategic step. You want to be "comfortable" with an investment, and investors seem to go both ways on the comfort scale. Some stay clear of anything that chances a loss, while others blithely sink money into high-risk ventures they know little about.

A sensible approach to worry-free investing uses the somewhat timeworn but still appropriate "pyramid of risk." The pyramid applies to your entire financial picture and is built on a broad base of financial security: a home and money salted away in insured savings accounts or certificates of deposits. As you move up from the pyramid's base, the levels get narrower and narrower, representing the space that is available for nest-egg investments that involve more risk. The greater the risk of an investment, the higher up the pyramid it goes and, thus, the less money you should put into it.

The best retirement investments start just above the base level and include mutual funds that own low-risk, dividend-oriented stocks and top-quality government and corporate bonds. Individual stocks and bonds that you pick yourself are on the same level. At the very top of the pyramid go investments that you should not consider for your retirement portfolio, such as penny (or microcap) stocks, most types of limited partnerships, and commodities futures contracts.

The amount of risk you decide to take with the money you've earmarked for retirement depends on several factors: your age and the number of years before retirement, the amount of money you need in order to reach your goal, your other resources, and your investment temperament. Recognizing the risks in every kind of investment can help you find your comfort level.

RISKS IN STOCKS. A company's stock price may drop because the firm hits the skids and the shareholders lose faith. It may also decline because large numbers of investors decide to move into bonds or cash on a particular day and sell millions of shares of stock of all kinds, thus driving the market down and dragging hundreds of companies along without bothering to differentiate the good from the bad.

RISKS IN BONDS. Bond prices track interest rates in reverse, rising when rates fall and falling when rates rise. Individual corporate bonds can be hurt if one of the rating services—Standard and Poor's and Moody's are the major ones—lowers its opinion of the company's finances. A bond that's paying an interest rate noticeably higher than similar bonds is likely to be riskier. That's the situation with "junk" bonds—lower safety ratings

A RISK-TAKING LINEUP

Here's how investors with different risk tolerances might divvy up their investments:

Investment Categories*	Super Cautious	Cautious	Moderately Aggressive	Aggressive
Safety and income	30%–40%	20%–30%	10%–20%	0%–10%
Growth with income	15%–35%	25%–35%	15%–25%	10%–20%
Growth	10%–25%	25%–35%	30%–40%	35%–45%
Aggressive growth	0%–10%	10%–20%	20%–30%	40%–50%

*Safety and income: Treasuries; CDs; short-term bond funds; guaranteed investment contracts (GICs); high-grade corporate bonds; zero coupon bonds
Growth with income: Utility shares and other dividend-paying stocks; real estate investment trusts (REITs); balanced, growth-and-income, and equity-income funds
Growth: Growth and international stocks and funds
Aggressive growth: Small-company/aggressive-growth stocks and funds

(or no ratings) translate to higher interest because of the higher risk of default.

RISKS EVERYWHERE. Real estate values rise and fall in sync with supply and demand in local markets, regardless of what's happening elsewhere. Gold, which is supposed to be a haven in inflationary times, has been decidedly unrewarding in times of tolerable inflation. Even federally insured savings accounts carry risks—not that Uncle Sam won't cover insured deposits, but that their interest rate won't be enough to protect your money from inflation, particularly after taxes get a crack at the earnings.

Because every individual's circumstances are different, there can't be a hard-and-fast formula for how retirement money should be allocated among different investment-risk levels. But as Chapter 9 pointed out, the stock market's big long-term performance edge points strongly in that direction. A portfolio mix of 70% to 100% stocks and zero to 30% bonds will likely produce the best results.

Besides risk, the other key element is time. Bear in mind that since your time frame is constantly changing, there is no fixed formula for how your nest-egg funds should be invested. What's more, because you are adding new money to your retirement cache—presumably each month—your strategy for divvying up those funds will change as investment conditions change, your nest egg grows, and you move closer to retirement.

For example, if you invested aggressively in small-company stocks early in the game but now want to take a more conservative stance, you can do so by placing most of your new money in blue-chip stocks, income funds, and Treasuries. No need to sell the small stocks to accomplish the shift. On the flip side, if you find you started out too conservatively, make your monthly additions to a more aggressive investment until you bring your overall nest egg in line with where you want it to be.

The point is that no investment portfolio is static. Even if you do nothing, it changes on its own as some investments do better than others, thus throwing your percentage allocations out of whack.

Also, the bulk of your nest egg may be locked up in a company plan that offers little investment choice. You can deal with that by investing money you do control—in IRAs and unsheltered accounts, for example—in the areas not available to you via the company plan. For example, if all your company 401(k) money is invested in GICs and other conservative categories, invest your IRA funds in stocks. Think of all your money as a single pie and divvy it up accordingly.

Here are three sample portfolio mixes for people in different stages of retirement planning that you can use as general guidelines.

Early in the Game: 20 or More Years to Go

PROFILE: A 40-year-old individual or couple wanting to retire in 20 to 25 years. Current nest egg is $50,000 or less, not counting a house if they own one.

APPROACH: There's a relatively small amount of money to spread around at this point, so keep it simple. Go for maximum growth in stocks, through strong emphasis on small-company shares as well as blue chips. Use mutual funds, not individual shares. No real estate other than home.

Full Speed Ahead: Ten to 20 Years Away

PROFILE: A 49-year-old couple looking toward retirement in 12 to 15 years. Current nest egg ranges up to around $200,000, not counting a house.

APPROACH: There's still a long way to go, so the goal continues to be maximum growth of capital. With an expanding portfolio, this couple has the ability to diversify further, especially buying individual stocks and by adding real estate to the portfolio in the form of REITs. A balanced fund can be a good, conservative choice, combining both stocks and bonds. For diversity, the couple can add more mutual funds, distributing small-stock holdings, for instance, among two or three

A LOOK AT THREE PORTFOLIOS

Years to Retirement	20	ten to 20	Less than ten
General allocation breakdown			
Stocks	100%	100%	75%
Bonds	0%	0%	25%
Specific breakdown			
Stocks			
Small companies	25%	20%–25%	15%
Blue chips	50%	45%	35%
Foreign	25%	20%–25%	15%
REITS	0%	5%–15%	10%
Bonds	0%	0%	25%

funds and some individual issues. Foreign-stock holdings can be further diversified among funds that invest in specific regions.

Closing In: Less than Ten Years
PROFILE: A 54-year-old, dual-income couple looking toward retirement in six to ten years. Current nest egg exceeds $200,000, not counting a house.

APPROACH: If this couple wants to retire at 62 they're only eight years away. Investments still need to concentrate on growth, though the shortening time frame calls for a more conservative approach. Stocks dominate, but with less emphasis on more volatile small-company stocks. As the couple gets within five years of retirement, they should increase their share of bonds and bond funds in their portfolio to about one-third.

Strategy #2: Plug Into the Mutual Fund Miracle

Mutual funds can be an investor's best friend. They let small investors hire professional money managers to take over the grunt work of investing—slogging through reports on thousands of individual companies to compile a suitable investment portfolio. By turning the dirty work over to mutual funds, you can make your retirement-investment portfolio as easy to manage as possible.

A mutual fund is an investment company that pools money from many investors and buys a portfolio of stocks and bonds meant to achieve a specific investment goal. The fund might own a selection of blue-chip stocks, small-company stocks, foreign stocks, a mix of stocks and bonds, or a host of other investment types or combinations. The key categories and some fund choices are presented later in this chapter. Each fund's goals and other details are divulged in detail in its prospectus—a helpful document you'll receive and should definitely read before investing any money.

Valued Features

Mutual funds offer a combination of services that are ideal for retirement investors. They are especially well-suited for beginning investors who worry about their own ability to select good stocks and who could benefit most from this brand of professional management. But even experienced investors and those with large portfolios can benefit from what mutual funds have to offer:

SIMPLE PROCEDURE TO BUY AND SELL. The process of selecting individual stocks and bonds can be complex, time-consuming, costly, and downright frustrating. Mutual funds offer an easy-buy, easy-sell concept. You can buy or sell with a phone call directly to the fund, through a broker, through the mail, or online.

The fund is required by law to buy back its shares when you want to sell them. The price at which shares are bought and sold is based on the fund's net-asset value. The NAV is the total market value of the fund's holdings, minus management expenses, divided by the total number of shares in investors' hands. Here there's a difference between "load" and "no-load" funds, which are discussed in more detail later. You can buy or sell a no-load fund at its net-asset value with no

> ## DIVERSIFICATION ADVANTAGE
>
> Because they provide automatic diversification, well-chosen mutual funds are a better choice than individual stocks or bonds for investors who have modest amounts of money or are just starting a retirement-planning portfolio.

commission. You buy a load fund that is sold at net-asset value plus a commission, but you sell shares back to the fund at net-asset value.

Because most mutual funds constantly issue new shares as investors send more money and redeem them as investors sell their shares back, the number of shares changes. These are "open end" funds.

But there are also "closed end" funds, which issue a set number of shares, then no more. Like their open-end cousins, these funds offer a diversified portfolio, but after shares are issued, they are listed and traded on the major stock exchanges, just like regular corporate shares. You buy and sell them through a regular broker and pay standard commissions, usually at a discount or premium to their NAVs.

PROFESSIONAL MANAGEMENT. Each fund has one or more portfolio managers whose job it is to direct the fund's buying and selling. These investment experts are hired by the management companies that sponsor the funds. While some individuals are more talented and successful at this than others, you can at least be assured that a knowledgeable individual is at the helm.

INSTANT DIVERSIFICATION. Each mutual fund share buys you an interest in whatever the fund owns. A typical large-stock fund, for example, will own shares in more than 100 companies, perhaps several hundred. This diversification doesn't insulate you from market movements. But if one stock dives, the impact overall is greatly softened. To gain the diversification advantages of most mutual funds, you'd probably need to invest at least $50,000 to $100,000 or more on your own—and you'd probably pay thousands in commissions to do so.

While diversification is a key strength of mutual funds, you still need to take it a step further by diversifying among several different funds as your nest egg grows. No single fund can meet all your retirement-investment needs (and even among funds with identical goals, some will perform much better than others). You can begin this process early. For example, a $5,000 nest egg can be split between two funds or even among three. A $50,000 portfolio might contain five types of funds, and a $100,000 portfolio could include six or eight funds. Even if you start out with just one or two funds, you can add others later on as you continue to add funds to your retirement nest egg.

SMALL MINIMUM INVESTMENT. Most mutual funds have a low minimum initial-investment requirement—typically $500 to $3,000. Some funds accept orders of as little as $25; a few have no minimum at all. Once the initial investment is made, most funds permit additional investments as small as $50 to $250. Since funds issue fractional shares, you can invest in round-dollar numbers. If you invest $200 in a fund selling for $11.50 per share, for example, you will receive 17.39 shares. Low minimums make mutual funds the perfect place

FINDING GOOD FUNDS

There are a number of good publications that can help you find good funds and keep up with fund performance. Popular periodicals covering funds regularly include *Barron's, Business Week, Forbes, Kiplinger's Personal Finance, Money,* and *Smart Money.* The most comprehensive coverage is available in Morningstar Mutual Funds, a 1,700-page compendium of mutual fund analyses and rankings updated every other week. It's unmatched for detail and timeliness. At $495 per year, it's expensive, but it can be found in many larger libraries. You may only need a single copy or a short-term subscription; a three-month trial with six updates is $55. Call 800-735-0700 or go to www.morningstar.com.

STRAPPED FOR FUNDS? NO PROBLEM

What if you're short on cash one month or need the money for other purposes? Not to worry. Most funds let you switch off the autopilot investment at any time with a phone call, and without penalty.

---

to invest small amounts of money on a regular basis for a long-term accumulation program.

AUTOMATIC REINVESTMENT OF EARNINGS. Dividends paid by stocks in the fund's portfolio, interest from bonds, and profits (called capital gains) earned when securities are sold are distributed to fund shareholders, usually once or twice a year. Most funds will automatically reinvest that money to buy you more shares of the fund. That's a way to give your long-term plan a big boost because it puts the power of compounding (described in Chapter 2) to work on your behalf. In effect, the fund invests more money in your retirement nest egg, even if you don't.

SERVICE PERKS. Mutual fund companies are eager to gain and keep you as an investment customer. The larger funds make it easy to inquire about your account, get current price and yield information, and make purchases, transfers, or redemptions. Funds love to have retirement account money in IRAs (Chapter 7), Keoghs, or SEPs (Chapter 8) because they know you are likely to keep the money there for the long term. So they've made the paperwork for opening these accounts (and any account, for that matter) virtually painless. Companies that manage a group of funds—a fund family—make it easy for you to switch your money from one member of the family to another, usually with a phone call.

EASY MONITORING. Keeping track of how mutual funds are doing is easy, too. Major newspapers publish fund prices daily, while personal-finance magazines regularly compare and rank mutual fund performance over a variety of time periods. *Kiplinger's Personal Finance,* for example, publishes a monthly list of top performers and an annual compilation of results for all funds, in the August issue. The funds themselves issue quarterly and annual reports, and most have toll-free numbers you can call for daily share prices. You can also check the mutual fund finder at www.kiplinger.com.

The Load/No-Load Choice

Mutual funds fall into two basic cost camps: those that charge commissions (load funds) and those that don't (no-loads). Front-end loads, charged when you first invest, typically range from 3% to 5.75%. Funds on the lower end of the scale are called low-loads. A back-end load, charged at the time you sell your shares, is also called a redemption fee. Numerous funds charge temporary or permanent redemption fees of 1% to 5%, which usually disappear for investors who hold the shares three to six years or more.

At first blush, it may seem foolish to pay a load if you can buy into another fund for free. And, indeed, there's no evidence that paying a load buys you better fund management or performance. That makes sense, in fact, because the load doesn't go to the managers—it goes to the broker or other financial professional who sells you the fund.

The key to the load/no-load decision is whether you have the time and confidence to pick the funds for your retirement portfolio. If so, no-loads are almost surely the way to go. If you don't want to take the time or feel you don't have the ability to evaluate funds, however, you should seek the advice of a broker or financial planner. And you should expect to pay for that service via a load.

Choosing the Right Funds

Note that we didn't say, "Choosing the *Best* Fund." It usually isn't enough to pick one good fund, or even two or three good funds. You will want to put together a good portfolio of funds that suit your needs. A portfolio is a group of funds, drawn from various fund types, that work together in all kinds of investing environments, so that while one fund might do badly, another may soar. By building a portfolio of funds, you reduce the risk that your overall holdings will be wiped out and at the same time maximize the growth of your nest egg.

To begin the task of finding the right funds for your portfolio, concentrate on the fund types whose objectives and willingness to take risks most closely match your own. Within each category, you can compare per-

---

THREE SAMPLE FUND PORTFOLIOS

Portfolio 1: Long Term

Best for investors who are at least six years from retirement or who won't need their money to meet other goals for at least ten years.

Legg Mason	
Opportunity Trust	30%
Harbor Capital	
Appreciation	20%
Artisan International	15%
Meridian Growth	15%
Dodge & Cox	
International Stock)	10%
Century Small Cap	
Select	10%

Asset Allocation
100% in stocks

Portfolio 2: Medium Term

Best for investors who plan to retire in fewer than six years or who have other goals five to nine years in the future.

Oakmark Fund	25%
Harbor Capital	
Appreciation	20%
Artisan International	10%
Dodge & Cox	
International Stock	10%
Century Small Cap	
Select	10%
Loomis Sayles Bond	25%

Asset Allocation
75% in stock funds (with 20% in foreign stocks), 25% in bonds.

Portfolio 3: Short Term

Best for investors in early retirement years, up to about age 75. After age 75, gradually sell off stock funds and put the proceeds into bond funds.

Selected American	
Shares	20%
Masters' Select Value	
Smaller Companies	10%
Tweedy Browne	
Global Value	10%
American Century	
Equity Income	10%
Harbor Bond	30%
(or Vanguard Intermediate-Term Tax Exempt)	
Loomis Sayles Bond	20%
(or Vanguard Intermediate-Term Tax Exempt)	

Asset allocation
50% in stock funds, 50% in bond funds.

formance records, costs, and shareholder services of individual funds to help make your final choices.

The categories used to describe mutual funds do a
pretty good job of indicating the kinds of investments
they make. For example, aggressive-growth funds take
the biggest risks by purchasing shares of fast-growing
small companies, international funds invest in shares
of companies based outside the U.S., balanced funds
balance their portfolios between stocks and bonds,
and so on.

Because the rate of return on your money must at
least keep up with the rate of inflation before and even
after you retire, you should keep a significant amount
in stock funds. Just how much depends on how much
time you have until retirement and your tolerance for
risk. For example:

If you have more than 15 years to retirement: You should
invest 100% of your money in stocks, whether your tolerance for risk is low or high. You could divide your
money between aggressive-growth, long-term growth,
and international funds—fund types offering the great-
est growth and risk—because you've got plenty of time
to ride out and more than make up for any slumps.

To cite a recent example, the 20-year annualized
return (the average annual return after compounding for the period ending December 31, 2004) for the
aggressive-growth fund category was 11.43%, even
though it suffered down years in which its return was
-9.16%, -4.54%, and -19.28%, and in 2002, in the aftermath of 9/11, it lost 28.11%. Likewise, the 20-year return for the long-term growth category was 12.44%,
whereas it had down years in which its return was only
-0.67%, -7.99%, and it lost 16.53% through December
31, 2002.

If you have six to ten years to retirement: You might
still keep 100% of your money invested in stocks if
you're comfortable with high risk, or reduce that
amount to 60% and invest the balance in bonds if
you're your tolerance is low. Either way, you would

still invest your stock money in aggressive-growth, long-term growth, and international funds.

With fewer than six years to retirement: Even the most risk-taking investors should begin to move some of their stock money into bonds—say, 25%. More conservative investors will increase the proportion of the portfolios devoted to bonds.

Once you're in retirement: You should continue moving your stock money into bonds—say 40% to 60% of your portfolio, depending on your tolerance for risk. You should also switch some or all of your remaining stock funds to less risky fund types, such as growth, growth-and-income, and real estate funds.

Here are details on the major mutual fund categories that you should consider for your retirement-plan investing, along with possible fund choices (keep in mind, these are not recommendations). Minimum purchase amounts are often significantly lower if you're investing in an IRA.

AGGRESSIVE-GROWTH FUNDS. These are swing-for-the-fences funds that go for big profits (that's "maximum capital gains" in investment lingo) by investing in small to medium-size companies, developing industries, or wherever rapid growth—and run-up in stock values—is expected.

Aggressive-growth funds seldom pay dividends. These funds carry higher risks than most other types of stock funds but can produce the biggest gains over the long term. Since 1926, small company stocks have posted an annualized return of 12.75% compared with 10.4% for large stocks (per Ibbotson Associates). And that includes 2001, when aggressive-growth funds were one of the hardest-hit broad fund categories.

Managers of these funds do a lot of buying and selling. And because that involves commissions, expenses tend to be higher than for other types of stock funds. Small-company funds work best when they are given ample time to strut their stuff.

Fund	Minimum Purchase	800# and Web site
Masters' Select Smaller Companies	$2,000	656-8864; www.mastersselect.com
Baron Small Cap	$2,000	992-2766; www.baronfunds.com
Century Small Cap Select	$1,000	321-1928; www.century.com
Fidelity Small Cap Stock	$2,500	544-8544; www.fidelity.com
T. Rowe Price Growth Stock	$2,500	638-5660; www.troweprice.com
Royce Premier	$2,000	221-4268; www.roycefunds.com

LONG-TERM GROWTH STOCK FUNDS. These funds seek long-term capital gains, usually by investing in larger companies than most aggressive-growth funds. This steady, inflation-beating growth feature makes these funds ideal for the heart of a long-term retirement portfolio, with less volatility than aggressive-growth funds. Here again, portfolio managers are unconcerned about dividends.

Fund	Minimum Purchase	800# and Web site
ABN AMRO Montag & Caldwell Growth N	$2,500	992-8151; www.abnamro.com
Clipper Fund	$25,000	776-5033; www.clipperfund.com
Harbor Capital Appreciation	$2,500	422-1050; www.harborfund.com
Jensen Portfolio	$1,000	992-4144; www.jenseninvestments.com
Legg Mason Opportunity Trust	$1,000	822-5544; www.leggmason.com
Meridian Growth	$1,000	446-6662; www.meridianfund.com
Oakmark Fund	$1,000	625-6275; www.oakmark.com
T. Rowe Price Capital Appreciation	$2,500	638-5660; www.troweprice.com
Third Avenue Value	$1,000	443-1021; www.mjwhitman.com

GROWTH-AND-INCOME FUNDS. These also emphasize growth, but are more conservative than long-term growth funds. They invest mainly in established companies, many of which pay dividends. The best of these funds achieve long-term growth but with more mild share-price swings than long-term growth funds. This type of fund tends to be less volatile than most other stock fund entries.

Fund	Minimum Purchase	800# and Web site
Fidelity Growth & Income Fund	$2,500	544-8544; www.fidelity.com
T. Rowe Price Equity Income	$2,500	638-5660; www.troweprice.com
T. Rowe Price Growth Stock	$2,500	638-5660; www.troweprice.com
Selected American Shares	$1,000	243-1575; www.selectedfunds.com
Vanguard 500 Index	$3,000	662-7447; www.vanguard.com

INTERNATIONAL AND GLOBAL STOCK FUNDS. International funds buy stocks in companies based outside the U.S., giving investors a chance to take advantage of growth opportunities in other parts of the world. Although they come with some inherent risks—foreign political upheaval, looser regulatory environments, and currency fluctuations—they can reduce your portfolio's volatility. That's because foreign markets don't usually move in tandem with the U.S. market; when one is doing poorly, the other may be doing well. Subcategories of international funds include emerging-markets, regional and single-country funds, which most investors will be wise to use sparingly, if at all. A broad-based international fund is the better choice.

Global funds (sometimes called worldwide funds) include some U.S. stocks as well, but they vary in just how much they keep invested in the U.S. Most investors will do better with international funds, because you can more reliably and easily track how much of your money is invested abroad.

Fund	Minimum Purchase	800# and Web site
Artisan International	$1,000	344-1770; www.artisanfunds.com
Dodge & Cox International Stock	$2,500	621-3979; www.dodgeandcox.com
Julius Baer International Equity A	$2,500	435-4659; www.juliusbaer.com
Oakmark International*	$1,000	625-6275; www.oakmark.com
Tweedy Browne Global Value	$2,500	432-4789; www.tweedybrowne.com

*Available only by direct purchase from Oakmark

SOCIALLY CONSCIOUS FUNDS. Many of these funds make their investment choices with an eye toward environmental awareness—investing only in companies that don't pollute. Others avoid investing in weapons makers, cigarette companies, nuclear-energy producers, and so on. Many also look for companies known for management that treats employees with respect. Still others describe themselves as promoting "conservative" or "Christian" values and eschew companies, for example, that promote sex and violence in the media. There are dozens of socially conscious funds to choose from, and it probably won't be difficult to find those that meet your social criteria. It may be harder to find well-performing ones. Once you've made your initial selection, look for funds whose returns are competitive within their investment category, such as long-term growth or growth-and-income.

Fund	Minimum Purchase	800# and Web site
Ariel Appreciation	$1,000	292-7435; www.arielfund.com
Ariel Fund	$1,000	292-7435; www.arielfund.com
Neuberger Berman Socially Responsive	$1,000	877-9700; www.neuberger berman.com
Pax World Balanced	$ 250	767-1729; www.paxworld.com
TIAA-CREF Social Choice Equity	$2,500	223-1200; www.tiaa-cref.org
Vanguard Calvert Social Index	$3,000	635-1511; www.vanguard.com

SECTOR FUNDS. Because they concentrate their holdings in a single industry sector—transportation, energy, health care, or precious metals, for example—sector funds are much more volatile than more diversified funds. As a result, these specialized funds are best suited for sophisticated investors who follow market signals and are prepared to switch funds often, or for long-term investors willing to assume above-average risk. Sector funds, except for some real estate funds, generally don't make good choices for retirement portfolios because of their higher degree of risk.

Fund	Minimum Purchase	800# and Web site
Columbia Real Estate Equity A	$1,000	426-3750; www.columbiafunds.com

HIGH-GRADE CORPORATE BOND FUNDS. These invest mainly in bonds issued by top-rated companies. Some specialize in short-term, some in intermediate-term, and some in long-term bonds. A few concentrate on zero-coupon bonds, signaled by the words "target maturities" in the name of the fund.

Fund	Minimum Purchase	800# and Web site
Harbor Bond	$1000	422-1050; www.harborfund.com
Loomis Sayles Bond	$2,500	633-3330; www.loomissayles.com
T. Rowe Price Spectrum Income	$2,500	638-5660; www.troweprice.com

U.S. GOVERNMENT BOND FUNDS. As the category name says, these funds buy U.S. Treasuries and other types of bonds issued by the federal government or its agencies. These, too, specialize in short-term, intermediate-term, or long-term maturities.

Fund	Minimum Purchase	800# and Web site
American Century Long-Term Treasury	$2,500	345-2021; www.americancentury.com
T. Rowe Price U.S. Treasury	$2,500	638-5660; www.troweprice.com
Vanguard Fixed-Income Intermediate-Term U.S. Treasury	$3,000	635-1511 www.vanguard.com
Vanguard Inflation-Protected Securities	$3,000	635-1511 www.vanguard.com
Vanguard Short-Term Treasury	$3,000	635-1511 www.vanguard.com

MORTGAGE-BACKED SECURITY FUNDS. These are more commonly known as Ginnie Mae funds, so named for the assets they own—mortgage-backed securities issued by the Government National Mortgage Association, or GNMA. Though these funds load up on Ginnie Maes, they own other kinds of mortgage-backed securities as well. Mortgage funds are more volatile than bond funds, especially when interest rates are falling and homeowners are refinancing and taking their higher-rate mortgages out of the pool. Funds that own adjustable-rate mortgages (ARM funds) are more stable, but they aren't immune to the same price pressures.

Fund	Minimum Purchase	800# and Web site
American Century GNMA	$2,500	345-2021; www.americancentury.com
Fidelity Ginnie Mae	$2,500	544-8544; www.fidelity.com
T. Rowe Price GNMA	$2,500	638-5660; www.troweprice.com
USAA GNMA	$3,000	531-8181; www.usaa.com
Vanguard GNMA	$3,000	635-1511; www.vanguard.com

INDEX FUNDS. The premise here is simple: If you can't beat the market, buy it. Portfolios are constructed so that they match the components of an index, such as the Standard and Poor's 500-stock index, small-company and international-stock indexes, bond indexes, and others. They offer these advantages for a retirement portfolio: predictability—your investments will do as well or as poorly as the stock market does; low costs, at least in theory, because there's little to manage; and above-average results, considering that just matching the S&P 500 makes your return above average—over the long haul, the S&P 500 has beaten roughly two-thirds of all stock funds. Index funds are a conservative way to hitch a ride on the market. Risk, because it matches the market's exactly, is average with these funds. However, because the S&P includes only large and midsized companies, index funds that track the Wilshire 5000, which mirrors the entire stock market including smaller companies, are usually a better bet.

Fund	Minimum Purchase	800# and Web site
Fidelity Spartan Extended Index	$10,000	544-8544; www.fidelity.com
Fidelity Spartan International Index	$10,000	544-8544; www.fidelity.com
Fidelity Spartan 500 Index	$10,000	544-8544; www.fidelity.com
Fidelity Spartan Total Market Index	$10,000	544-8544; www.fidelity.com
Vanguard Total Stock Market Index	$3,000	635-1511; www.vanguard.com
Vanguard Total International Stock	$3,000	635-1511; www.vanguard.com
Vanguard Index Total Bond Market Index	$3,000	635-1511; www.vanguard.com

Strategy #3: Add an Annuity Advantage

Variable annuities—which are investments sold primarily by life insurance companies—are another way to plug mutual funds into your retirement nest egg. Variable annuities are a convenient combination of a tax shelter for retirement money, mutual funds, and life insurance.

As life insurance, variable annuities don't offer a whole lot—no more than a guarantee that if you die before taking out your money, your heirs will get back as much as you put in. But as investments, they can be a solid supplement to a retirement plan. You invest as much money as you like in one or several funds within the annuity, where the money compounds without immediate taxation. Eventually, and after age $59\frac{1}{2}$ if you want to avoid a penalty, you can surrender the annuity and take a lump-sum payout Or you can take the money in installments over time.

The lure of variable annuities is the tax-deferred status of earnings. Plus, you can switch without tax consequences among the different funds offered within an annuity. Mutual fund holders, by contrast, pay taxes on income, capital-gains distributions, and profits from selling fund shares if they aren't held in an IRA or other tax-sheltered plan. Money inside an IRA, 401(k), Keogh, or SEP already benefits from untaxed growth, so variable annuities make sense only outside one of those plans—and only after you have fully funded those retirement vehicles.

Variable-annuity advantages do come at a cost. You face a 10% tax penalty on withdrawals of untaxed earnings before age $59\frac{1}{2}$, plus regular income taxes, plus surrender charges that can be as high as 9% to start with and gradually drop over a number of years. Terms vary and will be spelled out in the prospectus. Such penalties suggest extreme caution if there's even a remote chance that you might tap the annuity before $59\frac{1}{2}$.

Fees abound. The first one is an annual contract-maintenance fee—typically $30. Next come fees for managing the assets in each fund. These are akin to mutual fund expense fees and range between 0.3% and 2.5% of your investment annually. There's usually an assessment of about 1.25% per year to cover mortality and expense (M&E) risk and administration. The fees typically total 2.24% yearly on a $25,000 investment. By contrast, the average mutual fund investing in U.S. stocks would charge you 1.4%, and many come in at less than 1%. And finally, you may be faced with a surrender charge if you cash in the policy. Because of these fees, annuities are not a good choice for parking any rollover money from a company pension or 401(k) plan.

Annuity or Mutual Fund?

Can a variable annuity fit into the portion of your nest egg that's subject to tax? Or will plain old mutual funds work better? Here are the factors that will help you decide:

TIME FRAME. The longer you allow your assets to grow on a tax-deferred basis, the more advantageous the variable annuity becomes—a plus for retirement programs.

EXPENSES. The higher an annuity's operating expenses, the less likely it is to outperform a comparable but lower-cost mutual fund, even after taxes (we'll give you some low-cost annuity choices a little later).

TAXES. The higher your marginal tax rate while your annuity accumulates, the bigger the advantage of its tax deferral will be. This advantage is offset somewhat, however, by the fact that withdrawals from an annuity will be taxed as ordinary income in your top tax bracket, even if much of the gain comes from dividends and long-term capital gains (gains on investments held for more than 12 months). Long-term capital gains and dividends earned outside an annuity or other retirement plan get gentle treatment: The top tax rate on both is 15%; the top rate on ordinary income is 35%.

PAYOUT METHOD. Many of an annuity's advantages are lost if you accept payment in a lump sum on which taxes are due immediately. The annuity's relative attractiveness is enhanced if you draw a regular income from your kitty—a process that's called "annuitizing" the payout.

YOUR RISK TOLERANCE. An annuity works best with aggressive-growth stock funds that offer the highest potential long-term returns. If your risk tolerance tells you to shun such funds, you stand to gain less with an annuity. It makes little sense to use a variable annuity to invest in a bond fund, for example, because the fees and charges you will incur will claim too much of your money.

Picking the Best Variable Annuities

As with the other portions of your retirement nest egg, the key to success here is to think long term. Look for funds that consistently match or outperform the market, as opposed to those that sizzle one year and fizzle the next.

Here are some variable annuities with good investment choices and low expense ratios:
- **Fidelity** (800-544-2442)
- **T. Rowe Price** (800-469-6587)
- **Charles Schwab** (800-838-0650)
- **USAA** (800-531-4440)
- **Vanguard** (800-523-9954)

Annuities sold by Vanguard, T. Rowe Price, USAA, and discount broker Charles Schwab, all no-load mutual fund sponsors, have no front-end or deferred sales fees.

Before you buy, check such features of the annuity contract as minimum investment (generally $1,000 to $5,000), maximum ages for making contributions and for beginning payouts, limitations on and charges for switching among funds within the annuity, provisions for adding dollars at regular intervals, and availability in your state.

Strategy #4: Pick Your Own Stocks

Once your portfolio has grown to sizable proportions—say, at least $50,000—you may want to try your hand at picking some stocks. Don't abandon mutual funds, however. They have a place in portfolios of any size, and the long list of benefits they offer is still crucial to your plan. But well-chosen individual stocks, assembled alongside the other assets in your portfolio, can provide further diversification and long-term-gain potential.

The secret to selecting good stocks for your retirement portfolio is really no secret at all. The worry-free way to invest in the stock market is to invest for growth and "value." That means concentrating on stocks that pass the tests described below and holding them for the long term. These tests—while they don't work all the time—will help prevent you from making false and risky assumptions about the stocks you buy for your retirement nest egg.

Knowledge is power. Having the right information about a company and knowing how to interpret that information are the keys to selecting stocks. Predicting market movements is secondary for anyone with a long-term investment horizon—and no one has ever been able to do it on a consistent basis anyway.

Investment ideas can come from many sources—newspapers, magazines, television, newsletters—even your own personal experiences and observations can help you uncover terrific stocks. But an investment idea is only that—an idea. If you hear about a good stock, don't run out and buy it immediately. Before you act, gather the information you need to size up the company's prospects. Write to or call the company's investor relations department and ask for the last two or three annual reports and the latest quarterly reports. You can get company addresses and phone numbers from Standard and Poor's *Register of Corporations, Directors and Executives,* available in many public libraries.

Also request the company's "Form 10-K"—an extensive financial-disclosure document that must be filed annually with the Securities and Exchange Commission. A 10-K is similar to an annual report, absent the pretty pictures. It usually contains much meatier discussions. (See the box on the next page for more places to look for key facts on common stocks.)

Making Sense of It All

Instead of getting hung up on the price of a stock—which by itself makes the stock neither expensive nor cheap—look at key financial ratios that tell you the company's earnings per share or the value of its assets per share. We describe these measures below. You'll be ahead of the curve if you remember a few characteristics of common stocks.

DAY-TO-DAY PRICE CHANGES ARE PRACTICALLY UNKNOWABLE. Most stocks merely move in the direction of the overall market. Developments in an industry may also affect prices of the stocks within that sector, as may a host of unanticipated factors: An analyst downgrades the stock; the company unexpectedly wins (or loses) an important contract or lawsuit; a big shareholder sells a block of stock to pay for a divorce settlement.

OVER THE LONG TERM, THERE'S AN UNCANNY CORRELATION BETWEEN SHARE PRICE AND A COMPANY'S PROFITABILITY. Given this link, it's crucial to focus on a company's profits (also called earnings) before investing in its stock. The absolute size of a company's profits won't tell you much. What's important are profits in relation to the number of shares outstanding—in other words, earnings per share (EPS).

TO GET THE EPS FIGURE, DIVIDE EARNINGS BY THE AVERAGE NUMBER OF COMMON-STOCK SHARES OUTSTANDING DURING THE PERIOD BEING MEASURED. Look for companies with a pattern of EPS growth over at least five years and a habit of reinvesting 35% or more of earnings in expansion of the business. You can determine the reinvestment rate by comparing earnings per share with the dividend payout. Earnings that aren't paid out to shareholders get reinvested in the business. *Barron's, Value Line Investment Survey,* and stock reports issued by brokerage firms carry earnings estimates. So do a number of different services on the Internet.

STOCKS ARE NOT ALL EQUALLY VALUED. You can get an idea of which are cheap and which are expensive by checking how each stock is priced in relation to its

---

STOCK-SELECTION SOLUTIONS

Check out the gold mine of data and analyses on about 1,700 companies published in the *Value Line Investment Survey* ($75 for a 13-week trial subscription or $598 per year for a print version; an online version costs $65 and $538 respectively (www.valueline.com; 800-634-3583). The trial subscription, which comes with the complete set of stock reports offered with a full subscription, is a great deal. The historical earnings, dividend and price data, future projections, and pithy commentary can give you a good feel for a company. This survey also gives stock timeliness and safety ratings, on a scale of 1 (safest or most timely) to 5 (riskiest

or least timely). *Value Line* is the leading independent stock-analysis publication and is not affiliated with any brokerage firm. You'll find it in most good-size libraries.

The monthly *S&P Stock Guide* (Standard & Poor's, 55 Water St, New York, NY 10041; 800-221-5277) is a compendium of statistics (but no commentary) on more than 7,500 stocks. At $220 per year, *Stock Guide* has most of the hard facts you need to check out a company. Find it in libraries or order from S&P.

Another good informational move is to join the American Association of Individual Investors (AAII,

625 N.Michigan Ave., Suite 1900, Chicago, IL 60611; 800-428-2244; www.aaii.com). For $49 in annual dues, AAII's 150,000 members receive local chapter membership, a journal (ten times per year), a guide to low-load mutual funds, strategies for investing in stocks, and, at reduced cost, home-study courses, seminars, video-tapes, CD-ROMs, newsletters, and books.

Financial papers with the best stock listings are the *Wall Street Journal, Investor's Business Daily,* and the weekly *Barron's.* Available on newsstands, in libraries, and by subscription.

earnings. A key measure of a stock's price compared with others is its price-earnings ratio. The P/E, as it's generally known, is a key indicator of whether a stock is cheap or expensive and is probably the single most important number you can know about a stock. The P/E is the price of a share divided by the company's earnings per share. If a stock sells for $35 per share and the company earned $3.50 per share in the previous 12 months, the stock has a P/E ratio of 10. The P/E indicates how much investors are willing to pay for each dollar per share a company earns.

THE QUICKEST WAY TO FIND P/E RATIOS IS IN NEWSPAPER STOCK TABLES OR ON THE INTERNET ALONGSIDE THE STOCK'S PRICE. But what you see may not be too useful. For one thing, the numbers sometimes reflect one-time factors, such as earnings write-offs or asset sales, that temporarily deflate or inflate a company's profitability. Another problem is that P/E ratios in newspapers are based on the previous 12 months' earnings, whereas the investment world looks ahead. So analysts also calculate P/Es using forecasts of a company's profits over the next year and sometimes longer. That's why Value Line or brokerage projections of future profits come in handy. Many Internet sites also offer earnings projections.

THERE'S NO HARD-AND-FAST RULE FOR INTERPRETING P/E RATIOS. Investors use one or more of these analytical techniques:

Think small. A low P/E may indicate an undervalued stock. Over long periods, stocks with low P/E's deliver superior returns. But there's no rule that says a "cheap" stock won't simply get cheaper. If you invest in low-P/E stocks, make sure you're comfortable that the "E" part of the equation won't let you down.

Look at similar stocks. For example, if most drug companies have P/Es of 20 but Merck trades for a P/E of 12, then all other things being equal, Merck might be undervalued. But don't make such comparisons of companies in dissimilar industries.

Compare growth with P/E. You'll seldom see a company with steadily increasing earnings and a below-average P/E ratio because investors "pay up" for the likelihood the company will deliver higher profits. Those profits will later lower the P/E, based on today's price.

Deciding When to Sell a Stock

You don't want to cash in every time your stock moves up a few dollars—commissions would cut into your gain, and you'd also be stuck deciding what to do with the money. Likewise, you don't want to bail out in a panic if the market should take a temporary dive. But owning stocks long term doesn't mean owning them forever.

> **WORRY-FREE TIP**
>
> Here's a good move to make with earnings on retirement investments that are held outside of an IRA, Keogh, 401(k), or other tax-sheltered plan: Pay taxes on those earnings out of your pocket, rather than dipping into your nest egg for the money. Your retirement stash will grow much faster, aided by the compounding effect.

Brokerage firms are slow to issue "sell" signals unless a company faces dire problems. When stock analysts feel queasy about a stock, they often call it a "hold" or a "weak hold." You should take that to mean, "Don't buy any more shares and if you've got a profit, seriously consider selling this stock." As you manage your own portfolio, look for these clues that it's time to consider selling:

A change in financial fundamentals. How's the company doing? Are earnings growing? Are future prospects still bright, or are sales expected to flatten or even drop in coming years? If a company's long-term fundamentals start to weaken—whether it's a blue-chip stock or a small-growth company—it's time to reconsider your investment. If growth slows below the firm's long-term average, for example, and looks like it will stay slow, consider selling.

A dividend cut. A company that cuts its dividend is generally in trouble. Any signs that the dividend is in jeopardy—such as analysts' saying they don't think a company can maintain its payout to shareholders—can undermine the stock price and indicate a possible time to sell.

Your target price is reached. Many investors set specific price targets, both up and down, when they buy a stock. When the stock hits that target, they revisit the shares as a possible sell. A good target is to double or triple your money, or to limit a loss to no more than 20%. If the company's fundamentals and growth prospects are still strong, you can hang on. If it shows signs of peaking, the profits might be redeployed more profitably elsewhere. Those guidelines can prompt you to take your gains while the taking is good and to dump losers before the damage gets worse.

One useful strategy is to sell in stages after a strong run-up in price. You might, for example, sell half of your position, pocket those profits (or reinvest them elsewhere), and let the other half run. Other investors try to be contrarians by selling when everyone else is buying, on the theory that by the time "everyone" knows about an investment and starts buying, the smart money is headed for the exit.

Bigger fish lurk elsewhere. Another reason to sell is if you've found something significantly better. The potential of the new investment should probably be 40% to 50% greater, to make up for the additional commission costs, possible tax consequences, and risks of making a switch.

Strategy #5: Use Five Bond-Buying Tactics

Bonds can't match the performance record of stocks over the long haul. But they have proven their mettle over shorter time periods—particularly since the early 1980s.

For example, the 5.9% annualized (compound annual) return on corporate bonds since 1926 trails the

10.4% return for large stocks and withers next to the 12.7% showing for small-company stocks (per Ibbotson Associates). But take a look at the performance figures for the following investment categories between 1980 and 1995, a period in which bonds benefited greatly from a steep decline in interest rates: 15.8% for large-company stocks and 12.4% for long-term corporate bonds. You see little difference. That's a scenario that won't often be repeated, so it's no argument for abandoning stocks. But it does show that bonds, too, can have their day in the sun for investors who follow some basic bond-buying rules of thumb.

BUY BONDS WHEN YOU'RE GOING TO NEED YOUR MONEY IN A RELATIVELY SHORT TIME, OR YOU'RE RISK AVERSE. If you're investing for the long term and you can live with the ups and downs of the stock market, you'll likely do best by avoiding bonds altogether because their long-term returns are so much smaller than those of stocks. But when you're going to need your money in the next five years or so, it makes sense to put a large portion of your money in bonds. They serve as ballast for your portfolio, countering the swings of the stocks and stock funds you own. Unfortunately, no one can predict when interest rates will go up or down. A one-percentage-point drop in long-term interest rates will cause the share price of a long-term Treasury-bond fund to go up by about 11%, according to Vanguard, a fund group whose bond funds have done well because of their low expense ratios. But, notes Vanguard, a one-percentage-point increase in rates would cause that long-term Treasury fund's share price to drop by about 9%.

DIVERSIFY BY ACQUIRING BONDS WITH DIFFERENT MATURITY DATES OR BOND FUNDS WITH DIFFERENT AVERAGE MATURITIES. Short- and intermediate-term issues fluctuate less in price than longer-term issues and don't require you to tie up your money for ten or more years in exchange for a relatively small additional yield.

IN GENERAL, DON'T BUY ANY BOND WITH A SAFETY RATING LOWER THAN A, AND WATCH FOR NEWS THAT MAY AFFECT THE RATING WHILE YOU OWN THE BOND. The worst thing that can happen to a bond you own is that its issuer goes broke. To check the rating of any bond you're considering, ask the broker or look the bond up in the Moody's or Standard & Poor's bond guides found in many libraries, or check their Web sites (www.moodys.com or www.standardandpoors.com). For a mutual fund, the prospectus will describe the lowest rating acceptable to the fund's managers; annual reports should list the bonds in the fund's portfolio, along with their ratings.

FOR MAXIMUM SAFETY, STICK WITH BONDS ISSUED BY THE U.S. TREASURY. To buy them commission-free, set up an account through a program called Treasury Direct. For details, contact the Federal Reserve Bank branch nearest you; call the Bureau of Public Debt, in Washington, D.C. (800-722-2678.); or look for online information at www.publicdebt.treas.gov.

WATCH FOR "CALL" PROVISIONS. Some bonds can be called, which means they can be redeemed by the issuer before they mature. A company might decide to call its bonds if, for instance, interest rates fell so far that it could issue new bonds at a lower rate and thus save money. Call provisions are good for the issuer, bad for investors. Not only would you lose your comparatively high yield, but also you'd have to figure out where to invest the unexpected payout. Treasury issues are generally not callable.

Strategy #6: Dip into Dollar-Cost Averaging

Believe it or not, there is an investing technique that almost guarantees that your long-term investment plan will be a success. It takes only a tiny amount of money to launch, requires little time or effort on your part, and removes the worry of investing when prices are high.

The method is called dollar-cost averaging, and it's ideal for your retirement plan because it lets you invest with confidence regardless of where stock prices are headed. This may be the best retirement-investment strategy ever invented. Part of its beauty is that you needn't be a Wall Street guru or math whiz to use it. In fact, if you're making automatic deposits from your checking account into a mutual fund, reinvesting stock or mutual fund dividends in additional shares, or participating in a 401(k) plan at work, you're already involved in a form of dollar-cost averaging.

With dollar-cost averaging, you invest a fixed amount on a regular schedule—say, $250 per month or $500 per quarter. Nothing fancy. The trick for making this work as a nest-egg builder is to stick with your schedule, regardless of whether stock, bond, or mutual fund share prices go up or down. Because you're investing a fixed amount of money at fixed intervals, your dollars buy fewer shares when prices are high and relatively more when they are low. Result: Your average purchase price is lower than the average of the market prices on the same dates. Over time, dollar-cost averaging puts price swings to work in your favor.

(Note: The impressive performance of the stock market during most of the '90s resulted in what will likely prove an anomaly with dollar-cost averaging. Because prices in general steadily went up, dollar-cost averaging actually cost many investors more per share during this time.)

Because they charge no sales commissions, no-load funds are the absolute best deals for a dollar-cost-averaging plan. Buying $500 worth of stock regularly through a broker would be disastrously expensive. No-load funds let you invest small amounts to purchase even fractional shares with no commission.

If you have a lump sum to invest, such as a pension payout or an inheritance, you can still take advantage of dollar-cost averaging. You could temporarily park the cash in a money-market mutual fund and switch portions of the money to other investments on a monthly, quarterly, or other schedule. Investors with IRAs can set aside equal monthly installments throughout the year rather than waiting until the tax-filing deadline to scrape together the entire maximum IRA contribution.

How Dollar-Cost Averaging Works

If you invested $500 each quarter ($2,000 per year) for three years in a no-load, aggressive-growth mutual fund whose share price ranges between $15 and $28 per share, here's what would happen:

COMPARING THE DOLLAR-COST AVERAGING ADVANTAGE

Quarterly Investments: $500 (dollar–cost averaging)

Date	$ Amount	Share Price	Number of Shares Bought	Total $ Invested	Shares Owned	Account Value
Jan.	$500	$21.00	23.81	$ 500	23.81	$ 500.00
Apr.	$500	$21.00	23.81	$1,000	47.62	$1,000.00
July	$500	$20.00	25.00	$1,500	72.62	$1,452.40
Oct.	$500	$18.00	27.78	$2,000	100.40	$1,807.20
Jan.	$500	$16.00	31.25	$2,500	131.65	$2,106.40
Apr.	$500	$15.00	33.33	$3,000	164.98	$2,474.70
July	$500	$15.00	33.33	$3,500	198.31	$2,974.65
Oct.	$500	$18.00	27.78	$4,000	226.09	$4,069.62
Jan.	$500	$20.00	25.00	$4,500	251.09	$5,021.80
Apr.	$500	$22.00	22.73	$5,000	273.82	$6,024.04
July	$500	$26.00	19.23	$5,500	293.05	$7,619.30
Oct.	$500	$28.00	17.86	$6,000	310.91	$8,705.48

Market average price	$ 20.00
Number of shares owned if bought at market average	300.00
Year-end value if bought at market average	$ 8,400.00
Your average price	$ 19.30
"Free" bonus shares due to DCA	10.91
Dollar value of DCA bonus	$ 305.48

YEAR ONE: Your initial buy is at $21 per share, but the market drifts down during the year, with the fourth-quarter purchase at $18 per share. You own roughly 100 shares of the fund at year's end.

YEAR TWO: A better year for the fund, with the price starting out at $16 per share and ending at $18 with your fourth-quarter purchase. You now own 226 shares.

YEAR THREE: A great year for the fund—starting at $20 per share, the price moves up to $28.

Quarterly Investments: 25 Shares (no dollar-cost averaging)

Date	Number of Shares Bought	Share Price	$ Amount	Total $ Invested	Shares Owned	Account Value
Jan.	25	$21.00	$525	$ 525	25.00	$ 525.00
Apr.	25	$21.00	$525	$1,050	50.00	$1,050.00
July	25	$20.00	$500	$1,550	75.00	$1,500.00
Oct.	25	$18.00	$450	$2,000	100.00	$1,800.00
Jan.	25	$16.00	$400	$2,400	125.00	$2,000.00
Apr.	25	$15.00	$375	$2,775	150.00	$2,250.00
July	25	$15.00	$375	$3,150	175.00	$2,625.00
Oct.	25	$18.00	$450	$3,600	200.00	$3,600.00
Jan.	25	$20.00	$500	$4,100	225.00	$4,500.00
Apr.	25	$22.00	$550	$4,650	250.00	$5,500.00
July	25	$26.00	$650	$5,300	275.00	$7,150.00
Oct.	25	$28.00	$700	$6,000	300.00	$8,400.00

Market (and your) average price $ 20.00

Number of shares owned 300.00

Year-end value $ 8,400.00

Over three years you've invested $6,000 and have purchased about 311 shares that are worth $8,700 (not counting any dividend or capital-gains distributions paid by the fund along the way).

Compare that with other ways you could have acquired those shares. For example, if you had bought exactly 25 shares on the same dates, you would have invested the same $6,000, but you would have only 300 shares instead of 311. Those extra 11 shares are the "free bonus" you earned by employing a dollar-cost-averaging strategy.

Had you invested the entire $6,000 at the start, you would have purchased only about 286 shares, making the dollar-cost-averaging advantage even greater.

Good, Yes; Foolproof, No

Dollar-cost averaging doesn't always make you more money. But it does consistently add discipline, organization, and peace of mind to your investing for retirement. One key advantage is that dollar-cost averaging prevents you from being emotionally whipsawed by the market's ups and downs—a worry-free approach if ever there was one. It also saves you from sinking all your money into a mutual fund whose price has already risen dramatically. By spacing out the purchases with dollar-cost averaging, you develop an investment discipline that most people find hard to achieve.

But while dollar-cost averaging lets you put your retirement investments on autopilot, you shouldn't leave them there indefinitely. Inflation and increases in your income make your fixed-dollar contributions less meaningful over time. So fine-tune your saving schedule every couple of years. If you get a pay increase from your employer, try keeping a portion for yourself and investing the rest.

Putting a Dollar-Cost-Averaging Strategy to Work

You can take advantage of dollar-cost averaging by remembering to make investments on a regular schedule. Or, to put your plan on autopilot, here are two investment strategies that can simplify your life.

START AN AUTOMATIC-INVESTMENT PLAN. Many mutual fund companies will pluck money automatically from your bank account each month and invest it in a fund of your choice. (Some can do the same through automatic payroll deductions.) Signing up is simple. You fill out a short form that authorizes the fund to draw a set amount from your checking account at set intervals. Remembering that diversification is one of your investment plan's best friends, you may want to divide or alternate your monthly or quarterly investments among several types of funds.

REINVEST DIVIDENDS AND CAPITAL GAINS. This is another terrific autopilot approach. Most mutual funds sign you up automatically, unless you opt to take that money in cash payments. Don't. Your nest egg will grow much faster if you reinvest.

Take Advantage of DRIPs

Many individual stocks offer the opportunity to automatically reinvest dividends through direct investment plans, also known as dividend-reinvestment plans, DRIPs (or DRPs). About 1,300 corporations make it easy for you to invest through their DRIP programs. Instead of sending you a check for dividends your shares earn, a company with a DRIP will

---

THE TAX FACTOR IN DRIPS

Even though you don't receive dividends in cash, you will owe tax on them in the year they're paid, unless the DRIP is part of an IRA, Keogh, or other tax-sheltered vehicle. You'll get a record from the company telling you how many shares you've purchased, on what dates, and at what price. Save it—you'll need it to hold down the tax bill when you sell those shares.

use the money to buy more shares of the stock for your nest egg. With DRIPs you usually pay no commissions—money you'd pay to brokers can go instead to buy more shares. DRIPs let you buy only a few shares, or even fractional shares, a boon to small investors. And DRIPs even have an advantage over no-load mutual funds because you pay little or no management fee.

Most DRIPs let you make additional investments on your own, another way around brokerage commissions. And a handful of companies sweeten the pot even further by offering you the chance to buy DRIP shares at a discount of 3% to 5% from the market price. With most plans, you must already own at least one share of the stock, purchased through a broker, then sign up for the DRIP. A few firms allow you to buy the stock and sign up for the DRIP directly with the company, starting with as little as a single share or about $50, and with no commission. Companies with direct-purchase DRIPs include Johnson Controls, Texaco, and W. R. Grace. To join a DRIP, call the company's shareholder-relations department for an application.

Companies seldom promote their DRIPs, so unless you ask about them you may not know they exist. But most big-name firms, from Aetna to Xerox, have them. Netstock direct's Web site (www2.netstockdirect .com) lists companies that offer dividend reinvestment programs to current shareholders, as well as plans that let you buy initial shares directly from the company.

Don't buy a stock merely because it has a dividend-reinvestment plan or offers share discounts, direct purchases, or other DRIP features. Consider the company's fundamentals first. The company must have a solid balance sheet, good growth prospects, and other value features described earlier. Stocks with good long-term track records of steadily rising dividends make the best DRIP choices.

DRIPS do have some disadvantages:

■ **You usually cannot sell them quickly.** In the best case, the company will take your sale request over the phone and sell the stock sometime within a day or two. Otherwise, the company may sell shares only once a week; a few take up to a month. Add a few extra days if you're required to mail your request. If the price falls before your shares are sold, you're out of luck.

■ **Some companies tack on extra fees** when you sell.

DRIPs increase the amount of paper coming into your home. You may receive separate quarterly statements for each DRIP you own, whereas if you invested with one broker, the activity of stocks of several companies would be reported on one statement.

Dividend Dilemma

Stock dividends you receive but don't reinvest through a DRIP should still be invested elsewhere. Don't let this money escape from your retirement portfolio. Collect those dividends in a separate account, such as a money-market fund, earmarked for use in buying another stock when you have enough cash to do so. Or add dividend proceeds regularly to a stock mutual fund you own in which you may be able to invest amounts as small as $50 to $100 at a crack.

LOCATING DRIP DETAILS

Here are some helpful resources on dividend reinvestment plans:

The Directory of Companies Offering Dividend Reinvestment Plans lists details of over 1,000 DRIPs, including addresses and phone numbers, discounts, eligibility, and cash purchase limits. It is available for $36.95, plus $3 for shipping, from Evergreen Enterprises, P.O. Box 763, Laurel, MD 20707 (301-549-3939).

Buying Stocks Without a Broker: Commission-Free Investing Through Company Dividend Reinvestment Plans by Charles Carlson ($17.95, Horizon Publishing), or look for it at your public library. Carlson lists DRIP details and explains how to make the most of the plans.

Charles Carlson also edits a monthly newsletter, *The Drip Investor* ($69 for an annual subscription; Horizon Publishing Co., 800-233-5922, or order online at www.dripinvestor.com).

Strategy #7: Avoid These Investment Potholes

All investors goof, so one of the best things you can do is be aware of common investment potholes. Here are some of the pitfalls that cause investors to stumble . . . and some steps to help you avoid them.

Buying Only the "Beauty Contest" Winners

You see the lists everywhere: stocks or mutual funds that were "hot" last week, last month, last year. Often, that's a cue for you to sell, not to buy. Investments run in cycles. During a recession, the best stocks tend to be companies in noncyclical businesses—food, consumer goods, and drugs, for example—that are better able to weather a downturn. In a recovering economy, the list changes. By the time a fund or stock group makes the winner's circle, there's a danger that the cycle has already run its course and you'll be hopping on the bandwagon late.

For example, in 1999, Perkins Opportunity, a diversified U.S. stock fund, boasted a whopping annual return of 98.6%, only to suffer a down year in 2000 when its total annual return was -29.3%. For 2001, it rose again to return 17.7%, but then was down again in 2002 with a -16.7% return. According to Morningstar, every once in a while, Perkins Opportunity gets something right, and when its top holdings do well, it looks wonderful. But when there's a market selloff, this kind of high-flying aggressive-growth fund is likely to be clobbered. If you invest only by looking in a rearview mirror, you'll never see the potholes ahead.

ACTION PLAN: Some stocks and funds are perennial winners, so don't rule out everything that shows up on a list of top performers. But to pick future winners, look for investments with a proven long-term track record over five to ten years or more.

Underdiversifying / Overdiversifying

Diversification, like medicine, is good in the proper dosage. Too little is bad; so is too much. You want your nest egg divided among different markets—various types of domestic and foreign stocks, bonds, and mutual funds. But one increasingly common mistake, now that mutual funds have become so popular, is treating funds as if they were individual stocks. A mutual fund is already a diversified portfolio. Investors tend to add new funds each year but never sell the old ones, thus creating a portfolio stuffed with overlapping investments.

ACTION PLAN: Your retirement portfolio should include some blue-chip stocks and small-company stocks in a variety of different industries, government and corporate bonds in different maturities, and some foreign stocks. Unless you have a portfolio of at least $50,000, that means investing through mutual funds. Make one or two selections from different fund categories—you don't need two government-bond funds of the same maturity, for example. But with funds becoming increasingly specialized, you still need to diversify your holdings among a selection of funds and fund families.

Underestimating Inflation

The steady grind of inflation, which has averaged 3.1% per year since 1926, is a major long-term danger to your nest egg. Your investment return must match inflation just to stay even. Hoping to keep their nest eggs safe and guarantee their return, some investors lean heavily on such investments as CDs, GICs, and bonds in the belief that stocks are too risky. But over the long term, these investments have badly lagged the inflation-beating growth of common stocks.

ACTION PLAN: Put heavy emphasis on stocks in your retirement portfolio, consistent with your tolerance for risk. Look at the sample allocations on page 194.

Analysis Paralysis

Yes, gathering information is crucial to making wise investment choices. But at some point, you need to act. Some would-be investors study, study, and study some more, and never get around to buying the stocks or mutual funds they so love to read about.

PORTFOLIO TRACKER: HOW ARE YOUR INVESTMENTS DEPLOYED?

Complete this worksheet at least once a year, and preferably twice, so you'll know how your retirement plan's investment mix is changing. Then you can take action, if necessary, to keep it in line with your risk tolerance and long-term nest-egg goal. A particularly great year for small stocks or foreign shares, for example, could cause them to become a larger portion of the mix than you'd like, prompting you to sell some shares and redeploy the profits in other areas. If you own balanced funds, assign half the value to stocks, half to bonds.

Don't include your home as an investment for the purposes of figuring your asset mix, because selling it isn't an option, like switching from money-market funds to stocks. Disregard illiquid long-term investments, such as a piece of a family business, unless the investment is for sale.

These are general allocations. You may also want to further break down stock market allocations to include separate percentages for income stocks, blue chips, small-company stocks, or stocks by different industries.

	Current Value	% of Total		Current Value	% of Total
Cash and Cash Equivalents			**Bonds**		
Savings accounts	$ ____	____	Individual bonds		
Money-market funds	____	____	short-term	$ ____	____
Treasury bills	____	____	intermediate-term	____	____
Total Cash	$ ____	____	long-term	____	____
			Mutual funds		
Stocks			short-term	____	____
Individual shares			intermediate-term	____	____
domestic	$ ____	____	long-term	____	____
foreign	____	____	**Total Bonds**	$ ____	____
Mutual funds			**Real estate**	$ ____	____
domestic	____	____			
foreign	____	____	**Total Investments**	$ ____	100%
Total Stocks	$ ____	____			

They leave their money in a "safe" place—probably a money-market fund—while they search for the perfect investments for their nest egg. That analysis paralysis can cost plenty. The tendency toward over-analysis also leads to overspending on investment newsletters and reports.

ACTION PLAN: It's not a matter of picking the absolute best day or best investment; it's more a matter of doing something. Don't worry that your timing is off; over the long term you'll still be ahead. Keeping a favorite newsletter or two is okay. But investing that money instead of handing it over to the market "gurus" for advice will probably be the wiser move in the long run.

Swinging Only for Home Runs

Some people feel that no investment is worth bothering with unless it has the potential for "the big score." These are the same individuals who find their way into every hot investment scheme that comes along. You can achieve a terrific batting average by lofting a steady series of base hits just over the infield—you don't have to swing for the home run every time. Or ever, for that matter.

ACTION PLAN: Aggressive-growth stocks do have a place in an aggressive retirement portfolio—a move justified by their superior long-term performance. But they shouldn't occupy too large a portion—say, no more than 30% to 40% for the most aggressive, less for others. Owning them through mutual funds is the best way to spread the risk. And investors should be prepared to hold these investments for ten years or more.

Excessive Trading

If a stock you recently bought runs up in price, you may be tempted to take a quick profit by selling. If it drops, you may be discouraged and want to bail out. Remember your time frame. Your retirement investment program is not a short-term affair. Yes, a paper profit might evaporate over the short term. But a loss may disappear, too. If the company you selected does indeed have good fundamentals, you'll only be hurting your long-term plan by selling now, too quickly.

ACTION PLAN: Before you make any buy or sell decision, consider the impact of fees, commissions, and taxes.

Refusing to Sell Investment Dogs

Never selling can be harmful, too. It's a classic pitfall: An investor researches a stock or fund, falls in love with it, and out of stubbornness refuses to give it up, even if it turns in subpar performance year after year.

ACTION PLAN: The conventional wisdom is to hang on and wait for the price to come back up. That's no doubt the best approach to get past the inevitable ups and downs of the market. But it's also possible that a long-term laggard is no longer a good choice for your portfolio. Ask yourself: Would I buy it again today? If not, consider selling. (See the tips on when to sell a stock, starting on page 215.)

Failing to Monitor Your Portfolio

It may be a solid plan, but that doesn't mean you can ignore it. Any portfolio needs monitoring. The one constant in the stock market, for example, is change. As prices rise and fall, dividends flow in, or economic conditions change, your portfolio can become unbalanced.

ACTION PLAN: Give your holdings a periodic checkup—quarterly would be good, but yearly is a minimum. Keep your eye on maintaining top quality and diversification.

Make the Right Moves with a Pension Payout

Ageneration or two ago, you might have gone to work right out of college and stayed with the same company until you retired at age 65. Your devotion would have been rewarded with a tidy pension and perhaps the proverbial gold watch as well. But like so many other aspects of retirement planning, that storybook scenario is far less common today.

Americans jump jobs the way a track star jumps hurdles—fast and frequently. And with each job move (voluntary or otherwise), there may come a major decision: finding a new home for the retirement money you've built up in a 401(k) or other employer-sponsored retirement plan. If your money is in a defined-benefit plan (see in Chapter 4) you avoid this predicament because the company usually keeps the money until you reach retirement age and then pays you your due. With other kinds of plans, though, your vested benefit is yours to take when you leave the job.

If you've been with an employer for ten, 15, 20, or more years, the payout could be the largest sum of money you've ever received at one time. Even after just a few years, the payment can be impressive. But a misstep with that money could limit your flexibility, erase valuable tax benefits, and cost you out-of-pocket cash up front. (And thanks to changes in the tax law, you've got a new trap to avoid; we'll show you how to protect yourself later in this chapter.)

First, understand that most of the billions of dollars in retirement cash paid out by companies each year goes in lump sums to individuals under 55 who are changing jobs. But other events can trigger a distribution:

- **You accept an early retirement offer;**
- **The company you work for changes hands through a sale or merger;**
- **Your company terminates the retirement plan;**
- **You are laid off or fired;**
- **Your spouse dies and you're the beneficiary of his or her retirement plan; or**
- **You become permanently disabled.**

"Stop Me Before I Spend!"

No matter why retirement money becomes available to you early, your basic goal is to resist the temptation to spend any of the money. It's easy to get starry-eyed over a large check. Heck, why not blow just a bit of it on a few goodies? What's the harm?

Well, money from a company plan is generally subject to an immediate 10% tax penalty if withdrawn before age 55. Plus, each dollar withdrawn will be taxed at your regular income-tax rate for the year. That's money you'll never get back. Ultimately, someone in the 28% tax bracket in 2005 who receives a $25,000 payout from a pension plan and does not reinvest in another retirement plan will lose at least $9,500 of that sum to taxes and penalties. State and local taxes could make the bite even bigger.

The threat of losing so much to taxes and penalties should encourage you to roll over the money into an individual retirement account (IRA) where it will continue to grow for your worry-free retirement. That's the best choice for almost everyone, but you'd never guess that based on what actually happens: Almost two-thirds of the pension dollars paid in lump sums each year is spent outright.

Beyond what you lose immediately to taxes and penalties, the real pain of spending the money comes over the long haul to retirement. The dollar you spend now, if it had been left to grow free of taxes for another ten or 20 years or more, would have become many,

many dollars in the future. For example, with 20 years to go until retirement, a $25,000 payout would become $116,500 if it continued to grow at an 8% annual rate. A $10,000 payout invested at 10% for 15 years becomes $41,800; a $90,000 payout that earns 7% will become $177,000 in ten years. By spending the money, you throw away the growth potential that money had for your worry-free plan.

Avoid the Pension-Payout Trap

The latest attempt to convince workers not to make the mistake of spending retirement money early is a 20% withholding tax that applies to payouts made directly to employees whether they retire, quit, or lose their jobs. Fortunately, it's easy to dodge this confiscation. To avoid seeing 20% of your money go immediately to the IRS—as a forced down payment on a tax bill you may or may not owe—all you have to do is tell your employer to send your retirement money directly to an IRA or to your new employer's retirement plan if it accepts such rollovers. As long as the payout does not pass through your hands, there is no withholding.

If you're changing jobs and your new employer permits rollovers into its retirement plans, you can have the money shipped directly to the new employer's plan.

The direct rollover to an IRA is likely to be your best choice, even if you believe you may need to spend some of the payout. You can immediately tap your IRA without worrying about the 20% withholding. If you're

---

PENSION PAYOUTS

While the average departing worker exits with a payout of about $10,000, a $50,000 parting handshake for higher-level managers is not unusual, with top execs who sever their service often taking six-figure checks with them. Your first move is to find a home for the money; worry about specific investments later.

WORRY-FREE TIP

Is your financial future uncertain? Bank account slim? Do you worry that you might need part of the payout just to pay your bills until you find another job? You can still keep your options open. Just park your retirement-plan payout in a money-market fund through a rollover IRA. The IRA protects the tax-deferred status of your retirement money. The money-market fund keeps your cash liquid and at the ready should you need it in an emergency. Once your finances stabilize, shift the cash from the money-market fund to a growth-oriented stock fund to capture the higher long-term earnings potential.

---

under age 59½, you will still pay a penalty and taxes on what you withdraw, but by running the money through an IRA, you avoid withholding.

SPECIAL CIRCUMSTANCES. In some situations, however, opting for the IRA would be a mistake.

This applies, for example, if you are over age 55 but not yet 59½ and you know you need to spend part of the payout—to launch your own business, perhaps. No matter what your age, the part of the payout that does not go into an IRA will be taxed at your top rate. But age does play a role in whether you'll be stuck with the 10% penalty for early withdrawal of retirement funds. When company plans are involved, early is defined as before age 55. When it comes to IRAs, however, early is before age 59½.

Therefore, if you are over 55 but under 59½, having the money transferred to an IRA extends the threat of the early-withdrawal penalty. If you are in this age group and know you will need to use part of the company payout, ask your employer to split the payout. As much as possible should go directly to an IRA—to hold off both tax and penalty. Ask that the remainder be paid directly to you. Tax will be due on that amount and 20% will be withheld for the IRS, but you'll avoid the 10% penalty.

The other circumstance in which direct transfer would be a mistake is if you intend to take advantage of the ten-year averaging method for reducing the tax due on the payout. Averaging, which is currently available only to taxpayers who were born before 1936, is discussed later in this chapter. The trap, though, is that averaging is available only for payouts from company plans. If you have the money deposited in an IRA, you forfeit the right to use averaging. To take advantage of it, you must take the money directly from the company plan, and that means you're stuck with withholding.

Note that the withholding is not a new tax; it's a sooner-rather-than-later tax. If you wind up owing less than 20% of the amount in taxes, you'll get the excess back as a tax refund when you file your return for the year in question.

Transfer the Money Directly to a "Rollover" IRA

Clearly, the best bet for most taxpayers is to have the payout transferred directly to an IRA. The law that imposed the 20% withholding rule also demands that employers offer to make the direct transfer and warn employees about withholding if they turn down that offer.

The introduction of the Roth IRA in 1998 could cause some confusion here. Should you roll over the company-plan payout into a traditional IRA or a Roth? Actually, you have no choice—it must go to a traditional IRA. You could immediately roll the money from the old-fashioned IRA into a Roth, but doing so would trigger a tax bill on the full amount of the rollover, as discussed in Chapter 7. Using this two-step method to roll part or all of your company plan into a Roth could make sense, depending on your circumstances. After all, all future earnings would be tax-free rather than simply tax-deferred. But for our purposes here, the key is keeping your options open. The way you do that is to have your money transferred directly to a traditional rollover IRA.

As noted above, using the direct transfer to put off paying taxes can put a ton of money in your retirement plan's pocket. The advantage is worth repeating.

Say, for example, you're 45 and about to leave your job with a $50,000 payout from a profit-sharing plan. If you took it as spending money instead of rolling it into an IRA, you'd owe a $5,000 penalty plus $14,000 in taxes if you're in the 28%-tax bracket. But if you roll the money into an IRA, that $19,000 remains a part of your nest egg, free to continue growing tax-deferred. Over 20 years, that $19,000 alone will become $156,600 if it earns the average historical return of 10.4% for large-company stocks—and that's not counting the rest of the payout. The larger the lump sum, the bigger the benefit of continued tax-deferred compounding. There's no limit on how large a pension distribution you can transfer into a rollover IRA.

HOW THE ROLLOVER WORKS. A rollover is a tax-free shift of assets from one "qualified" (IRS-approved) retirement plan to another—commonly from a company profit-sharing or 401(k) plan to an IRA. These are the key rollover rules:

If the transfer is made directly from your employer to a new trustee (the bank, brokerage firm, mutual fund, or insurance company that establishes your account), no tax is withheld from the payment.

But if the money is paid to you in a lump sum, it is subject to a 20% withholding tax taken out by your employer. Thus, on a $50,000 lump payment, you would receive only $40,000; the other $10,000 would go to the IRS. You would still have the right to roll over the full $50,000 to an IRA yourself, and doing so within 60 days would avoid taxes and penalties. But you'll have to come up with the $10,000 that was withheld, then apply to get it back as a tax refund at tax time.

Only money from a retirement plan can be rolled over to continue to grow tax-deferred for your retirement.

Severance pay and bonuses are not eligible for an IRA rollover.

Any money representing after-tax contributions to a plan may not be rolled over to an IRA. You do, however, get to take that money tax-free. There's no tax, penalty, or withholding on that portion of the payout, since you paid tax on the funds before they went into the company plan. Earnings on those contributions can be rolled over into a IRA.

As noted above, if you select an IRA rollover, you forfeit the right to use ten-year averaging. However, if your payout is shipped to a new employer's plan you retain that right. And, if the money goes to an IRA and is later rolled into a new employer's plan, you regain the right to use averaging when you exit from that plan.

Rollover versus Standard IRA

A rollover IRA—one specially created to receive a pension payout—differs only slightly from a standard IRA. Even if you already have a regular IRA, your company-plan payout should go into a separate, newly established rollover IRA. This preserves your right to later roll the entire amount, including earnings, out of the IRA and into a new employer's pension plan. If you blend rollover funds into an existing standard IRA, or make any additional deposits to the rollover IRA, you lose the option to make that move even if the new employer's plan permits it.

A rollover is your best choice if you don't need the money now and aren't likely to need it in the foreseeable future. The younger you are, the more you'll benefit from putting the entire distribution into an IRA because there will be more time for your nest egg to grow tax-deferred.

Rollover to Another Qualified Plan

If your new employer has a retirement plan, you may be able to have your payout transferred directly from the old company to the new. This, too, avoids any

Even if you already have a regular IRA, your company-plan payout should go into a separate, newly established rollover IRA account.

penalties or tax bite for now. Plus, you preserve your ability to use forward averaging later on.

If the new plan permits rollovers, a deciding factor will be the choice of available investments in the new plan. Find out what investment options the new company's plan offers and how they performed in the past. The choices should include at least a couple of stock funds, an income fund, and perhaps an international fund. If the plan offers little choice, or poor investment performance in the past, you'll be better off in a rollover IRA where you can make your own investment selections.

Tap the Keogh Advantage

If you have a Keogh plan—funded, for example, with income you earned moonlighting as a self-employed consultant while keeping your day job—you have another rollover option. Instead of rolling the funds into an IRA or a new employer's plan, roll them directly into your Keogh account, tax- and penalty-free.

This move keeps the IRS at bay and lets you retain the right to save taxes later with forward averaging. You also have the flexibility to invest the funds as you wish. A rollover to your Keogh will not affect the size of your regular annual contribution to the plan. What's more, Keogh money can be withdrawn penalty-free after age 55 if you decide to retire early, while money pulled out of an IRA will generally be penalized if you are under age 59½.

Stay Put

Unless your plan is being terminated, you probably have the option of leaving the money in your ex-employer's 401(k) or other retirement program. Companies are required by law to allow employees whose accounts total more than $1,000 to leave their money right where it is or to provide an automatic rollover into an IRA account, unless the participant chooses otherwise. The plan administrator must notify the participant in writing that the distribution can be transferred to an IRA. Some companies allow employees to leave their funds in the company plan until they reach 70 1/2.

In some circumstances, staying put might be the best choice. For example, if a portion of your money is invested in company stock—and you expect the company to do well—you can leave your money alone. You still have the right to roll it over into an IRA at a later date. Or you might leave it and take the payout at a later date—paying the 10% early-withdrawal penalty if you're under age 59 1/2 when you make the withdrawal—and perhaps take advantage of forward-averaging tax benefits, too. Your money will continue to grow, tax-deferred, although you give up the kind of investment flexibility you would gain by rolling the assets into an IRA.

On the flip side, leaving money invested in shares of a company you no longer work for can boost the risk level a notch. Since you'll no longer be involved with the firm day to day, you may not have as good a feel for the company's prospects. A common mistake is falling in love with your own company's stock and leaving your nest egg invested in it out of loyalty. Such a move can turn sour if the company's fortunes turn south.

If you decide to stay put, keep close tabs on this part of your plan. Once you start building assets in a new plan elsewhere, there may be a tendency to let this one slide. Figure on reconsidering your stay-put decision once a year.

START PERIODIC PAYMENTS. Your employer's plan may also allow you to start receiving periodic payments keyed to your life expectancy, no matter what your age. Even if you're under age 55, there won't be a penalty as long as the steady payments continue for at least five years and until you reach age 59 1/2. The money you receive will be taxed as income, but it won't be subject to withholding.

Choosing periodic payments is a good way to help fund early retirement. Even if you roll the money directly into an IRA, you can take it out later using periodic payments (Chapter 7 details on how this escape

> A common mistake is falling in love with your own company's stock and leaving your nest egg invested in it out of loyalty.

hatch works). And, as noted earlier, there's no mandatory withholding if the money goes first to an IRA.

Forward Averaging to the Rescue?

Ten-year forward averaging is a special computation method—available only to taxpayers born before 1936—that taxes a payout all at once, but the bill is figured as though you received the money over a number of years. Although you must actually pay the tax right away, the amount due will be significantly less than if the full amount was heaped on top of your other taxable income. To use forward averaging, your lump-sum distribution must:

- **come from a qualified plan** in which you have participated for at least five years before the distribution;
- **represent your entire interest in the plan** and be paid to you within a single tax year; and
- **be paid after you leave your job** or after you reach "normal" retirement age for your company's plan.

So what's the big deal? Well, it could greatly reduce your tax bill. If the payment is less than $70,000, current rules make part of the money tax-free. And the bill on the taxable portion is figured as though you got the money in equal chunks over five or ten years. That means more of it is taxed in lower brackets than if you lumped it all on top of your other income in the year you receive the payout. You have to pay the tax bill all at once, but averaging could reduce what you owe.

WHAT'S EARLY?

There's a lot of confusion over when the 10% early-withdrawal penalty applies. If you are pulling money out of a regular IRA, the penalty usually applies if you are under age 59$\frac{1}{2}$. When the money comes out of a company plan after you leave the firm, however, the penalty applies only up to age 55. No matter why you leave the job—whether you quit, are fired, or take early retirement—if you're over 55 when you get the payout, there is no early-withdrawal penalty.

Averaging makes sense if you need to spend a good part of your payout quickly. Otherwise, it's usually better to ignore this tax break and roll your money over into an IRA. The longer you keep that tax shelter going, the more likely the benefits will exceed those of averaging.

The key point: Whenever you have a lump-sum payout coming, be sure to check on the status of averaging and weigh the possible advantages if you qualify.

Planning for Change

Planning a job jump soon? If so, start asking questions and gathering information about your current employer's pension plan and possible new homes for your money. Request investment and IRA account information from banks, mutual funds, and brokerage firms that are candidates for your rollover IRA business. You'll want answers to these questions about your plan at work:

■ **Must the payout be in cash** or can securities be rolled directly (without being liquidated) into an IRA or other qualified plan? If your employer is a major corporation—an Exxon, IBM, or Procter & Gamble, for example—and you own company shares in your retirement account, you may want to hold on to that stock. Find out whether shares can be transferred with little or no cost. If taking your money means the stocks must be liquidated, however, you may want to stay put.

■ **Can you leave the money where it is?** If your current investments are performing well, and the rules permit you to stay in the plan even if you leave the company, that's an option you'll want to consider. Do some comparison shopping with similar types of investments offered elsewhere before you decide. If the money's in a growth-stock fund, for example, how are other growth-stock funds performing?

■ **How long will it take** to complete the payout/transfer process?

■ **What portion of the payout,** if any, represents voluntary after-tax contributions you've made? This portion can't be rolled over into an IRA, but it won't be taxed when you withdraw it.

Investing the Payout Cash

Once you've kept the IRS at bay and found a new home for your retirement-plan money, you can turn your attention to where specifically the payout should be invested. Chapters 9 and 10 describe your best choices and investment strategies. The basic idea is to keep the money on the growth track for the ten, 15, 20, or more years you still have to go until retirement.

The great opportunity in a rollover IRA is the freedom to choose a diverse array of investments for this portion of your retirement nest egg. Stocks are the best bet for long-term growth. The historical 10.4% annual return for large stocks, and an even better 12.7% for small-company stocks, stands head and shoulders above the 5.5% historical return on long-term government bonds and inflation's average 3.0% annual bite.

For payouts of less than $50,000, mutual funds are an ideal vehicle because of their built-in diversification. Go with one of the major fund groups and you can choose among several conservative stock funds, small-company funds, international funds, and balanced funds that hold both stocks and bonds.

Keep the big picture in mind when you make your investment selections. For example, if your spouse's 401(k) plan money is invested in highly conservative

---

KEEPING IT IN THE FAMILY

If your 401(k) money is managed by one of the major fund families, such as T. Rowe Price or Fidelity, and you've been happy with your investments, you may be able to exit your company plan but stay within the fund family. Some fund firms will arrange an inside rollover—a quickie transfer from your 401(k) into a rollover IRA at the same firm.

---

guaranteed investment contracts, you can weight this portion of your total nest egg more heavily toward small-company and other growth-oriented stocks.

The Golden Handshake: Sizing Up an Early-Payout Offer

One reason you might have to deal with a payout decision is an offer from your employer to, in effect, take your money and run. Thanks to the phenomenon of "corporate downsizing," these payouts, or early-retirement offers, can be a big opportunity to advance your plans for a worry free retirement. Here, however, the choices become more complex as companies attach a variety of incentives to sway your decision to move on.

Should you bite if an early-retirement payout is offered? Maybe. Some early-retirement plans are super deals. One may give you the opportunity to launch a new career or start a business. In effect, an early-retirement incentive is a bribe to get you to quit your job so your employer can cut its long-term costs. But analyzing an early-retirement offer isn't easy—especially because early-exit deals can be one-time offers good for a short "window" period of a few months or even weeks. Financial incentives in the offer might include the following:

- **Enhanced defined-benefit pension.** Early-retirement deals commonly increase the monthly pension checks you have coming by as much as a third. Often that's accomplished by adding three to five years or more to your tenure at the company for purposes of the formula that calculates your monthly benefit.
- **A lump-sum payment** pegged to your salary level and length of service. Be aware that any such severance payments could not be rolled over into an IRA and would be taxed as regular income.
- **A social security "bridge"** to provide extra income until social security benefits kick in at age 62.
- **Extended health and life insurance benefits.**

Golden Handshake Checklist

If your employer makes an early-retirement offer, here are the key points to consider when making your decision:

- **What will your pension benefits be** if you accept the offer? Get the dollar details. How does that compare with what you'd get if you continued working at the company?

- **What are your employment prospects elsewhere?** If you've considered moving on anyway, this is a good time to polish your résumé and look around. With luck, you'll walk away with a golden handshake from your current employer and capture a better job.

- **If you plan to take an early-retirement offer before landing another job,** take stock of your financial standing now. Do you have ample savings, without dipping into retirement funds, to get by until you land another position?

- **Where will you put your early-retirement lump-sum payout?** Your choices are spelled out earlier in this chapter.

- **Will any part of your payout**—in the form of severance or a bonus, for example—be counted as ordinary income and thus be fully taxed?

- **What happens if you reject the offer?** This may involve some guesswork and sleuthing on your part. Just how badly is the company doing? Will salary increases stop if you stay? What about bonuses? If there's a chance that the ultimate early-retirement "offer" will be in the form of a layoff, consider taking the money now.

- **If the company's "voluntary" plan doesn't seem so voluntary for older workers,** you should know that federal law prohibits companies from discriminating against older employees. If you decline early retirement, it should not affect your future opportunities or working conditions.

Monitor Your Retirement Plan's Pulse

Chapter 12

Y ou're not in clover yet. Setting your plan in motion was the hardest part. But now you have to make certain it stays healthy and on track. And to do that you'll have to keep taking your plan's pulse. Here are the vital signs you need to check and adjustments to make along the way to your worry-free retirement.

Watch Out for Inflation

Like termites eating silently and steadily away at the framework of your house, inflation can inflict irreparable damage by steadily chewing up a chunk of your nest egg's value. Even seemingly low levels of inflation cause big-time damage. At a "modest" 4% annual inflation rate, a 40-year-old earning $50,000 today will need an income of $109,500 to enjoy the same buying power 20 years from now. If inflation averages 5%, the figure will jump to $132,500.

Owning stocks and stock mutual funds will be your best long-term defense against inflation. Large-company stocks have managed to gain a yearly average of 10.4% since 1926—a comfortable margin above the rate of inflation. Sure, you may have to pay tax on some of your stock earnings each year if the investments aren't held in a tax-sheltered account. But stocks will generate the bulk of their return as appreciation, and there's no tax due on that gain until you sell. When taxes are due, you should consider paying the bill from separate funds rather than using the money in your retirement nest egg. That keeps your retirement money compounding at top speed and puts you well ahead of those inflation termites.

Reassess Your Plan When Changes Occur

A job change, a big promotion, an inheritance, a divorce or marriage, a child who wants to attend Harvard, or a child who doesn't—all these events and many others can change the shape of your retirement finances. To keep your plan on track, recalculate your retirement-income goal and the assets you have available to meet that goal whenever a major change happens. The worksheet in Chapter 2 can help you do this. It's a good idea to recalculate every couple of years even if there haven't been any big changes.

Go for Some High-Tech Help

You can also put a personal computer and some special software to work helping manage your retirement plan. Of course, you don't have to enter the computer age just for this purpose: an old-fashioned pencil, paper, and this book can get you the same results. But if you're comfortable at the keyboard, a couple of retirement-planning software packages can be especially helpful at plugging "what-if" scenarios—featuring various inflation, income, and investment assumptions, for example—into your plans. The computer is also good for helping you organize the numbers you need to put your plan in focus.

Track Your Investment Performance

It's crucial to keep taking the pulse of your investment portfolio—primarily the stocks and stock mutual funds you own. Don't be fanatic about it; no need to eyeball the stock and fund tables every day. This is a long-term proposition, after all, and paying too-close attention can cause needless worry. But long-term or no, you can't ignore investment performance and the fact that everybody makes a bad choice now and again.

Your approach can be as simple as reading the quarterly and annual reports you'll receive from the stocks and funds you own as well as a few of the investment publications listed in Chapter 10. Or you can plug all that info into a general money-management software program that will make all the key calculations for you. Two popular, easy-to-use programs are *Quicken* and *Microsoft Money*. Both are available in Windows and MacIntosh versions.

For a quick read, use the Portfolio Tracker worksheet on page 228 to help calculate your portfolio allocations; make adjustments if they're out of whack.

Keep Tabs on Your Debt and Savings Schedule

Damaging debt—in the form of credit card-balance creep—can sap funds that could otherwise go to retirement savings. Watch those plastic balances to avoid paying needless interest, and channel the savings into your nest egg. Consider a plan to pay off your mortgage early and save thousands of dollars in interest costs. Chapter 3 has the details.

Check Your Social Security Record

The Social Security Administration has begun doing this work for you. If you're age 25 and over, it will send you an annual report. If you're under age 25, you can ask for a report. Call 800-772-1213 and ask for a "Personal Earnings and Benefit Estimate Statement" (PEBES) or order one online at www.ssa.gov. About four to six weeks after you return the form, you should receive an estimate of your retirement benefits, along with a year-by-year listing of your social security wages. Check for mistakes and request a change if you find any. For details on the benefit you'll get, see Chapter 5.

Review Your Insurance Coverage

This includes coverage you buy yourself and what you have at work. Coverage at work is subject to change. For example, a promotion could boost the amount of life coverage you receive. And a job change could completely alter your insurance picture. Review your insurance every two years; fill any gaps and cancel overlapping policies.

Monitor Your Company's Pulse, Too

Your own retirement plan's pulse may be closely linked to your company's health. That's especially true if you participate in a profit-sharing plan at work, hold any of your retirement assets in company stock, or participate in an employee stock-ownership plan (ESOP). Read the company's annual and quarterly reports and outside media or analyst reports on the firm. If the company's growth prospects dim and other investment options are available for that money, consider switching your assets elsewhere.

Try for an Early Exit

If your plan is going well, you may be considering an earlier exit. To have a realistic shot at early retirement, you'll need to make some calculations, much as you did in Chapter 2 to figure your goal and potential retirement-income gap.

One of the obstacles to early retirement is that you can't count on all your long-term savings and invest-

---

EARLY RETIREMENT WORKSHEET

First calculate your income goal at retirement. Multiply your current salary by a future-growth factor from the table below. For example, use 4% estimated annual inflation and add that to the amount you expect your salary to rise each year—say, 3%—for a total of 7%. If you want to retire early in 15 years, look where 7% intersects 15 years and you find the multiplier 2.76. Multiplying that by your current salary—say, $50,000—tells you what you'll be earning ($138,000 in this example) at the point you want to retire. Figure on needing 80% of that once you retire, and you arrive at an annual income goal after early retirement of $110,400.

A. $_____$ × $_____$ × 0.80 = $_____$
    Your current income   *multiplier from table below*   *your goal*

Example: $50,000 × 2.76 = $138,000 × 0.80 = $110,400

FUTURE-GROWTH MULTIPLIERS

Years to Early Retirement	Annual Yield on Savings and Investments								
	4%	5%	6%	7%	8%	9%	10%	11%	12%
5	1.22	1.28	1.34	1.40	1.47	1.54	1.61	1.69	1.76
10	1.48	1.63	1.79	1.97	2.16	2.37	2.59	2.84	3.11
15	1.80	2.08	2.40	2.76	3.17	3.64	4.18	4.78	5.47

ments to kick in with income right from the start. The worksheet below reflects the fact that employer pension benefits are rarely available before age 55, that social security benefits can't start before age 62, and that IRA funds, while generally tied up until age 59½, can be tapped earlier, as discussed in Chapter 7. A shortfall at any stage presents you with a series of choices: beef up your savings, adjust your standard of living, plan to work part-time in retirement, or delay your early out.

PLUGGING IN THE NUMBERS. The following guidelines will help you determine what numbers to use on the worksheet.

1. Savings. Assume you can get this money whenever you want it, although you may face a penalty if you break a CD or cash in an annuity early. Begin with

		TARGET AGE			
		50-54	55-59	60-62	62-plus
1. Savings	$_____ × 0.08 =	$_____	$_____	$_____	$_____
2. Home equity	$_____ × 0.08 =	$_____	$_____	$_____	$_____
3. IRAs*	$_____ × 0.08 =	$ NA	$ NA	$_____	$_____
4. Keoghs*	$_____ × 0.08 =	$ NA	$_____	$_____	$_____
5. 401(K)s*	$_____ × 0.08 =	$ NA	$_____	$_____	$_____
6. Pension**		$ NA	$_____	$_____	$_____
7. Social security**		$ NA	$ NA	$ NA	$_____
B. Column totals		$_____	$_____	$_____	$_____
C. Shortfall (A minus B)		$_____	$_____	$_____	$_____

*See the discussion for these lines for an exception that allows penalty-free access to your money before the age shown.
**When they become available, your pension and social security benefits form the cornerstone of your retirement income. It's assumed you will not be investing them.

A "loophole" provides a penalty-free escape hatch if you want to take your regular IRA money early.

what you have today in your personal savings and investment fund (not counting tax-sheltered plans) earmarked for retirement. Use a future-growth multiplier from the table in the worksheet to see what the savings will be worth when you think you'd like to retire. For example, if you have $50,000 now, plan to retire in 15 years and expect your savings and investments to yield 6% a year (after taxes) until you retire, multiply $50,000 by 2.40—the figure at which the 15 years and 6% columns intersect. That's $120,000. If that nest egg generates 8% a year (before taxes) after you retire, you can count on $9,600 toward your retirement needs.

2. Home equity. We show home equity becoming available at 55, on the assumption that that's the earliest you'll want to tap your home to finance your retirement. In the past, that was also the earliest you could take up to $125,000 of profit tax-free. Now, as discussed in Chapter 9, homes can be sold for tax-free profit at any age. For this line, begin with the current value of your home and apply the future-growth multiplier to estimate its value when you'll sell it. Then subtract any mortgage you'll still have outstanding at that time and any of the proceeds from the sale you'd use to buy a retirement home. The result is the figure that goes on line 2. Multiply it by 8% (.08) to see roughly how much annual income you can expect.

3. IRAs. For this line, apply a future-growth multiplier to what's currently in your IRAs. Remember that because your IRA will grow tax-deferred (or tax-free for a Roth IRA) you should use a higher multiplier than you did for your savings and investments.

If your money's in a regular IRA, it's basically tied up until you reach 59½. But as Chapter 7 spelled out, a "loophole" provides a penalty-free escape hatch if you want to take your regular IRA money early. The table on page 120 gives you a rough idea of how large a penalty-free withdrawal you'd be able to get from a regular IRA starting at various ages and with different rates of return. The dollar figures in the chart represent the approximate amount of withdrawal for each $10,000 of assets in the IRA. Thus, a 55-year-old with $100,000 in an IRA could withdraw about $8,350 per year if the presumed annual return was 8%.

If you're hoping to retire early, consider starting a Roth IRA, or converting a regular IRA to a Roth. You can withdraw the total of your investments at any age without tax or penalty, and the Roth offers ways to tap earnings early without penalty under certain conditions, as explained in Chapter 7.

4. Keogh accounts. You can tap a Keogh without penalty as early as age 55, or at a younger age if you follow the life-expectancy-based payout schedule explained in the discussion of IRAs.

5. 401(k) accounts. Money in 401(k) and profit-sharing plans can be withdrawn without tax penalty as early as age 55, too, if you leave the job. (If you leave earlier and have the money rolled over into an IRA, you can take penalty-free withdrawals even earlier based on the life-expectancy schedule discussed above.) Once again, remember when you pick a future-growth multiplier that these retirement savings grow tax-deferred.

6. Employer pension benefits. Defined-benefit plans rarely provide benefits before age 55. Your personnel office should be able to estimate what you can expect at the age you plan to retire. You can probably expect your benefits to increase for each year past age 55 that you delay retirement.

7. Social security benefits. Social security retirement benefits can't begin until age 62, and at that age checks will be reduced by at least 20% of what you'd get if you waited until 65 to start collecting. Look at Chapter 5 for an idea of what to expect from social security. Remember that social security benefits will increase with inflation after you retire and start receiving them. As with all categories, if you are married, calculate what will be available to your spouse, and when.

INTERPRETING YOUR NUMBERS. For most people, this worksheet will paint early retirement as a swan dive into poverty. But the bottom line isn't that quitting early is an impossible dream. Instead, the worksheet shows what it will take to make it come true.

Take heart. In a sense, the worksheet is stacked against you because it does not take into account any additional savings from this point forward. If you're regularly putting money into an IRA, Keogh, 401(k) plan, or other retirement investment account and plan to continue to do so, a part of the shortfall will be covered with the earnings from these future savings.

Say, for example, that you're 45 now and your early-retirement goal is age 60—15 years away. If you plan to put the maximum of $3,000 into an IRA each year (the maximum IRA contribution will rise to $5,000 by 2008) and expect it to earn 8% annually, you can add $87,973 to the IRA line in the worksheet. Figuring that it will earn 8% a year once you retire adds more than $7,000 to your annual retirement income.

Continued funding of a 401(k) plan can do even more to make your early-retirement dream a reality. Say you're making $40,000 now, making 6% contributions to your 401(k) and your employer is kicking in a 50% matching contribution. If you maintain that savings level over the next 15 years, get 5% annual salary increases, and your account earns an average annual rate of 8%, it will wind up holding about $135,000 more than shown on the worksheet. At 8%, that would generate another $10,800 of interest income each year.

The worksheet doesn't take into account the fact that inflation after you retire will demand steadily increasing amounts of income to maintain your lifestyle. But two things work in your favor on this point. First, as the years go by, other sources of retirement income may kick in, and second, the income figures shown on the worksheet assume that you're not touching your principal. As the years go on, you would be able to dip into principal as well as spending the income it generates.

Look at Living Costs Where You Plan to Retire

You'll need to do some homework if you plan on pulling up stakes at retirement. Research such things as an area's cost of living, local taxes, and housing costs before making any decisions. An inexpensive way to do this is to subscribe to the area's newspaper. You're likely to get a good picture of the local economy, taxes, and home prices.

These sources, available at your local library and in bookstores, can also help you research prospective retirement locations:

- *Where to Retire* magazine (Call 713-974-6903, or order online at www.wheretoretire.com; $18.00 for a one-year subscription)
- *Retirement Places Rated,* by David Savageau (John Wiley & Sons, $23.99)
- *50 Fabulous Places to Retire in America,* by Lee and Saralee Rosenberg (Career Press, $16.99)
- *America's Best Low-Tax Retirement Towns,* by Eve Evans and Richard L. Fox (Vacation Publications, $16.95)
- *America's 100 Best Places to Retire,* edited by Richard L. Fox (Vacation Publications, $17.95)

One major consideration when selecting a place is state taxes. Are you moving to a higher-tax state or a lower-tax state? The difference could mean thousands of dollars per year. Each state has a different mix of income, property, sales and other taxes. A few states—Alaska, Florida, Nevada, South Dakota, Texas, Washington, and Wyoming—have no income tax, at least for now. New Hampshire and Tennessee do tax income from dividends and interest only. Most states (35) tax all or part of pension income, but the others don't. State and local sales taxes combined range from zero (in New Hampshire, Oregon, and a few others) to around 9% (in parts of Tennessee). And 15 states tax social security benefits, just as the federal government does.

Tax information will help you manage your move. If you are going to a more highly taxed state, for example, you might want to complete the sale of your home

Before you pull up stakes, research such things as an area's cost of living, local taxes, and housing costs.

before making the move. That way, if any profits were taxable, you'd pay the lower state rate. One way to avoid being tripped up is to have an accountant in the new state review your tax situation before making any major financial decisions. You may check a state's income and sales tax at www.kiplinger.com/managing/taxes.

Resist Retirement Money Myths

The closer you get to retirement, the more you'll start to hear these three common retirement investment myths. To build your resistance, remind yourself that your goal is a long-term strategy that protects your nest egg from swings in interest rates as well as the possibility of renewed inflation.

MYTH: You should switch all your savings to income-producing investments.

WRONG. Don't assume that you need to eliminate all investment risk at the point you retire. Financial planners generally recommend that as a new retiree you keep anywhere from 35% to 60% of your nest egg in stocks and stock mutual funds. Then, over the next ten or 15 years after retirement, you could begin a gradual shift toward 30% stocks and the rest in bonds and cash.

MYTH: CDs and bonds are the best choices for steady income, rain or shine.

MAYBE. But if inflation clouds gather, you're going to get soaked. An inflation rate as low as 4% will slash your purchasing power by half in 18 years. People who invest for income often blithely assume that the interest rate they start out with is the one they'll always earn. But when a bond or CD matures, you'll have to reinvest the principal at whatever rate prevails at the time. The way to guard against unfavorable fluctuations in interest rates is to diversify your holdings so that declines in interest income will be offset by growth in other investments—namely, stocks. Stock funds that pay regular income in the form of dividends are a good complement to fixed-income investments such as CDs, bonds, or bond funds. (See growth-and-income fund discussion on page 203.) Utility stocks and blue chips with long, unbroken dividend-paying records are also good choices.

MYTH: Never touch your principal.
WRONG. That only works if you are superwealthy, and such thinking will lead you to overemphasize fixed-income investments when you need to keep a large hunk of your nest egg where it still has an opportunity for growth. A better strategy is to build a mix of stocks and bonds, then decide on a set percentage of the portfolio that you will spend each year, regardless of your actual rate of return. Yes, you may have to dip into principal to supplement income when the stock market performs poorly. But on the other hand, you'll be ahead if the stock market has a stellar year.

Consider a Post-Job Job

Wait just one darned minute! You've spent the past umpteen years planning so you can enjoy a worry-free life of leisure during your retirement years. Why would you want to go back to work? Well, maybe in spite of everything you've been doing to prepare, it appears that you'll come up a few bucks short of your goal. Perhaps you just want to live better. Or maybe there's a new career you've always wanted to tackle. If you're among the growing numbers of Americans accepting early-retirement offers, you may figure you're entirely too young to hang it up.

In this new era of 20- and even 30-year retirements, the post-job years are an opportunity to launch another part-time profession. Many retirees today are healthy and energetic. They'd rather retire to a second career—be it a job or a business of their own—than to a rocking chair. Working part-time can erase two common post-retirement worries: boredom and money. Here are a few ideas for your post-job job search:

■ **See whether your company has flexible retirement options.** Some companies rehire retirees part-time. Other businesses allow employees to phase in their retirement by working 40% of the time.

> **Many retirees today would rather retire to a second career—be it a job or a business of their own—than to a rocking chair.**

> **Don't start your business at the expense of your nest egg. Earmark an affordable amount to bankroll your business— no more than you can afford to lose.**

■ **Check with the National Executive Search** (a division of the National Executive Service Corps), which places retired executives in full- or part-time positions across the country in not-for-profit organizations. Its mission is to strengthen the management of these organizations. Salaries for these high-level positions, such as chief financial officer, vice-president of finance, or directors of marketing and development as well as board members, vary with the organization, ranging from $100,000 to $300,000. For details, call 212-269-1234 ext. 126, or send a current résumé to 29 West 38th Street, 8th Floor, New York, NY 10018, or go to www.nesc.org.

■ **Contact National Able Network** (Ability Based on Long Experience), an umbrella agency for senior-employment programs around the country. This not-for-profit organization has been around since 1977. Offices in several cities have telephone hotlines for job-search assistance, and some have computerized job-matching systems. But they may go by different names. To find the location nearest you, call the job hotline at 312-782-7700, write to National Able Network, 180 North Wabash Ave., Chicago, IL 60601 or log onto www.nationalable.org.

■ **Consider temping.** Temporary agencies actively recruit older workers for a wide variety of positions, and temping is ideal for those who like flexible hours. Kelly Services (www.kellyservices.com), which has 2,500 offices worldwide, offers job opportunities ranging from engineering assignments to in-home care for the elderly. Adecco (www.adecco.com), another major temp agency, also has an extensive placement program for retired workers, consisting mainly of secretarial and clerical work.

Start Your Own Business

The idea of starting a business after retirement has a lot of appeal for many retirees. You can be your own boss, set your own hours. It's a way to slip back into the employment harness, yet move at your own pace.

But don't start your business at the expense of your nest egg. It's easy, and tempting, to sink a lot of money into getting a new business off the ground. The "big break" seems to always be just around the corner, if only you had a few more dollars to get there. Earmark an affordable amount to bankroll your business—no more than you can afford to lose. And be sure the other elements of your retirement plan are firmly in place before putting any money at risk.

If you're thinking of starting your own business, contact the Service Corps Of Retired Executives (SCORE), which is a nonprofit association comprised of 10,500 volunteer business counselors throughout the U.S. and its territories. There are nearly 400 SCORE chapters around the country staffed by volunteers—themselves retired—who will help you start a new business or expand an existing one. They'll provide you with a mentor who is knowledgeable in your prospective field. SCORE also sponsors workshops and seminars. Call 800-634-0245 or search the Web site (www.score.org) to find the location nearest you.

Bookstore shelves are packed with helpful resources on starting and operating a small business. These are especially apropos:

- *Home Business, Big Business: The Definitive Guide to Starting and Operating On-Line and Traditional Home-Based Ventures,* by Mel Cook (MacMillan Publishing Company; available used on Amazon.com)
- *Steps to Small Business Start-Up,* by Linda Pinson and Jerry Jinnett (Dearborn Trade Publishing, $22.95)
- *Home-Based Business For Dummies®,* by Paul Edwards, Sarah Edwards, Peter Economy (Wiley Publishing, Inc., $21.99)

If You Work and Collect Social Security

You should be aware that if you work and collect social security after age 62 but before the year in which you reach full retirement age, the government takes away $1 of your social security benefits for every $2 you earn over certain earned-income limits ($12,000 in 2005). In the year you reach full retirement age you lose $1 for each $3 earned above a different threshold

If you own your home outright and plan to stay put when you retire, consider tapping the equity through a reverse mortgage.

($31,800 in 2005); thresholds change annually. Starting with the month in which you reach full retirement age, you will receive your full benefits with no limit on your earning. You won't be alone if you view that as an unfair tax of 50% and 33⅓% respectively on top of your regular income taxes. Once you've reached full retirement age (currently age 65), you can earn as much as you want from a job and still collect your full social security benefits.

Tap Your House for Retirement Income

If you own your home outright and plan to stay put when you retire, you may be able to tap the equity in your later years through a reverse mortgage.

A reverse mortgage lets you convert equity into cash in the form of a monthly check that a lending institution sends to you. The money changes hands in reverse. As the checks roll in, the loan balance increases. When the homeowner sells, moves, or dies, the loan comes due. The borrowed money, plus interest, would be paid from the proceeds of the sale of the house.

Sounds attractive, but understanding the fees and costs involved has daunted even financially savvy individuals. Recent abuses have forced HUD (the Department of Housing and Urban Development) to issue new rules regarding these mortgages. You must meet with a HUD-approved counselor before you can receive a reverse mortgage, and that counselor can not charge you a commission. Consumers were getting charged up to 10% commission rates in the past by some counselors. The counseling session may be done in person or over the phone.

Reverse mortgages are available in all 50 states, the District of Columbia, and Puerto Rico. Generally, you must be at least 62 years old to take advantage of these loans. The older you are when you apply, the more money you'll be able to get because the lender figures you won't be around as long to collect checks, so each monthly installment can be larger.

Because of the costs involved in obtaining a reverse mortgage, it's usually not wise to get one for a short period of time. Selling your home after a year or so will stick you with a big bill and you will have enjoyed few of the benefits of the loan. Another drawback to reverse mortgages is a relatively high interest rate. A conventional home-equity loan or second mortgage is probably a better choice for retired homeowners who can afford the monthly payments.

■ **For more details on reverse mortgages,** check the Web site of the National Reverse Mortgage Lenders Association at www.reversemortgage.org. In addition to downloadable consumer information, you'll find a reverse-mortgage calculator that will tell you how much cash flow your home could generate, based on how much equity you've accrued and the house's age and location. You can also order *Just the FAQs: Answers to Common Questions About Reverse Mortgages* by calling toll free, 866-264-4466. The publication divides questions into three groups: those appropriate to ask before getting a reverse mortgage; those applicable while a reverse mortgage is in effect; and those applicable at the end of the reverse mortgage period.

■ **The AARP Home-Equity Information Center,** a unit of the American Association of Retired Persons, offers materials that explain home-equity conversion plans in great detail. Of particular interest is *Home-Made Money: Consumer's Guide to Reverse Mortgages* (download from the Web site Publication #D15601), a 72-page guidebook describing the various home-equity conversion options, risks, benefits, and availability. The guidebook and other brochures on reverse mortgages are available from AARP's Home-Equity Information Center, 888-687-2277, or write to AARP, Consumer Affairs Section, 601 E St., N.W., Washington, DC 20049. Information is also available on their Web site (www.aarp.org/revmort).

Need More Help? Hire a Financial-Planning Professional

A financial planner can be a valuable ally in keeping your retirement-planning mission on schedule. You can link up with a planner on a continuing basis or pay for advice periodically as a kind of second opinion

Start your search for a financial planner with a referral of some kind — lawyers, accountants, and insurance agents are good people to ask.

on your program. A good financial-planning pro can see to it that your investments are diversified and consistent with your retirement goals. A good planner can also help you anticipate the tax consequences of any financial decisions that affect your retirement nest egg.

Many planners are registered with the Securities and Exchange Commission as investment advisers. This means they can serve as money managers for their clients, creating and managing investment portfolios and charging a fee comparable to that charged by mutual funds. If you are going to turn your investment decisions over to a planner, it is crucial that you choose an able one, that the planner keep you informed about what's happening to your nest egg, and that you not hesitate to speak up when you aren't comfortable with what's being done with your money.

Financial planners earn their keep in different ways. Some work on a fee-only basis, charging you by the hour or for performing a specific task. Others collect commissions on the investment products they sell you, such as stocks, bonds, mutual funds, and insurance policies. Many planners fall in between, charging a mixture of fees and commissions.

A planner's fee structure is no indicator of competence, although fee-only planners insist that commission-based planners have a built-in conflict because they have a stake in selling you something whether you need it or not. That's something to think about.

Start your search with a referral of some kind—lawyers, accountants and insurance agents are good people to ask.

■ **The Financial Planning Association** (FPA; 800-322-4237) will provide you with a list and background data regarding five members who are doing business in your area, or you may search online at their Web site (www.fpanet.org) for this information and other helpful tips.

■ **For a directory of fee-only planners, contact the National Association of Personal Financial Advisors** (3250 North Arlington Heights Road, Suite 109,

Arlington Heights, IL 60004; 800-366-2732; www .napfa.org).

■ **For names of certified public accountants who are also financial planners, contact the American Institute of CPAs** (Personal Financial Planning Division, 1211 Avenue of the Americas, New York, NY 10036; 888-777-7077 0r 212-596-6200; www.aicpa.org).

Index

Share the message!

Bulk discounts
Discounts start at only 10 copies and range from 30% to 55% off retail price based on quantity.

Custom publishing
Private label a cover with your organization's name and logo. Or, tailor information to your needs with a custom pamphlet that highlights specific chapters.

Ancillaries
Workshop outlines, videos, and other products are available on select titles.

Dynamic speakers
Engaging authors are available to share their expertise and insight at your event.

**Call Dearborn Trade Special Sales at
1-800-621-9621, ext. 4444,
or e-mail trade@dearborn.com**

Dearborn™
Trade Publishing
A **Kaplan Professional** Company